ROCK-CLIMBING

IN THE

ENGLISH LAKE DISTRICT

By OWEN GLYNNE JONES, B.Sc.Lond.

MEMBER OF THE ALPINE CLUB

SECOND EDITION

*With a Memoir and Portrait of the Author, thirty-one full page
Illustrations in collotype, nine Outline Plates of the chief routes,
and an Appendix by George and Ashley Abraham.*

'But ever when he reach'd a hand to climb,
One, that had loved him from his childhood, caught
And stay'd him, "climb not lest thou break thy neck,
I charge thee by my love," and so the boy,
Sweet mother, neither clomb nor brake his neck,
But brake his very heart in pining for it,
And pass'd away.'
                                        —*Gareth and Lynette.*

E. J. MORTEN (Publishers)
DIDSBURY MANCHESTER
ENGLAND

First published 1900
G. P. ABRAHAM & SONS
Keswick, Cumberland

Republished 1973
E. J. MORTEN (Publishers)
6 Warburton Street, Didsbury
Manchester, England

ISBN 0 85972 998 2

Printed in Great Britain by
The Guernsey Press Co. Ltd., Vale, Guernsey, Channel Islands

PUBLISHERS' NOTE.

THE rapid exhaustion of the first edition of Mr. OWEN GLYNNE JONES' book on "Rock-climbing in the English Lake District," and further numerous enquiries for copies of this unique and invaluable work, induced us to make arrangements for the publication of another issue.

Since the first edition appeared in 1897, several important new climbs have been made, most of which have been written about by the author, and are here found just as they left his pen. Of some of the other climbs nothing had been written, so, in response to the request of several climbing friends, an appendix, bringing the book up to date, has been added. The memoir by Mr. W. M. Crook, which is accompanied by an excellent portrait of Mr. Jones, will, we are sure, be welcomed by all as a valuable addition to the work.

We are glad to avail ourselves of this opportunity of acknowledging the kindness of several friends for much valuable advice and assistance given.

Our best thanks are due to Messrs. W. H. Fowler, W. M. Crook, John Graham, H. C. Wilmot, and, last but not least, the author's cousin, Miss Winifred E. Davies. That this volume may meet with the warm and cordial reception accorded to the first edition is the earnest wish of the publishers.

G. P. ABRAHAM & SONS,
KESWICK.

PREFACE.

I FEEL I owe a word of apology to the readers of this brief and inadequate memoir of a dead friend. At the request of Jones' most intimate friends I have compiled it in the scanty leisure moments of a few weeks of a busy life, too few to do justice to my theme. I wish to return my heartiest thanks to those of his friends who have so quickly and generously aided me with the materials at their disposal, especially to Mr. F. W. Hill, Dr. W. E. Sumpner, the brothers Abraham, of Keswick; Mr. W. J. Williams, Mr. Harold Spender, and M. Spahr, of Evolena. I hope if any inaccuracies are detected by these or other friends, they will communicate with me. It has been difficult to avoid them, for all the written documents do not agree in facts and dates. I trust, however, that this brief record of great effort, great achievement, and great tragedy will be more acceptable than no record at all.

W. M. CROOK.

National Liberal Club,
  Whitehall Place, London, S. W.
    Feb. 26th, 1900.

Region separate, sacred, of mere, and of ghyll, and of mountain,
Garrulous, petulant beck, sinister laughterless tarn ;
Haunt of the vagabond feet of my fancy for ever reverting,
Haunt and home of my heart, Cumbrian valleys and fells ;
Yours of old was the beauty that rounded my hours with a nimbus,
Touched my youth with bloom, tender and magical light ;
You were my earliest passion, and when shall my fealty falter ?
Ah, when Helvellyn is low ! Ah, when Winander is dry !

William Watson.

OWEN GLYNNE JONES.

CHAPTER I

EARLY LIFE AND FIRST CLIMBS

OWEN GLYNNE JONES was born on November 2nd, 1867. A Welshman by blood, he was a Londoner by birth, for he first saw the light of day in Clarendon Street, Paddington. His father, Mr. David Jones, was a carpenter and builder, and the son commenced his education at a local school. Of his early life there is little to tell. He seems to have spent his holidays in Wales, and there to have developed, among what may without inaccuracy be called his native mountains, that passion for climbing which made him famous, and which led to his early and much lamented death.

In 1881, when not yet fourteen years of age, Owen Jones was sent to the Central Foundation School in Cowper Street, City Road, of which Dr. Wormell was head master. Those who knew him there speak of him as 'a bright, promising schoolboy.'

He remained at Dr. Wormell's for three years (1881-1884). He distinguished himself in science and won several prizes while at the school. On leaving he was awarded the Holl scholarship, and passed to the Technical College at Finsbury, under the City and Guilds of London Institute.

Jones spent two years (1884-1886) at Finsbury. During that time he passed through the complete course of instruction in the Mechanical department there. He worked with conspicuous ability and success at mechanical engineering, mechanical drawing, mathematics, and chemistry, as well as in the mechanical laboratory and in the wood and iron workshops. When he left, his teachers spoke of him in the highest terms. ' Mr. O. G. Jones,' said Professor Perry, ' was as able, as earnest, as promising as any other whom I can now remember.' Mr. John Castell-Evans speaks of his 'eager enthusiasm and scrupulous conscientiousness ; ' and Professor Silvanus Thompson wrote of him : ' He is imbued with modern methods, . . . and is possessed of a healthy enthusiasm for his work that is infectious.' At the close of his course he passed with a Clothworkers' Scholarship to the Central Institution in Exhibition Road, South Kensington, where he passed the next three years of his life.

The three years (1886-1889) he spent in the Engineering Department, and at the end of his course he had attained the highest position in the class-list of any student of his year, and he received the diploma of Associate of the Institute. On the completion of his course he was appointed assistant in the Mathematical Department. During his life at South Kensington he made the same impression as heretofore on all with whom he came in contact. Intellectually alert, diligent, energetic, enthusiastic, he seemed bound to make some mark in the world.

In the year following the completion of his course, and while he was an assistant at South Kensington, I first met him.

It was during the Easter holidays of 1890. Having broken away from the party with whom I had been spending most of my holiday in Borrow-dale, I made my way to Wastdale Head Inn. I picked up a chance acquaintance with two young fellows in the inn, and we agreed to go together to climb the Pillar Rock—with the aid of a 'Prior's Guide' which I had in my pocket.

When we commenced the ascent, which proved very easy—I believe we went up the easiest way— the dark, slim young fellow somehow naturally assumed the lead. Before we started he had discovered that I had been to Switzerland and had done some climbs there, so he was very modest about his own powers. A few seconds on the rocks dissipated all doubt. With great confidence and speed, climbing cleanly and safely, he soon showed he was no ordinary climber. I had been out with some very tolerable Swiss guides, but never before with a man to whom rock-climbing seemed so natural and easy. My curiosity was excited. He could not be one of the great climbers, for he had never been out of the British Islands, but he could climb.

On the top we found a small, rusty tin box, in which were a number of visiting cards. One of these belonged to Mr. A. Evans, of Liverpool, and a subsequent visitor had written on it the date of his death in the central gully of Llewedd. One of us produced a card, on which the other two wrote their names. The dark young fellow signed his name 'O. G. Jones.' I wonder if that card is there still.

That afternoon and the following day he plied me with questions about Switzerland. How did the climbing there compare with these rocks? Had I climbed the Matterhorn? Did I think he could do it?—absurd question—and so on. Restless, eagerly active, very strong, good-tempered, enthusiastic, he was a man one could not forget. We parted after a day's acquaintance. I never dreamed I should see him again.

His companion on that occasion was another South Kensington man, Dr. Sumpner, now of Birmingham. The next time we met was at Jones's grave in Evolena. During our conversations at that first brief meeting I learned that Jones was at South Kensington; he told me he first learned serious climbing on Cader Idris; I marvelled at his wonderful grip of the rocks, his steady head, his extraordinary power of balancing himself on one foot in what seemed to me then almost impossible positions, and I felt that his enthusiasm would soon lead him to the Alps, if any opportunity offered.

His heart was already there. Yet he was so ignorant of the 'lingo' of the climbing world that my use of the words 'handholds' and 'footholds' considerably amused him.

The following Easter he was again among the Lake Mountains, having devoted the Whitsuntide and Christmas holidays of the preceding year to his favourite pursuit, the last mentioned period being spent in North Wales. I hurry over his climbing in the Lake District for the very sufficient reason that in this volume, so characteristic of its author, his work there is described by himself with all the accuracy of a trained scientist, and with all the enthusiasm of an ardent mountaineer. Descriptions of all these climbs were kept by him in numerous small notebooks, full of neat shorthand with dates, proper names, &c., written in, and with occasional pen and ink sketches of his routes up crags and gullies to illustrate the shorthand notes. Full of mournful interest are these touches of a vanished hand, these silent echoes of a voice that is still.

It was, I believe, during this Easter of 1891 that he met Mr. Monro, to whose enthusiasm he was subsequently wont to attribute his first visit to the Alps, which took place in the autumn of that year. The result of that meeting and the wonderful amount of climbing in 'the playground of Europe' that Jones managed to cram into eight short years must be reserved for another chapter.

CHAPTER II

CONQUERING THE ALPS

In the autumn of 1891 Owen Jones was an unsuccessful candidate for the Professorship of Physics at University College, Aberystwyth, and almost immediately afterwards he was the successful candidate for the post of Physics Master in the City of London School, which he was occupying at the time of his death. In the previous year, 1890, he had taken his B.Sc. degree in London University, coming out third in the list of First Class Honours in Experimental Physics. These facts are mentioned here now, somewhat out of their proper chronological order, because, with the exception of a few papers he contributed to magazines (the *Alpine Journal*, the *Climber's Journal*, and *Cassell's Magazine*) and sundry newspaper articles, they are the only facts that need be mentioned in his otherwise uneventful, though busy, life.

Jones' real life was lived among his beloved mountains. His devotion to them was unsurpassable, his zeal was consuming, his enthusiasm knew no bounds. In the summer holidays of 1891 he had his first introduction to the Alps. His most original work was undoubtedly done among the rocks of his native Wales and in the English Lake country, but he flung himself into Alpine work with all the ardour and energy of which his peculiarly ardent and energetic nature was capable. He spared neither time, money, nor comfort in his devotion to the noblest and most exacting of all sports—that of mountaineering.

The following table—very imperfect, I fear—compiled by his own hand up to the close of 1897, and for 1898 and 1899, from letters kindly sent to me by his friends, will give some idea of his marvellous physical endurance and the extent of his knowledge of the Alps. His own portion of the list was found in his handwriting in his copy of Cunningham and Abney's 'Pioneers of the Alps':—

1891	Dent des Bosses	1892	Fénètre de Saleinoz
	Grande Dent de Veisivi		Col de Chardonnet
	Pas de Chèvres		Pic du Tacul
	Col de Seilon		M. Redessan
	Col de Fénètre		
	M. Capucin	1893	Dent Blanche
	Tête de Cordon		(This was in April, 36 hours.) No summer season in Alps.
	Tête d'Ariondet		
	Grand Combin		
	Grivola	1894	Piz Languard
1892	Thälihorn		Piz Morteratsch
	Rossbodenjoch		Zwei Schwestern
	Matterhorn		Piz Bernina
	*Mittaghorn and Egginerhorn		Croda da Lago
			Kleine Zinne
	Punta di Fontanella		Grosse Zinne
	2 cols to Prerayen		M. Pelmo
	Col d'Olen		M. Cristallo
	Combin de Corbassière		Sorapis
	Col de Boveire		Cinque Torri (3 ways)

* Not in Jones's List.

1895 Rothhorn from Zermatt
        „   „   Zinal
      Traverse Zinal and Zermatt
      Riffelhorn from Glacier
      Dom from Randa
      Täschhorn and Dom (traversed from the Mischabeljoch to Randa— first time by this route—in one day)
      Monte Rosa
      Rimpfischhorn (from Adler Pass)
      Matterhorn (traverse)
      Weisshorn
      Obergabelhorn
      Grand Cornier
      Triftjoch
      Furggenjoch
      Lysjoch
      Süd-Lenzspitze (traverse)
      Nadelhorn
      Hohberghorn
      Steck-Nadelhorn (?)

1896 Little Dru
      Blaitière
      Col du Géant (twice)
      Charmoz (traverse)
      Aig. du Plan
      Aig. du Midi
      N. peak Périades (by the Arête du Capucin)

1897 Schreckhorn (in January)
      Finsteraarhorn
      Jungfrau
      Aletschorn (traverse)
      Beichgrat
      Bietschhorn

1897 Lötschenlücke
      Mönch
      Mönchjoch
      Eiger
      Aig. d'Argentière
      Aig. Moine (traverse)
      Aig. Tacul (traverse)
      Col du Midi
      Portiengrat } In one day
      Weissmies
      Fletschhorn } In one day
      Laquinhorn

1898 In winter : From Grindelwald to Rosenlaui by the Wetterhorn-Sattel, Finsteraarjoch, and Strahlegg
      Two Drus (attempted traverse)
      Big Dru
      Grèpon (traverse)
      Dent de Requin
      Aiguille du Chardonnet
      Aiguille du Midi
      Mont Maudit
      Mont Blanc (traverse)
      Aiguille du Géant
      Two Drus (traverse)
      Riffelhorn
      Wellenkuppe and Gabelhorn
      Lyskamm and Castor
      Alphubel, Rimpfischhorn, and Strahlhorn
      Allalinhorn
      Dent Blanche by South Arête
      Täschhorn by Teufelsgrat
      Dom, Täschhorn, and Kienhorn, descending by Teufelsgrat

1899 Riffelhorn
      Pollux   } In his
      Breithorn (traversed from Schwarzthor)   } first five days
      Six chief points of Monte Rosa   } at Zermatt.
      Matterhorn
      Cols d'Hèrens and Bertol
      Petite Dent de Veisivi   } In 12 hours
      Grande   „   } from Kurhaus
      Dent Perroc   } Hotel and back
      Aig. de la Za (by face)
      Aig. Rouges (traverse of all peaks)
      Mt. Blanc de Seilon in one day
      Dent des Bouquetins
      Mt. Collon
      Pigne d'Arolla in one day
      Dent Blanche (West Arête attempt)

I cannot pretend that this list is perfect, and the
brief notes I append are intended rather to give in a
small space some of the points of human interest in
the above bald list of names than for his mountaineering friends, to whom anything that could be
printed here could convey little or nothing that was
new.

It is a coincidence that he commenced his
acquaintance with the Alps in the very valleys—
Ferpècle and Arolla—in which he spent the last
days of his life, and down which his friends mourn-
fully escorted his body eight years later. It was on
one of the Dents de Veisivi (the Petite Dent) that,
in 1898, Professor Hopkinson, one of Jones' numerous climbing friends, met his death with his two
daughters and his son. As we walked down the
Arolla valley the day before he fell from the Dent

Blanche, Owen Jones was chatting, with a wonderful freshness of recollection of detail, of his climb up the Grand Combin during his first season in the Alps, and I believe the guide who led him up then was one of the search party from Evolena who found his body on the rocks of the Dent Blanche.

The earlier climbs of 1892 were described by him in a paper entitled 'The Dom Grat and the Fletschhorn Ridge,' which appeared in the *Alpine Journal* in 1898. A brief quotation from his own account will give some idea of the easy vivacity of his style.

Speaking of the Saas peaks which 'were designed in pairs,' he writes :—

'It is, perhaps, to our credit that we took an easy pair first—the Mittaghorn and the Egginer —but our stay at Saas that year was to be short, and we could not afford to fail at higher work. A couple of Saas loafers undertook to guide us, but proved to be lamentably weak. They shed tears and ice-axes, and required much help from us dismayed amateurs. Then we left the district, and before my next visit my comrades were scattered over the globe, beyond the seductive influence of axe and rope.'

How characteristic of poor Jones the whole of that passage is ! The unconcealed evidence of his own great physical strength, the playful sense of humour—his friends will remember how he used to explain his own initials, O.G., as standing for the 'Only Genuine Jones'—in the words 'they shed tears and ice-axes,' and the touch of pathos, in the light of after events, of the phrase ' beyond the seductive influence of axe and rope.'

The omission of the names of the Mittaghorn and Egginerhorn from Jones's own list in 1892 shows that even his own record cannot be regarded as complete, a thing not to be wondered at considering the enormous amount of work he did.

It will be noticed that in this year, as in the year before and in 1894, Jones has entered the names of peaks and passes that in the succeeding years he would have considered quite unworthy of serious notice.

But next year he ventured on a feat that, so far as I know, was not only extraordinary for one with comparatively so little experience of the higher Alps, magnificent climber though he was, but it has remained, I believe, unique in the annals of the great mountain on which it was performed. At Easter, 1893, Jones climbed the Dent Blanche, the mountain with which his name will be for ever associated in the climbing world. The ascent was made on the 25th and 26th April, and the expedition took thirty-six hours, a wonderful feat of strength and endurance. M. Adrien Spahr, the landlord of the Hotel de la Dent Blanche at Evolena, and of the new Kurhaus at Arolla (from which Jones started the day before his last, fatal climb), has kindly favoured me with the following brief note in reference to that expedition :—

'C'est bien le 25 Avril, 1893, que Monsieur Jones a fait l'ascension de la Dent Blanche avec les guides Pierre Gaspoz et Antoine Bovier père d'Evolène. Je suis redescendu moi-même avec lui depuis Evolène à Sion.'

In an interview which appeared in the press in 1894 Jones said of this climb, one of the most difficult things he ever did :—'The longest day I ever had afoot was at Easter, '93, doing the Dent Blanche. We took two guides and a porter, and had great difficulty in getting them to attempt the last two hundred feet. We were out in the open for thirty-six hours, with very short rests, no sleep, and excessive labour, but we revelled in every minute of it. The mountain was in a dangerous condition, and the last five hours on the way home we spent in wading, waist-deep, through soft snow. It was rather painful, of course, but there was a certain pleasure even in our pain, for it helped to make philosophers of us. We agreed to think of other things in the midst of our sufferings, and we succeeded creditably well. I believe now that I could stand almost anything in the way of pain or exposure.'

In 1894 he commenced in the Engadine and then went on to the Dolomites, where his great skill as a cragsman and his familiarity with all sorts of rock-work made him much more at home than he yet was among the snow-peaks, as his list shows. On rocks I think it is not using the exaggerated language of friendship to say that he probably had no superior among his countrymen at the time of his death, and comparatively few equals. Among the great snow-peaks he had not attained so high a level. Had he lived he would, I believe, have ranked with the greatest, for he had not done all he was capable of; and when he met his death he was still in his prime, and he was a man of great courage, immense resourcefulness, and phenomenal physical endurance.

In 1895 he devoted himself largely to the reduction of the great peaks in the Zermatt district, some of which he already knew. In that year also he returned to the Dom Grat and the Fletschhorn Ridge, whose acquaintance he had made in 1892. The following passage from the *Alpine Journal* derives an added interest from the fact that Elias Furrer was his guide then, as he was his guide on the last, fatal climb :—

' In August, 1895, Elias Furrer took me from the Täsch Alp to the Mischabeljoch, and thence over the Täschhorn and Dom to Randa, a course of seventeen and a half hours, including halts. Shortly after-wards Mr. W. E. Davidson followed our route from the Mischabeljoch. During the same week Furrer showed me a third pair of the Saas peaks. We bivouacked on the Eggfluh rocks one bitterly cold night, and next day traversed the Südlenspitze and Nadelhorn. The usual *grande course* is to include the Ulrichshorn, and descend to Saas again; but Furrer had business and I fresh raiment at Zermatt, and we hastened over the Stecknadelhorn (or was it the Hohberghorn ?), and thence by the Hohberg

Pass and Festi glacier down to Randa in fourteen hours from the start.'

His energy in climbing this year was remarkable, I had almost said stupendous. In addition to the long climbs referred to in the above extract, it will be seen from the list given above that he twice ascended the Zinal Rothhorn, traversed the Obergabelhorn and Matterhorn, and did two important climbs without guides. The ascent of the Rothhorn from Zinal was the first that Mr. Hill and he made together in Switzerland. The traverse of the Rothhorn and the ascent of the Weisshorn he did without guides, in company with the Hopkinsons, who perished in 1898 on the Petite Dent de Veisivi. Mr. W. J. Williams, who climbed much with Jones in the Alps, has kindly placed in my hands a very characteristic post-card of Jones's, giving, in his own brief, vivacious way, a clearer idea of his boundless enthusiasm and energy in his favourite sport than anything that anyone else could write. It is dated 'Bellevue, Zermatt, Monday, Sept. 2, 1895,' and reads as follows:—'The Hopkinsons and I traversed the Rothhorn without guides in grand style. Reached the summit from the Mountet in $4\frac{1}{4}$ hours, including $\frac{3}{4}$ hour halt. Had a shock of earthquake on the top. Next day we went up to the Weisshorn, bivouac in open air, and the day after managed the Weisshorn. It was delightful. Then they went off to their people at the Bel Alp, and I stayed on at Zermatt ever since. The weather was bad at the end of the week (Weisshorn on Friday), but on Monday I crossed the Furggenjoch with Elias Furrer, whom I took on for 14 days at 20 francs, and Tuesday traversed the Matterhorn; Wednesday, the Monte Rosa hut; Thursday, Monte Rosa from the Lysjoch, a lengthy expedition, but magnificent; I carried my camera the whole time; Friday, the Fluh Alp; Saturday, the traverse of Rimpfischhorn from the Adler pass, dangerous by falling stones, but very jolly; Sunday, I rested and photographed down here. To-day I go to the Täsch Alp, and to-morrow shall attempt the traverse of Täschhorn and Dom in one day. If the weather still holds I shall then traverse the Dent Blanche, which is now in fine condition, like ourselves. Love to all.—Owen.'

Lived there ever a keener mountaineer? On the day before he was killed, as we were walking down the Arolla Valley together, I expressed surprise at the vast amount of eager work he was crushing into every week. He replied, 'You see there are only a few years in which I can do this sort of thing, and I want to get as much into them as possible.' Alas! Owen Jones had not twenty-four hours more; the years were ended.

The season of 1896 was a terribly bad one and Jones suffered with less energetic and less daring mortals. In the *Alpine Journal* he laments that he only did six peaks, but he crossed the Col du Géant twice, traversed the Aiguille de Charmoz, and did the North peak of the Périades by the Arête du

Capucin.   And the disappointments of that summer
season had the effect of sending him to the Alps in
the following winter—his first winter visit.   He
deserted his favourite Christmas hunting grounds,
Wastdale Head Inn and Pen-y-gwrwd, for the Bear
Hotel at Grindelwald.   It so happened that I was
there when he arrived.   On the last day of 1896 I
had made an unsuccessful attempt on the Schreckhorn after being out fourteen and a half hours,
and after an accident to the leading guide, which
confined him to bed for three weeks.   I returned to
Grindelwald and thence to England.   Jones, who
had just come out, determined to climb the Schreckhorn.   The first attempt failed, as the snow was in
very bad condition, and he only got as far as the
hut, where he spent a far from comfortable night.
A few days later, however, he made a second
attempt with successful results.   Both in print and
in manuscript he has left an account of the two
expeditions.   I quote a short passage—it has not
too close a relation to the climbs, but it illustrates
the playful humour which made Jones so charming
and vivacious a companion, alike in an alpine hut or
in the smoke room of ' P.Y.G.'

'I approach for a moment with some delicacy
the threadbare topic of the insect population of
alpine huts, the fauna of the alpine bed.   In
summertime the traveller must not assume that the
straw on which he lies is more dead than alive.
Carelessness in this respect may cost him his peak

next day; he should bring Keating and use it liberally. But in winter he is almost safe and unmolested. Some say that the fleas go down to the valley with the last autumn party, and come up in the early summer with the first tourists. Others think that they hibernate in the warmest corners of the hut and make it a rule to emerge only when it is well worth while. An occasional winter tourist is probably too tough, his attractions too few. The solution of the problem I must leave to others. It will probably be offered by some conscientious German biologist, in an exhaustive illustrated monograph, published in the Mittheilungen.'

The autumn holidays of this year were again very busy ones. Jones spent them in the Alps, and, as his list shows, his climbs included the traverse of the Aletschhorn, Aiguille du Moine, and Pic du Tacul. He did the Portiengrat and Weissmies in one day, and the Fletschhorn and Laquinhorn in another. Young Emil Imseng was his guide, and he found Jones rather too hungry for peaks to be the easiest sort of patron to travel with. When they had done the Portiengrat he had had enough for one day, so he suggested that Jones should rest. But he did not know his 'Herr;' the Weissmies was taken that day likewise.

In 1898 Jones again paid a winter visit to the Alps. Grindelwald was a second time his centre. He crossed from there to Rosenlaui by the Wetterhorn-Sattel, and crossed the Finsteraarjoch and the Strahlegg.

In the Summer of 1898 he went first to Chamounix, and afterwards to Zermatt, and got through a portentous amount of work. He began by attempting the traverse of the two Drus, but failed owing to bad weather. However, he climbed the Grand Dru, and then in rapid succession the Grépon, Dent du Requin, Aiguille du Chardonnet, Aiguille du Midi, Mont Maudit, traversed Mont Blanc, climbed the Aiguille du Géant, aud finished up in that district by accomplishing his formerly thwarted purpose, and traversing both the Grand and the Petit Dru.

Then he came on to Zermatt. He climbed the Riffelhorn again (by the Matterhorn Couloir), did the two peaks of the Lyskamm (in conversation with me the last time I met him he seemed to think this the most difficult thing he had ever done) and Castor, Strahlhorn and Rimpfischhorn, Wellen Kuppe and Gabelhorn, Allalinhorn and Alphubel, Dent Blanche (by the south arête), the Täschhorn by the Teufelsgrat, and the traverse of the Dom, Täschhorn and Kienhorn.

I was standing outside the Monte Rosa Hotel, in the main street of Zermatt, one bright sunny day, that summer, when early in the afternoon Jones, with his two guides, came in from one of these climbs. He had been frequently doing two peaks in one day (I believe he had once done three). All the party showed signs of wear and tear, but Jones was the freshest of the three. His face and hands were as brown as berries, covered with dust and sweat; his clothes were literally in rags, torn to pieces on the rocks. Yet in a few minutes he had washed, changed into the garb of civilization, and reappeared as fresh in body and as vigorous and vivacious intellectually as if he had undergone no fatigue at all. Twenty hours' physical work did not appear to take as much out of him as five hours does out of humbler mortals.

It was just about this time that his friends the Hopkinsons were killed in the Arolla Valley. Jones was a good deal upset by the news, and knocked off climbing for a couple of days, a wonderful thing for him; but then he resumed as busily as ever. Of the climbing skill both of Dr. Hopkinson and of his young son, who was killed with him, he spoke in the highest terms. He had frequently climbed with both.

I have said little of Jones's British climbs, for the simple reason that the fullest and best record of his work in Lakeland is contained in the book to which this brief memoir is prefixed, and his work in Wales (which he also intended to describe in a volume) is not so easily accessible or so fully recorded in any published documents as is his work in the Alps. Apparently there does not exist among his papers any list of his Welsh climbs, though he kept voluminous shorthand notes of almost everything he did in the climbing world; but it is not possible, in the short space and time at my disposal, to attempt to give from them any complete picture of the work he did in Wales. The Messrs. Abraham, however, have kindly placed in my hands the following brief notes of some of the most remarkable experiences they have had in company with Jones, both in Wales and in the Lake District:

'Two climbs with Mr. Jones are most strongly impressed on our memories, and these two would probably rank as the two finest rock climbs made in our district.

'These are Scawfell Pinnacle from the second pitch in Deep Ghyll in 1896, and the conquest of the well-known Walker's Gully on the Pillar Rock in January, 1899.

'Both of these were generally considered impossible, and it is probably no exaggeration to say that no leader excepting Mr. Jones would have had confidence to advance beyond the ledge where the last *arête* commenced on the Scawfell Pinnacle climb.

'The same thing might be still more emphatically said of the last pitch in Walker's Gully, and to those who know the place it is almost incredible that the climb could even be commenced under such conditions as prevailed during the first ascent.

'We visited North Wales with Mr. Jones in 1897, and explored the climbs in the Cader Idris district. The finest climb in this district is the Great Gully above Llyn-y-Cae on Mynydd Pencoed, and Mr. Jones was the first explorer and climber of this and most of the Cader Idris climbs. Some time was also spent at Penygwryd during this visit, but unsuitable weather prevented any climbs of importance being done.

'Shortly after Easter, 1899, Mr. Jones paid his next visit to North Wales, and on this occasion much new and first-class climbing was done from Ogwen Cottage as centre.

'The second ascent of Twll Du was made by a party led by Mr. Jones, and shortly afterwards the two great gullies to the right of Twll Du were first ascended under Mr. Jones' leadership. Amongst several minor first ascents the gully in the Eastern Buttress of Glyder Fach and the first direct ascent of the Northern Buttress on Tryfaen from Cwm-y-Tryfaen are most worthy of note.

'The following Whitsuntide again saw Mr. Jones at Ogwen Cottage, but the weather conditions were such as to prevent any very notable climbing being recorded.

'Of course it is impossible to give in the space at my disposal any idea of the large amount of climbing done in these various districts by Mr. Jones.

'To one with his abnormal physical powers, and true love and enthusiasm for the mountains the most was generally made of every opportunity to climb.

'He was never so happy as when in a really 'tight' place, and to many climbers the spirit and energy shown by him under most trying circumstances will act as an incentive to worthy imitation.

'As a climber he was unique, and many years must elapse ere another can hope to fill his place worthily ; but, as a friend under all circumstances, he was always to be depended upon, for the weakest and heaviest members in every party were generally his special care, and many can never forget his true unselfishness and the kindly way in which personal blunders were criticised.

'Whether the party was struggling up a waterfall or resting shivering and wet under a huge chock-stone, or clinging desperately to a wind-swept ridge or icy couloir, everyone felt happy with Jones as their comforter and leader.

'The musical gatherings in the evenings seem now to lack one voice, and nought but sadness can be left for many of those who remember companion-ships which can never be replaced.'

CHAPTER III

THE LAST SEASON IN THE ALPS

I COME now to the last season in the Alps, the season of 1899. The first part of his holiday was spent at Zermatt, and then he and Hill met by arrangement at the Kurhaus at Arolla. They soon got to work, beginning with the two Dents de Veisivi (the scene of the accident to the Hopkinsons the previous year) and the Dent Perroc, in twelve hours from the Kurhaus and back. Then followed the Aiguille de la Za by the face, a traverse of all the peaks of the Aiguilles Rouges, Mont Blanc de Seilon and the Pigne d'Arolla in one day, the Dent des Bouquetins, and the traverse of Mont Collon. A slight accident to one of the party of which I was a member, necessitated an unexpected descent on the evening of August 26th to Arolla, in the hope of finding a doctor. There was none there, but we found many friends and acquaintances, among them being Owen Jones. On the morning of Sunday 27th, our party left for Evolena just after breakfast, as we heard there was a German doctor there, and we wanted our wounded member attended to without delay. Just as we were starting we found Jones and Hill leaving also, intending to traverse the Dent Blanche, climbing it by the west arête, which had only been done twice before, and we all hoped shortly to meet again in Zermatt.

It was a bright sunny morning, hot and dusty. For a good part of the way from Arolla to Haudères I chatted to Jones. We did not go very fast on account of the damaged member of our party, about whom Jones was very solicitous. He himself seemed very fit, and was full of life and enthusiasm for his favourite passion. He chatted freely of all his climbs, of our first meeting nine years before, of all that had happened since, of frostbite on the Dom, and the remedy—sticking his fingers into boiling glue—worse than the disease. His traverse of the ice arête between the two peaks of the Lyskamm and his Easter ascent of the Dent Blanche seemed to me to have made the deepest impression on him of all his achievements in the mountains. He was rather inclined to underrate his wonderful rock-work in North Wales and in the Lake District, a department in which, in my opinion, he was really greatest, though his feats of endurance in the Alps were something off the common. He told me that his ambitions inclined towards a tour in the Himalayas, if circumstances allowed of his realising that dream.

At Haudères we parted company. Hill and Jones, with their guides, who met them at Haudères, turned up to Ferpècle ; we went on to Evolena. If my friend's health permitted, I had arranged to see Jones in Zermatt on Tuesday afternoon. Difficult as was the expedition he was undertaking, the awful reality of the morrow never crossed my mind even as a possibility. A stronger or more well-equipped party I had never seen start on an expedition. It was about 12-30 when we all said good-bye.

At Evolena the doctor ordered our invalid a day or two of complete rest. So on Monday morning the third member of our party, with his guide, started for the Col de la Meina to return to his wife, whom he had left in the Val des Bagnes, from which we had come. For the sake of the walk I accompanied them to the top of the Col. About 9-15, just before we lost sight of the west arête of the Dent Blanche, I searched the arête with my field glasses to see if any trace of Jones and Hill's party could be detected. None of us could see anything, so we concluded, as the mountain was in very good condition, that they had probably already got to the top, and were then descending by the south arête. But they were still on the arête, though we failed to see them on the dark rocks. Had it been three-quarters of an hour later we might actually have been witnesses of the accident.

On the top of the Col de la Meina we were caught by a storm of mist and rain, blowing up from the west. I bade adieu to my friends and hastened back to Evolena. That was the mist which caught Mr. Hill on the gendarme in his descent after the accident and detained him 22 hours alone on the great mountain.

But of the accident no one dreamed. No pre-
monition, no presentiment, troubled our thoughts.
Monday and Tuesday passed quietly and unevent-
fully for us.

On Wednesday morning my friend got permission
from his doctor to walk up to Arolla for lunch. We
gladly availed ourselves of the new freedom.

At Arolla we found many of Jones's friends
hoping to meet him shortly in the Zermatt Valley.
On our way back to Evolena we passed the body of
the Tiroler guide, Reinstadler, of Sulden, which was
being carried down the valley. He had been killed
on Monday, August 28th—that black and fatal day
in the Evolena Valley—by falling into a crevasse on
the Pigne d'Arolla.

As we re-entered the garden of our hotel, M.
Spahr met us looking very grave. 'Had we heard
of the great accident on the Dent Blanche?' For
the first time the thought of danger to Jones and
Hill crossed my mind. I quickly asked him for
details, telling him why I was apprehensive.

He had had a telegram from Dr. Seiler from
Zermatt, which he showed me. It was in French
and ran something like this: 'A tourist and three
guides have fallen from the Dent Blanche. A caravan of guides is starting from Zermatt to look for
the bodies, which will reach Haudères about six
o'clock to-morrow evening. Have four coffins
ready at Haudères. I am coming round myself.—
SEILER.'

Four bodies! This could not be Jones and Hill's party, there would be five or three, for they had intended to make the ascent on two ropes, three and two respectively on each. If all five had been roped together, one could not have been saved. My mind grew easier. So we reason when we do not know.

But I could not avoid thinking of the awful accident, and as I thought my fears returned. No other party had left the Evolena Valley for the Dent Blanche that week. The bodies had fallen on the Evolena side. It was improbable they had climbed from the Zermatt side. Could it be that the fifth body had not been seen? One climber and three guides was a most unusual party? I grew uneasy again, and finally telegraphed to Dr. Seiler: 'Have Messrs. Jones and Hill arrived?'

While we were waiting for dinner and a reply, a voice hailed me by name out of the gathering gloom. It was that of Mr. Harold Spender, who had just driven up the valley with his sister and a younger brother, Mr. Hugh Spender. We exchanged greetings and discussed the accident. I told them what I feared.

We were sitting in the balcony outside the hotel in the summer darkness when a villager put a yellow telegraph envelope in my hand. I hastily tore it open, and this is what I read: 'M. Hill arrived safely this morning, but Jones and three guides fell an hour and a half from the top on Monday morning.—Seiler.'

Owen Glynne Jones was dead. My mind almost reeled at the fact. Intellectually I knew it must be so, but I was utterly unable to realise it. I could almost hear the sound of his voice and the rattle of the nails of his dusty boots on the stones that last Sunday morning. But his voice was stilled for ever.

And Hill! He had escaped, but how? Where had he been since Monday morning? Out on the mountain alone, without guides, or food, or drink. The thing was incredible, impossible. But the impossible and the incredible was true.

At eleven o'clock fifteen guides and Mr. Harold Spender started as a search party. My injured friend and myself went with them as far as we could. The little village was already in darkness, swathed in sorrow. For the telegram that brought me news of Jones's death announced the death of a village guide too.

In the chapel only lights burned. It was the vigil round the body of Reinstadler. Silently and sadly we tramped up the valley along the carriage road to Haudères. Then in single file, like an army on a night march, we marched up the steep and narrow path to Ferpècle. Far below us, on our right, the torrent roared. We picked precarious steps by the light of our lanterns and the aid of our axes. We talked little and in muffled tones.

We reached Ferpècle about 1-30 a.m. on Thursday. The hamlet was asleep. The guides broke eight huge poles out of the fences of the fields and

from the outbuildings.   Grim duty ! The poles were
to make four rude biers on which to carry the bodies
down.

Between 3 and 4 a.m., we gained the Bricolla
Alp, where Jones and Hill had slept the night
before the fatal climb. The kindly shepherd provided us with milk and a fire—it was now very
cold—and we produced provisions from our rücksacks
and had a much-needed meal. It was a curious
sight—the little stone hut, a big wood fire blazing
in a hole in the floor, pails of milk all round the walls
on shelves, a circle of rough weather-beaten men,
their faces lighted by the flickering flames and by
the uncertain light of one or two of our lanterns.
Rembrandtesque—and profoundly sad.

A little after four we went out. The grey dawn
was just breaking, but a cold, thick, clammy white
mist had swept down on the alp and chilled us to
the bone. At the top of the moraine my friend and
I had to turn back. We should only have been a
hindrance had we gone on, as both of us were
damaged. Spender and the guides went forward.
Let Mr. Spender describe the rest.

'At four the column resumed its way. Rain
had begun to fall and a dense mist was closing down
upon us. But it was soon light enough to put out
our lanterns and courage came with the dawn. We
rounded the alp, and then began to climb the long,
dreary moraines which lead up to the glacier. The
guides went at a terrific pace. But it was good to

be taken into this noble fraternity—to be accepted as a comrade and not as a " climber "—to be honoured by a share in the generous quest.

'But the pace soon slackened. We halted on the edge of the glacier, roped in fours, and began to search gingerly for a way through the terrific ice-fall of the glacier. We were mounting by the old approach to the Dent Blanche, up the ice-fall, now long since abandoned. The glacier was, of course, quite changed since any of these guides had last visited it. The ice was split and rent into every conceivable shape. We were surrounded with leaning towers of ice, threatening at any moment to fall on us and crush us.

'A great pile of seracs on the Northern ice-fall, across the ridge, fell with a mighty crash. Away to the right we could hear the thunder of avalanches. But never for a moment did the guides hesitate. Steadily and unflinchingly they threaded their way between the menacing seracs. Crossing broken fragments of ice, balancing between profound crevasses, not thwarted but ever searching for a way. At last we suddenly struck upon the tracks of Jones's party away to the North side of the glacier close to the rocks. There we scrambled up, half by the rocks and half by the ice, and then at last, after many hours, found ourselves on the great plateau beneath the long snow couloir running down from the West Ridge. There, if anywhere, they were likely to be. And there, high up among the rocks, we could just see, with the aid of a good telescope, some dark objects which were not rocks.

' " There are our friends," said the guides.

' Yes, there was no doubt of it. It was now ten o'clock and the sky had cleared. A party was formed, and mounted the rocks to fetch the bodies. As they climbed, suddenly another army of men appeared below us, above the ice-fall, advancing swiftly. They were the party of the Zermatt Guides. They came on unroped, climbing fast. It was a magnificent sight to see this troop of giants in their own element, a troop of equals, masters of peril. They halted below the rocks and sent up another small band to join the Evolena Guides. There was a long pause, and then they all began to descend, bringing the bodies.

' I will draw a veil over what we found. Men cannot fall many thousands of feet and lie in artistic attitudes. . . . But it was four o'clock before the Bricolla hut was reached, and darkness had fallen before the bodies came to Haudères. The Zermatt Guides were out for twenty-four hours, and the Evolena Guides over twenty.'

Mr. W. R. Rickmers, a German resident in England, and a member of the Alpine Club, sends the following to the *Alpine Journal* :—

' Mr. Seiler sent out thirty guides under Alois Supersaxo. Dr. R. Leuk, Mr. K. Mayr, and Mr. W. R. Rickmers joined them. We left the Staffelalp at 10 p.m. on August 30th, reached the Col

d'Hérens at 6 a.m. on the 31st, in fog and snow,
which cleared away later on. Descended Ferpècle
Glacier towards termination of W. ridge of Dent
Blanche, and ascended the small glacier which comes
down from point 3,912 on the S. *arête*. At the spot
under the "g" in "Rocs rouges" this glacier forms
an icefall (moderately difficult), and besides that a bit
of the Glacier de la Dent Blanche hangs over the
narrowest part of the W. ridge. We then came to
the foot of a great gully. On the map it is the first
one from W., and it is very clearly indicated. In
the rocks to the right of the couloir (looking down)
and about three hundred feet above the rim of the
glacier, the bodies were found. It was about 10 a.m.,
and a party of Evolena guides, accompanied by Mr.
Harold Spender, was already on the spot.

'The height above sea-level was ca. 3,600-3,700 m.
Straight above, on the ridge, one saw a smooth cliff
(ca. 400-500 feet below summit), and if that was the
fatal *mauvais pas* the fall must have been about
1,500-1,700 feet in a series of clear drops of many
hundred feet. The rope was intact between Furrer
and Zurbriggen.

'The guides did their work well; the icefall, of
course, caused a great deal of trouble.'

While the search party was crossing the glacier
and the snow-fields, I watched them through my
glasses. Presently the sun got the better of the
morning mist, and the pure white snow gleamed
beautifully. Then from the Col d'Hèrens there

swept a tiny, serpentine black line, moving fast. It was men. I turned my glasses on them. They were the Zermatt party, some thirty strong, advancing at a rare pace. It was a beautiful sight, so masterful, so sure was their progress.

As the long, hot hours of mid-day passed, I descended to Ferpècle, and sent up a boy with food and drink for the certainly wearied searchers when they returned from their sad duties. At length they came, drawing the bodies over the grass slopes till they reached a path where they could be carried on their shoulders. Darkness had fallen when we reached Haudères.

Late on Friday night Mr. Hill came round for the funeral. His voice seemed to me strangely altered. Otherwise he had come through his terrible experience wonderfully, thanks to a splendid constitution and nerves of steel. Then first I heard the true story of the accident. I reproduce his own account from the *Alpine Journal*. All had roped together early in the climb, and the accident took place about ten o'clock. Mr. Hill says :—

'When I reached the level of the others, Furrer was attempting to climb the buttress, but, finding no holds, he called to Zurbriggen to hold an axe for him to stand on. Apparently he did not feel safe, for he turned his head and spoke to Jones, who then went to hold the axe steady. Thus we were all on the same level, Vuignier being some twenty-five or thirty feet distant from them and also from me.

Standing on the axe, which was now quite firm, Furrer could reach the top of the buttress, and attempted to pull himself up; but the fingerholds were insufficient, and before his foot had left the axe his hands slipped, and he fell backwards on to Zurbriggen and Jones, knocking them both off, and all three fell together. I turned to the wall to get a better hold, and did not see Vuignier pulled off, but heard him go, and knew that my turn would soon come. And when it did not I looked round, and saw my four companions sliding down the slope at a terrific rate, and thirty feet of rope swinging slowly down below me.

'It is difficult to analyse my sensations at that moment. My main feeling was one of astonishment that I was still there. I can only suppose that Vuignier had belayed my rope securely to protect himself and me during our long wait on the traverse.

'It must be admitted that Furrer did not choose the best route; but his choice is easy enough to understand, for the only alternative did not look inviting. At all events, it is certain that he acted on his own initiative. I say this reluctantly, and solely for the purpose of contradicting a statement I have read in an account of the accident—that he was induced by Jones to climb straight over the gendarme instead of going round it. It is a pity that historians, who must of necessity be ignorant of the facts, should go out of their way to make such conjectures.

'The problem before me was a difficult one. It was quite impossible to climb down alone, and I could not expect to succeed where guides had failed; the only course open was to attempt to turn the gendarme on the right. This I succeeded in doing with great difficulty, owing to the ice on the rocks and the necessity of cutting up an ice slope in order to reach the ridge. In about another hour I gained the summit, and was greeted with a faint cooey, probably from the party we had seen. I could not see them nor make them hear, so made my way down with all reasonable speed, hoping to overtake them. When I reached the lowest gendarme—the one with a deep narrow fissure—a sudden mist hid everything from view. It was impossible to see the way off; and while I was trying various routes a snowstorm and cold wind drove me to seek shelter on the lee-side of the rocks. There, tied on with my rope, and still further secured by an ice-axe wedged firmly in front of me, I was forced to remain until mid-day on Tuesday. Then the mist cleared, and, climbing very carefully down the snow-covered rocks I reached the snow arête, where most of the steps had to be re-cut. The next serious difficulty was the lower part of the Wandfluh; I could not remember the way off, and spent two or three hours in futile efforts before I found a series of chimneys on the extreme right, leading down to the glacier. The sun set when I was on the high bank of moraine on the Zmutt Glacier, and in the growing darkness it was far from easy to keep the path. The light in the Staffel Alp inn was a guide as long as it lasted, but it went out early, and, keeping too low down, I passed the inn without seeing it, and being forced to stop by the nature of the ground, spent the night by the side of the torrent. It was late in the morning when I awoke, and then a scramble of a few minutes brought me to the path, near the sign-post, and I reached Zermatt at half-past eleven.'

Mr. Hill's escape is one of the most wonderful in the history of mountaineering. His endurance and courage are not less remarkable. To have been out alone, in bad weather, without anything to eat save five raisins, and with nothing to drink but ice and snow, on a difficult and dangerous mountain, and to have returned safely is, I believe, a record in climbing annals. I may add a few details, given me by Mr. Hill when I first met him after the accident, which he has not reproduced in the above narrative.

He thinks his companions were killed instantaneously. They uttered no sound ; they made no apparent attempt to save themselves. With arms outspread they rolled helplessly down the awful face of the mountain. He watched them for a few seconds, powerless to help, if help would indeed have availed, and then turned from the sickening sight.

During the last part of his descent, even his great strength began to fail. Once, on the Wandfluh, he lost his axe and had to spend an hour in climbing down to recover it, as it was absolutely essential to his safety. After he left the Zmutt glacier in darkness, he appears to have become delirious. He was constantly talking to imaginary companions. He fell into holes in the ground and went to sleep without strength to rise. He wakened from cold, called to his companions to go on as it was time to be leaving, stumbled, and fell asleep again.

On Saturday morning Dr. Sumpner arrived, having travelled straight through from Birmingham to Evolena. Friends tramped down from Arolla, others had come from Zermatt, the secretary of Jones's section of the Swiss Alpine Club came from near Neuchâtel. A carriage bore Jones's plain black coffin, with a gilt cross on it, down from Haudères. We buried him and the Evolena guide, Vuignier, in the little graveyard of the Roman Catholic church, almost in sight of the glorious, but terrible, mountain on which they met their fate. The scene in the village almost baffles description. All the villagers, men and women, attended the funeral, clad in coarse white robes. The grief of the women, especially of Vuignier's poor old mother, was heart-rending to witness. The little Roman Catholic chapel was crowded, the congregation all in white, save the acolytes, two village boys, who served the altar in their coarse brown, everyday clothes, and the choir, whose strong voices rang through the whitewashed, humble building. A little knot of Englishmen, sun-browned, of another faith or of no faith at all, joined in the impressive and solemn service. It was a sight that no one present can ever forget.

After the service, we bore the two coffins to the graveyard. Rev. Mr. Scott, the Anglican chaplain,

read the English burial service over Owen Jones's
grave.   Mr. Hill sent a beautiful wreath of edelweiss
and the foliage of the Alpine rose.   A rude wooden
cross marked the spot till Jones's friends erected
a suitable gravestone.   The lovely warm sunshine
and the bright blue sky, and the gleaming snows on
the slopes of the Dent Blanche, formed a curious
contrast to the mourning of the village in that
Alpine valley.

Thus perished, as he would, I doubt not, like
to have died, Owen Glynne Jones, a brave and
dashing mountaineer, a cheery and kindly friend,
whose presence will be long missed by all who
had the privilege of knowing him.   His death was
due to a pure accident, occurring when he was in
the plenitude of his powers, and when he seemed
just about to reap the reward of long years of
patient, ardent toil.

W. M. CROOK.

CONTENTS

LIST OF ILLUSTRATIONS

OUTLINE DRAWINGS OF THE CHIEF ROUTES

INTRODUCTION

SOME eight years ago chance led me to the Lake District for the first time, and a kindly acquaintance whom I then met at Wastdale taught me something of the joys of rock-climbing. Since that occasion every holiday has been spent on the mountains, either in Cumberland or North Wales or Switzerland, and they have taught me much that is worth knowing and that when once learnt can never be forgotten. Men with the highest literary qualifications have written of the charm of mountaineering, and every aspect of the subject has been touched upon with fullest justice and with a grace of style that has captivated many a non-climber in spite of his prejudices. Yet I cannot refrain from adding my own humble tribute of praise to the sport that has done so much for me and my best friends.

It satisfies many needs; the love of the beautiful in nature; the desire to exert oneself physically, which with strong men is a passionate craving that must find satisfaction somehow or other; the joy of conquest without any woe to the conquered; the prospect of continual increase in one's skill, and the hope that this skill may partially neutralize the failing in strength that comes with advancing age or ill health.

Hunting and fishing enthral many men, but mountaineering does not claim the sacrifice of beasts and fishes. Cricket and football are magnificent sports, and it is a perpetual satisfaction that the British races are becoming enthusiastic in their appreciation of keen contests in these games. Yet there is something repulsive in the spectacle of five thousand inactive spectators of a struggling twenty-two, and the knowledge that the main interest of many players and observers is of a monetary character does not tend to convince one of the moral benefits that these sports can offer. On the other hand, it is scarcely fair to judge a sport by those who degrade it in this manner, and we all know that genuine cricketers and footballers play for love and honour.

The mountaineer does not reap any golden harvest by his exertions—even if he writes a book on his subject. He does not exhibit his skill to applauding thousands; and his vanity is rarely tickled by the praise of many. He must be content with the sport itself and what it offers him directly.

Probably the scientific mountaineer gains most. He is certain to acquire rare and valuable knowledge of facts in zoology, botany, or geology, if he starts with the necessary intellectual equipment. The physicist's mind is perpetually exercised by the natural phenomena he witnesses; mist bows, Brocken spectres, frost haloes, electrical discharges of the queerest description, mirages, all these offer him problems of the most interesting kind. But the fact is, there is so much to do that is directly connected with the climbing itself that the natural sciences are usually left to themselves, and their consideration reserved for special expeditions.

On the other hand, science can often assist the climbing. The engineer can triumph with applications of the rope. He can tell us some facts worth knowing on the value of friction as an aid to stability, on the use of an axe as a support or as a lever, or on the safe methods of negotiating loose stones. The man who knows something of geology is a useful member of an exploring party; he is often able to guess correctly where available passages occur in a wilderness of rock, and can judge at a distance what quality of climbing the party may expect. The expert in mountain weather does not exist; perhaps he does not dare to, or perhaps the subject is too complicated for a nineteenth-century scientist. However this may be, it is worth while paying a little attention to meteorology and noting the quality of weather that follows any definite condition of the wind, the barometer, or the atmospheric temperature.

The causes that have resulted in the publication of this little book are as difficult to define as those that produce a rainy day in the Alps; and, now that the book is written and nothing remains but an introduction, I wish that the reverse order of pro-

ceeding had been adopted, and that the introduction
had been written as a peg on which succeeding
chapters might have been definitely hung.

From the outset the illustrations have been
regarded as the chief feature of the book, and it was
my good fortune early to obtain the co-operation of
Messrs G. P. Abraham & Sons in the production
of good photographs of the most interesting pieces of
rock scenery that the Lake District affords. Messrs.
George and Ashley Abraham have accompanied me
on several climbing excursions with the express
purpose of obtaining artistic and yet accurate photographs of the main difficulties that beset the cragsman's course, and I am bound to add that they are
as skilful in tackling severe pitches as they are in
taking successful pictures. The practical troubles in
manipulating heavy photographic apparatus where
most people find work enough in looking solely to
their own safety, the frequent impossibility of finding
a sufficient contrast in light and shade among the
crag recesses, and the subsequent difficulties in
development of such awkward subjects, will convince
the reader that theirs has been no light task, and at
the same time will offer sufficient excuse for certain
small defects that we have been unable to eliminate
from the photo-mechanical reproductions. These are
in collotype on platino surface paper; their preparation has been undertaken for the most part by
Messrs. Walford and Co., Mill Hill Park.

For the benefit more particularly of climbers,
several outline diagrams have been introduced to

explain the outlines of those more important crags up each of which many different routes have been found, lines of ascent that cannot be readily recognised in the photographs themselves, and that cannot be briefly described in words. Some of these are purely diagrammatic, where it has been found impossible to base them on good general views. The others are outlined from photographs, and can in most cases be compared directly with the corresponding views from which they are derived.

With the knowledge that I was getting substantial aid in the illustrative portion of the book, the management of the rest has been much simplified. There are very many people who come regularly to the English Lake District to ramble about on the fells and to make the ordinary ascents. Of these, by far the greater number steer clear of the precipices and other steep parts, wisely recognising the danger that attends the inexperienced in such places. Nevertheless they enjoy the mountains and are charmed with the scenery. They do not know much about the innermost recesses of even their favourite peaks. To many of them Mr. Haskett Smith's little book on 'Climbing in England' must have been a revelation; for it indicates with sufficient clearness that every crag in the country of any considerable dimensions has been explored with wonderful thoroughness by Alpine climbers, and that these abrupt walls and gloomy gullies are the happy hunting-ground of many an enterprising athlete. If my accounts of the different ascents were briefly stated in the orthodox climbing-guide form, the book could appeal to none but the elect; only an athlete in excellent training could digest such solid diet. If, on the other hand, they were recorded in narrative form, with a little expansion of detail where serious difficulties occurred during the expeditions, the book might at the same time appeal to many a tourist who loves the country and who likes to learn more about it. The latter course has been adopted, and it is sincerely to be hoped that the succeeding chapters will interest such tourists.

There was another and more important consideration which helped to decide on the form actually taken. Our Alpine climbers of the highest rank are born, not made. But most of the others, taking with them some natural aptitude and plenty of money, are made abroad. Why do they not take their preliminary training for a year or two in Wales, or Cumberland, or on the Scottish hills? It would be much wiser and cheaper to support the 'home industry' so far as it goes, before making their *dèbuts* on the high Alps. Our British hills can give them no glacier practice, but they can learn a vast deal concerning rock-climbing before they leave the country. To such as these the book is primarily dedicated. There are no professional guides in Cumberland who know anything about the rocks. The amateur must come out and manage for himself. But it is here intended to show that the Cumberland

school is a well-graded one; that the novice can
start with the easiest and safest of expeditions, and
can work his way up to a standard of skill comparing
favourably with that of the average Swiss guide.
There is nothing so instructive as guideless climbing,
be it ever so humble in character. It makes the man
wonderfully critical when taken in hand by guides
later on, and renders him also much more able to
profit by their practical instruction.

For such beginners, the mere statement of the
position of a gully and the number and character
of its chief obstacles would be quite useless. He
requires something more; a suggestion here and
there of the manner in which the troubles can be
avoided or overcome, and a comparison of these
difficulties with others. It is natural that every man
has his own way of employing the limbs; my way of
dealing with a pitch might not at all suit another
climber, who perhaps relies less upon balance and
more on strength of arm than myself, or *vice versâ*.
It is therefore unwise to appear dogmatic in describing methods, and I hasten to assure those knowing
critics that I have never meant to appear so. And
yet it is none the less a definite object throughout to
render the accounts in sufficient detail for those who
want assistance in repeating the ascents. I have not
hesitated to draw on old experiences, gained when
the ground was comparatively new to me; for there
is a tendency to depreciate, or indeed to overlook
entirely, the difficulties in any familiar route after

constant practice has removed those elements that
introduce risk or uncertainty of success, and a novice
can often explain to a novice far more effectively
than an expert.

The Lake District is becoming more popular every
year as a centre of operations for cragsmen. Yet
there is no corresponding development of a set of
professional guides out there, though I believe they
would thrive exceedingly, and all stock information
about the mountains is confined to a few manuscript
books, and to Mr. Haskett Smith's little publication
already referred to. The new comer is continually
at a loss for details; he has no means of learning
what is difficult or easy, how to circumvent dangerous
obstacles or to discover the safe points of attacking
them; he is dependent for such facts on chance
acquaintances made in the country or on correspon-
dence more or less painfully elicited from authorities.
When unsuccessful in these ways he is sometimes
tempted to launch out on his own account and wrest
the information from the mountains themselves.
This heroic method is undoubtedly the most effective,
but it involves too much risk for the unpractised hand,
and the wonder is that so few serious casualties occur
in its application. Such accidents do occur through
ignorance of the district, and always will so long as
the necessary knowledge that gives safety to the
explorer is confined to the few.

Mr. Haskett Smith's book serves in the fullest
manner to indicate where good scrambling can be

obtained, to define the few technical terms in the cragsman's vocabulary, and to give general advice concerning the best centres. It has been of the greatest use to the climbing fraternity, who owe their thanks to him. But he gives no detail of the scrambling itself. He has appealed more particularly to the expert, who can manage all his pioneering for himself. Notably is this the case with the Pillar Rock—practically his own particular preserve— where most of the routes have long since been made out by him. For years he knew the Rock as no one else knew it; every chimney and ridge and wall was within his ken. Yet in his little handbook there is scarcely an indication of the possession of all this unique knowledge. Most climbers expected some expansion in the description of his early explorations; but he has kept rigidly to his scheme of treatment, and dealt but scant justice to himself throughout the work. This book, then, is to be regarded in some ense as supplementary in character, the cordials witness of the good sport obtainable by following his advice and general directions.

There are many men who think well of the sport, but speak slightingly of the narrow field offered for it by the Lake District. No doubt the Alps offer far more scope both in range and quality. But we cannot very conveniently reach Switzerland at every season of the year. At Christmas and Easter it is entirely barred to most people. The expense of foreign travel is a consideration, and the question of

length of holiday is rarely negligible. Cumberland
can be reached in a night from London ; the district
is an inexpensive one for tourists. The fact that
there are hundreds of climbs at our disposal in the
Alps is no great inducement in itself; we can never
climb more than one or two at a time, and for most
of us there will always remain scores of ascents that
we shall never have the opportunity of accomplishing.
One can learn how to swim as effectively in a swim-
ming-bath six feet deep as in an ocean ; and one can
gain an extensive and practical acquaintance with
rock-climbing in a district where the whole set of
climbs can be accomplished by the expert in a few
short holidays, as in a country where the choice is
unlimited. Personally I should always go to the
high Alps when the chance offered itself, but Cumberland serves remarkably well to allay the desire for
mountain air and vigorous exercise when Switzerland
is out of the question.

What does it matter that a climb has been done
before ? Climatic conditions and the members of
one's party introduce sufficient variety. Years ago
an expert reporter was trying to teach me shorthand. His method was to induce me to copy out
the same report again and again ; it was an excellent
idea, and the system was well vindicated with apter
pupils. Likewise in climbing, an apt pupil will
learn rapidly by repetition of the same ascents.

This introduces a point on which I am scarcely
qualified to speak, that of physical aptitude on the

part of the would-be climber. Mr. Clinton Dent in the
Badminton volume bestows a chapter on the subject
of 'Mountaineering and Health.' Here we have an
authoritative summary of the physical qualifications
required by the mountaineer, and of the bodily ail-
ments he may possibly incur. A perusal of the
chapter will convince the reader of the suitability of
a mountainous region such as our own country can
offer for preliminary training before the high Alps
are approached. There is much less likelihood of
over-strain; snow-blindness, frost-bite, and mountain
sickness are rarely met with here.

Climbers are absolutely incapable of any sustained effort when they reach certain altitudes, and
the limit depends on the individual. It is the mis-
fortune of some to feel an uncomfortable perturbation
of the heart when once a definite level is passed.
They are well enough able to exert themselves below
that level, but can hope for no pleasurable exercise
above it. With every desire to climb, with muscle
and mind enough to excel in the sport, they are
nevertheless debarred from enjoying the high Alps.
Let them therefore make the best of our British hills
for a while, and then perhaps proceed to the
Dolomites in the Austrian Tyrol for fuller applications at a safe low level of what they have here
learnt.

Solitary scrambling is universally condemned.
Most climbers of experience have learnt something
about it, and are unanimous in their unfavourable

judgment. Nothing teaches the scrambler so quickly, if his nerve is sufficiently strong; but the penalty paid for slight mistakes is often extreme, and the risk is too great for him to be justified in deliberately choosing the single-handed venture. A party of two makes the strongest combination for most of the ordinary Cumberland climbs; three are generally better for the severest courses. Any beyond that number will to a greater or less extent increase the difficulty of the ascent and the time spent in effecting it.

A rough classification is here appended of some seventy-five of the well-known courses judged under good conditions. They are divided into four sets. The first are easy and adapted for beginners, the second set are moderately stiff, those of the third set rank as the difficult climbs of the district, and the last are of exceptional severity. Some attempt has been made to arrange them in their order of difficulty, the hardest ones coming last; but the variations of condition of each due to wind, temperature, rain, snow, or ice are so extensive that no particular value should be attached to the sequence. But even if only approximately correct, the lists may help men in deciding for themselves where to draw the line that shall limit their own unaided performances. As for the items in the fourth class, they are best left alone. Mark the well-known words of an expert (Mr. C. Pilkington) : 'The novice must on no account attempt them. He may console himself with the reflection that most of these fancy bits of rock-work are not mountaineering proper, and by remembering that those who first explored these routes, or rather created them, were not only brilliant rock gymnasts but experienced and capable cragsmen.'

Easy Courses :

Deep Ghyll, by the west wall traverse.
Cust's Gully, Great End.
Traverse across Gable Crag.
'Sheep Walk,' Gable Crag.
D Gully, Pike's Crag.
Broad Stand.
Needle Gully.
'Slab and Notch' Route, Pillar Rock.
Great End Central Gully (ordinary ways).
South-east Gully, Great End.

Moderate Courses :

C Gully, Pike's Crag.
A Gully, Pike's Crag.
Westmorland Crag, Great Gable.
Penrith Climb.
Scawfell Chimney.
Deep Ghyll (ordinary route).
Scawfell Pinnacle (short way up).
West Climb, Pillar Rock.
Raven Crag Chimney, Great Gable.
Bottle-shaped Pinnacle Ridge.
Gable Crag Central Gully (ordinary way).
Pendlebury Traverse Route, Pillar Rock.
Combe Ghyll.
Walla Crag Gully.
Arrowhead Branch Gully.
Professor's Chimney.
Needle Ridge.
Arrowhead Ridge Traverse from East Side.
Pavey Ark Gullies.
Eagle's Nest Ridge (ordinary way).

Difficult Courses :

Deep Ghyll West Wall Climb.

Great End Central Gully (chimney finish)

Pillar Rock by Right Pisgah.

The Doctor's Chimney.

Pillar Rock by Left Pisgah.

Gable Crag Central Gully (direct finish).

Oblique Chimney.

Gable Needle.

Arrowhead Ridge (direct climb).

Kern Knotts Chimney.

Doe Crag Great Gully.

Eagle's Nest Ridge by the Ling Chimney.

Pillar Rock by the Great Chimney.

The B Chimney, Pike's Crag.

Scawfell Pinnacle by Steep Ghyll.

Keswick Brothers' Climb.

Sergeant Crag Gully (ordinary way).

Mouse Ghyll.

Moss Ghyll (by branch exit).

Pillar Rock (by north face).

Keswick Brothers' Climb, Variation Finish.

Deep Ghyll (by variety routes).

Doe Crag North Gully.

Collier's Climb, Scawfell.

Raven Crag Gully, Glaramara.

Moss Ghyll (by direct finish).

West Jordan Gully, Pillar Rock.

Shamrock Gully (ordinary route).

Engineer's Chimney, Gable Crag.

Kern Knotts West Chimney.

Pisgah Ridge, by the Tennis Court Ledge.

Iron Crag Chimney.

Exceptionally Severe Courses :

Doe Crag Intermediate Gully.

Screes Great Gully (direct).

Shamrock Gully (new route).

Doe Crag Central Chimney.

Scawfell Pinnacle by Deep Ghyll.

Scawfell Pinnacle by Professor's Chimney.

Kern Knotts Crack.
Doe Crag Easter Gully.
North face of Pillar (by hand-traverse).
Sergeant Crag Gully (direct route).
Walker's Gully.
C Gully of the Screes.
Eagle's Nest Ridge.
Scawfell Pinnacle direct from Lord's Rake.

In every expedition the party should be provided with a sufficient length of rope—varying from twenty to fifty feet for two men, thirty to eighty feet for three—according to the character of the climb and the lengths of its individual pitches. It is very unwise to dispense with the rope, even on simple courses; the fact is patent in the Alps that amateurs take a long time to learn how to look after their portion of the rope when busily engaged on rocks; they are apt to leave all such details to the guides in front or behind them, and would do well to practise regular independence in that respect.

Ice-axes are generally necessary during the colder months of the year. They are inconvenient to manipulate on very difficult rocks, whether the climber is going up or down. But in the rapid descent of easy crags, face outwards, they are invaluable as aids to balancing; and steep grass or scree can undoubtedly be descended better with their assistance. The Cumberland crags are too smooth to make *scarpetti* (*Kletterschuhe*) worth trying. These are rope-soled shoes that grip better than nailed boots when the texture of the rock-surface is sufficiently rough, but our expeditions are best made without them.

For more general information on the climbing-kit, and for the best possible advice to those wishing to commence British hill-climbing, the reader is referred to the chapter in the Badminton volume on Mountaineering, discussing 'Hill-climbing in the British Isles.' It was written by Mr. Charles Pilkington, a former President of the Alpine Club, whose last words on the subject may fittingly be quoted in closing this introduction :

'In conclusion, let us sum up the lessons that the mountains of the British Isles can teach us. That they can give healthy exercise, and cultivate in us the power of appreciating the beauties and grandeur of nature, has long been known to the many, but apparently only the few have hitherto recognised what it is the purpose of this chapter to point out to others—namely, that they form a good and safe training ground where men may learn and practise nearly all that is necessary in the art of mountaineering. Amongst them we may learn the proper use of our legs ; the balance of our bodies, and so to regulate our movements that distances may be traversed and heights scaled with the least possible expenditure of force. We can learn to discriminate between the real and apparent angle and difficulty of a steep mountain face, how to judge of pace and distance, and to steer by map and compass even in the worst weather. We may learn to climb difficult rocks, to avoid dislodging loose stones, and to guard against those dangers that are peculiar to grassy mountains. We can practise carrying a pack, and to a great extent learn the use of the ice-axe and rope, and something also of the varying conditions and appearance of snow. We can cultivate perseverance, courage, the quiet uncomplaining endurance of hardships, and last, but not least important, those habits of constant care and prudence without which mountaineering ceases to be one of the finest sports in the world, and may degenerate into a gambling transaction with the forces of nature, with human life for the stake.'

ROCK-CLIMBING

CHAPTER I

PIKE'S CRAG

THE Pikes of Scawfell are bold and picturesque, but their precipices are slight and climbers can find but little on them that needs the use of a rope. One genuine exception must be made in favour of Pike's Crag, the rock that guards the Pikes end of Mickledore. Here a good deal of practice may be obtained, and although in comparison with Scawfell Crag over the way we may feel that everything is in miniature, yet the quality of the work is good and some of the pitches really severe. Few people seem to have troubled to examine the detail of the cliff until September, 1894, when Messrs. Fowler and Wilberforce spent a few days on it, and prepared the effective diagram of the lines of route that they subsequently transferred to the Wastdale book.

The crag is visible from the road near the head of Wastwater, and its three chimneys show up as black recesses of inviting steepness and difficulty. These retain their interesting appearance all along the walk up Brown Tongue, and it is surprising that at Hollow Stones everybody turns off to the right towards Deep Ghyll, when straight ahead they cannot but observe the opportunity for novelty that Pike's Crag can offer them.

Between the Pulpit rock that overlooks the Mickledore screes and the main mass of the Pikes is a little *col* or neck that can be reached with ease from either side. A gully runs up to it behind the Pulpit from the Mickledore screes, with no difficulties whatever to obstruct the walker. Another (D) leads to the same spot from the Lingmell side, starting near the foot of the great buttress of the Horse and Man rock, and boasting of two pitches. Between D and a scree gully well away to the left lie the three chimneys, A, B, and C, and the best climbing of these crags is here concentrated.

It is true that we can get some pleasant scrambling up the outside of the Pulpit. A grass gully shows well in the illustration, close to the right-hand edge of the picture. The square tower of rock to which its left branch leads overlooks the D gully and offers fair sport. There are probably a few interesting problems in the short gullies leading from D towards the Horse and Man ridge. But to cover the best ground in a single expedition I can recommend the ascent of A and descent by C, then the direct climb up the right branch of B and a return down the two pitches in the D gully. Such was an afternoon's work that I was advised to undertake when inquiring

PLATE I.

THE PIKE'S CRAG GULLIES.

AA is about 300 feet high.

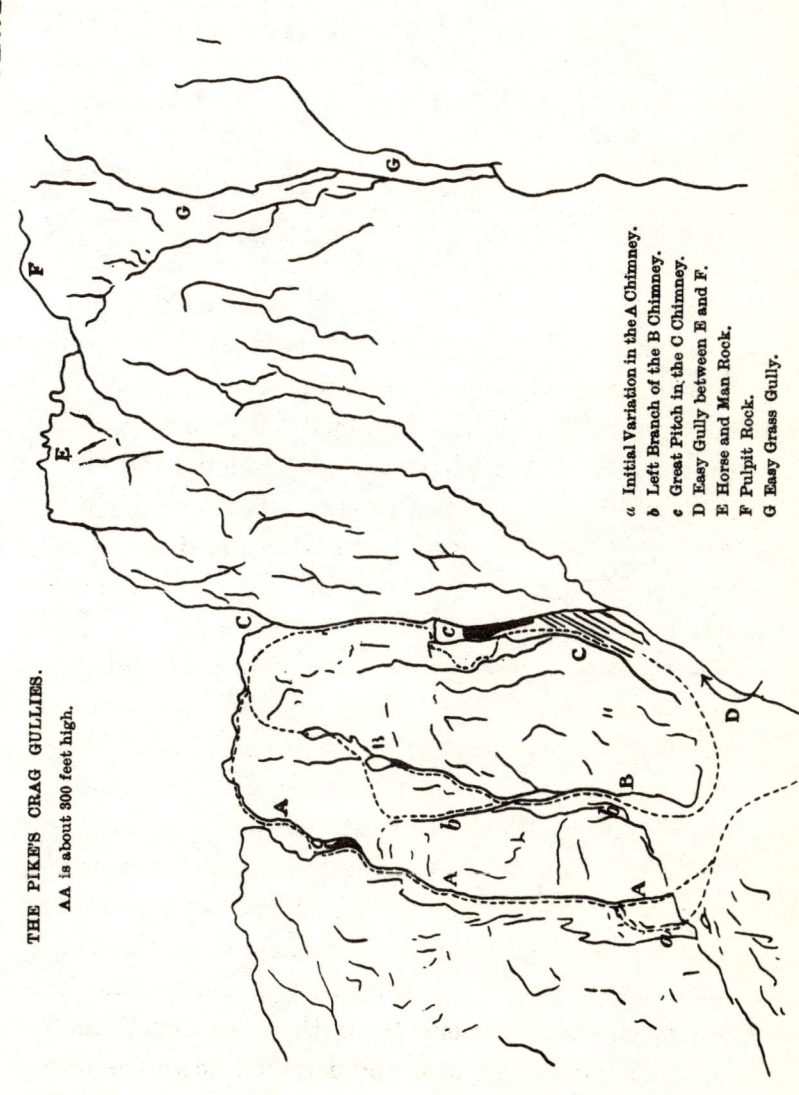

a Initial Variation in the A Chimney.
b Left Branch of the B Chimney.
c Great Pitch in the C Chimney.
D Easy Gully between E and F.
E Horse and Man Rock.
F Pulpit Rock.
G Easy Grass Gully.

of those who knew best how to gain a general knowledge of Pike's Crag. My companion was unac-
quainted with Lake District climbing ; it was his first
day in Wastdale, and during our walk homewards,
after following as rigidly as we could the directions
given us, he was reluctantly compelled to admit
that Cumberland climbing had good points that he
had never hitherto attributed to it.

We bore up from Hollow Stones directly towards
the A chimney, over a good deal of rough ground and
an occasional snowslope. It is the longest climb of
the three, and the hand-and-foot work commenced at
once. A block at the bottom, some fifteen feet in
height, was turned by a vertical crack on the left, with
excellent holds on the side wall. An easier way is by
the right, up a series of steep, wet, and mossy ledges.
This block was crowned by long tufted grass, and more
moss in the bed of the gully indicated clearly that we
were not on a much frequented route to Scawfell
Pikes. A few feet higher we noticed a grass terrace
stretching across the face of the crags to the right.
There proved to be several such terraces on the same
buttress between us and the B chimney, and we
concluded that it would be possible to climb up from
one to the other and so avoid the chimneys altogether.
Soon our route became steeper and careful clambering
was necessary. The gully was narrow and its walls
smooth, and no chance of further side-exit was open
to us. Then came the first genuine pitch, in three
portions of increasing severity, though the hardest

is not in any way difficult or dangerous. We worked first over a small boulder, then a bigger one followed, and we were brought to a standstill at the entrance of a narrow cave. We decided in favour of the right wall, which showed good holds up near the level of the roof. It looked a bad bit to surmount, but when once the right leg of the climber had been swung on to a sloping ledge on the wall, it was only needful to edge along towards the jammed boulder and step off into the bed of the gully again. The whole pitch is about thirty feet high. Walking up the scree that now presented itself, we were rather disagreeably impressed by the appearance of the second pitch that confronted us. It was a mossy wall about ten feet high, and water streaming down it gave us but little hope of continuing the climbing beyond it with dry garments. Nevertheless the reality was not so objectionable. The wall stretched from side to side of the gully and offered many routes up. Taking a course to the right of the middle, we found small footholds beneath the moss that gave the chance of using the fingers and toes only. Clammy embracing we avoided, and our satisfaction on reaching the top was altogether disproportionate to the actual difficulty we had overcome, and will be unappreciated by those who tackle the gully in drier weather. It seems to be still better to work up the left corner.

Forty feet higher we could see the third and last pitch. The gully is now very much more open. We made a digression on the right again, and peered inquisitively down the hole at the top of the B chimney—the hole that was said to discriminate nicely between a thin man and a thick. The buttress was considerably broken about here, and offered admirable scrambling of a heterogeneous description ; but we had yet one more stage in our own direct course, and returned to finish it. Several boulders had combined to form another cave, whose interior appeared to be rather complicated—judging by the number of times I knocked my head in exploring its upper regions. We tried hard to force a route up the right wall, but after twenty minutes had been wasted in futile attempts we decided to take the regulation route to the left, and leave the variation for another day that might find us there with an ice-axe. The left wall is sufficiently provided with holds to make the climb easy ; but at the top there were several stones to be passed that report said were in a shaky condition. We were not troubled by them, and after passing over, a glance at the screes that remained above gave assurance that the presence or absence of a few loose stones at the head of the pitch would be quite fortuitous.

After a short halt called for photographic purposes we made for the head of the C gully, the next to the west that actually reaches the sky-line when viewed from below. It was nearly all scree at a steep angle, and we had good reason to be thankful that no exploring parties were further down. There were two or three places passed in our descent where the craggy bed of the gully jutted out through the layer of loose stones, and at such spots, though no actual climbing was necessary, the danger of one man bombarding the other with projectiles made us both proceed with an excess of caution. The one difficulty in the gully, which we were now preparing to descend, is by far the finest looking pitch on Pike's Crag. A large boulder with square edges roofs in a cavern thirty feet high; a stream of water pouring down the gully spreads over the boulder, and forms a thin curtain of spray stretching from side to side of the cave entrance. The two walls of the gully are black and glistening, the floor of the cave is slippery, and slopes steeply down to the foot of the ghyll. The only safe way up or down the pitch is by a series of ledges in a square recess on the left, well marked in the opposite illustration.

We were ignorant of the character of the climbing here, but there was no resisting the conclusion forced upon us by a peep over the edge of the pitch, that the recess on our right offered us the only chance of descent. The ledges were tufted with thick grass that now and again threatened to give way. But on the whole we felt very safe, and when the actual corner of the recess was reached, the difficulties vanished and we had a simple traverse back towards the waterfall. The descent of six or eight feet to the foot of the fall was partially under the spray, but haste on such slippery ground was out of the question, and we moved one at a time with a

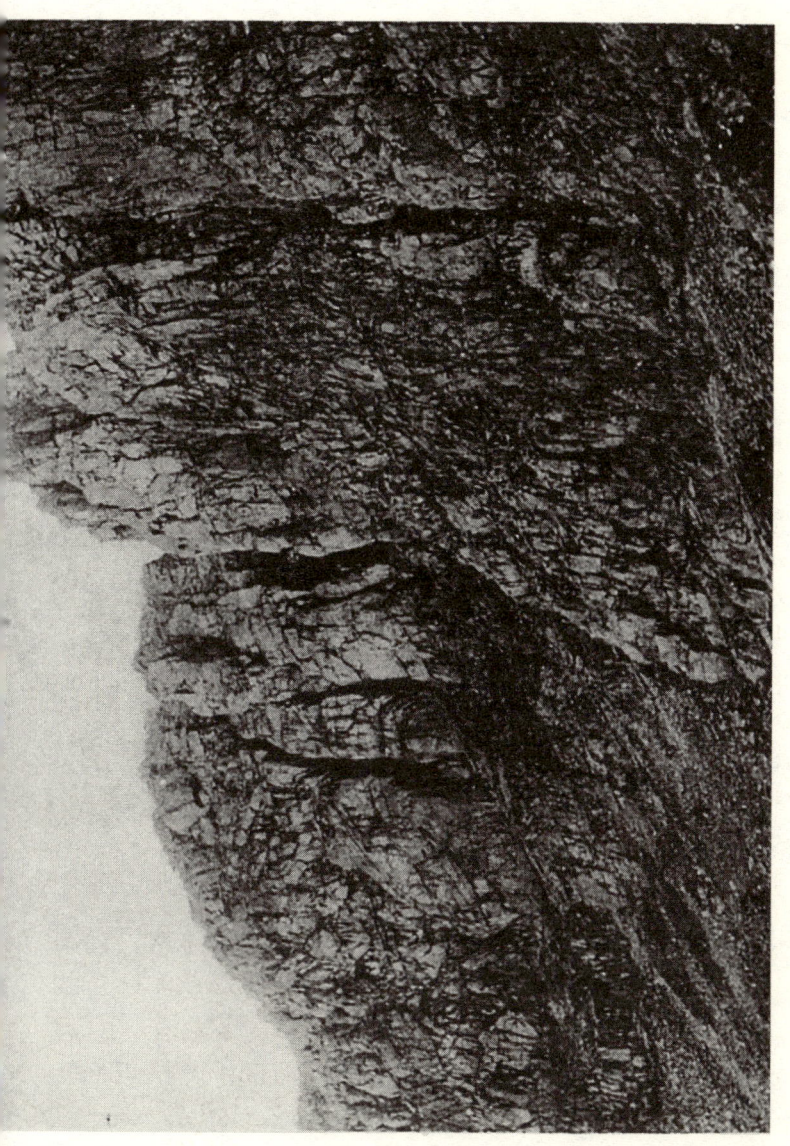

G. P. Abraham & Sons, Photos.

Keswick

THE PIKE'S CRAG GULLIES

solemn indifference to the damping influences around us, that might have argued a whole day's previous exposure and the absence of a vestige of dry clothing. We had a steep slide down the snow banked up at the foot of the gully, and then picked a way across to the B chimney, the centre of the series and the most attractive.

A and C may be reasonably called easy. They are not too hard for muscular novices, and are comparatively safe. But the central chimney is decidedly stiff, and should not be indiscriminately recommended with the others. It is very narrow all the way to the jammed stone at the top; it is about as difficult to get out, when half-way up, as it is to continue the direct ascent, and suitable belaying for the leader or his followers cannot be found at the hardest parts of the climb. I tried the chimney once when there was a considerable quantity of water coming down, and was compelled to give it up : it is probable that even with a second man to help me I could not have managed it.

We found our way safely to the entrance of our chimney and started up. Almost immediately we passed the branch gully on the left. It looks very formidable, and indeed its first pitch is undoubtedly hard. It consists of a two-storied cave, the first floor composed of three jammed stones, which are passed by backing up the crack and traversing outwards. The second pitch is of a simpler character, consisting of a cave that can be passed on either side. We had no designs on this variation, and were contented to throw a casual glance towards the lower obstacle as we proceeded up the rocky bed of our central chimney. Our field of view soon became very limited, for the clean-cut parallel walls on either side were scarcely five feet apart, and the average slope of the gully exceded forty-five degrees. During the first hundred feet the work was distinctly safe and easy, but a glance backward at the point whence we had started, seemingly the first stop in the event of our falling, made us both inclined to imagine dangers in our way. The side walls in intense gloom formed a fitting frame to the narrow picture of the distant sunlit fells. The general aspect of the situation closely resembled that of the upper half of Collier's climb on Scawfell, and of the Oblique Chimney on Gable Crag, though in each of those cases the chimney is at a considerable angle to the vertical, whereas here the fissure in the rocks is almost perpendicular. We were a little perplexed by some ice that had frozen in large rounded knobs to a thickness of eight or ten inches over a steep six feet of the gully. An axe would have summarily disposed of any icicles of doubtful security, but we had not expected any such evidences of cold and were unprovided. The ice was not absolutely continuous ; here and there we could kick out levels for our feet, and to our relief the trouble was passed in a few minutes. Then came the worst bit of the ascent—the scene of my discomfiture eighteen months before. First came a vertical wall stretching across the gully, and rising twenty feet above our somewhat insecure standing. Beyond that the gully sloped evenly to the dark recesses of a cave, the jammed boulder of which almost appeared vertically above our heads. We mounted an upright block at the foot of the wall, and prospected for holds. None were visible. I peered at the sides in search of scratches, which would show whether the earlier party or parties had backed up the chimney. No! they had not availed themselves of that process. Then, with the conviction that an indirect way must exist, we examined the walls a few feet below the pitch, and at last hit upon a way of mounting higher. I was belayed by a rope passing round the upright block already referred to, and proceeded to walk along the horizontal edge of a thin crack on the right wall, leaning across to the other side of the gully for general support on the hands. I had implicit trust in the rope and the man at the other end of it, or the manœuvre would have given me agonies of apprehension. Just as the second step was being made along the crack, its thin edge broke away under my foot and I slipped a few feet down the gully, till the rope tightened and brought me to a stop. A second attempt was more successful. The edge was followed till it expanded into a respectable foothold, and then, holding myself straight, I was able to reach good ledges for the hands. It was now easy to stride across to the left wall and climb directly upwards

along its crest to a platform large enough for both
of us; hither my companion followed me, adopting
almost the same tactics and taking but half the time.
We were now virtually out of the gully, and found
the sunshine pleasant after so much darkness. But
the joy that might have attended our remaining
efforts in working up to the head of the chimney was
marred by the reflection that we had not conquered
the chief difficulty; we had only avoided it. This is
right and proper for snow-climbers, but distinctly
unorthodox for cragsmen. Our doubts grew as we
advanced, and at last I proposed to descend again
and settle them finally. This suggestion was met
with a very prompt approval, and ten minutes later
found me at the foot of the vertical wall again. It
did not look any easier, and I am not prepared to
say how narrowly I missed a second failure. After
leaving the upright block the scanty holds soon disappeared, and with some desperate struggling I
found myself backing up the chimney with the feet
thrust hard against the left wall. Both sides seemed
dangerously smooth, but cautious wriggling for a
distance of two or three feet brought a handhold
within reach, and the top of the wall was gained.
The only other ascent known to me was by a man
with a singularly long reach, and in some marvellous
way he managed to climb the wall without any
backing up.

Thence to the cave was fairly easy after a few
mossy loose stones had been flung down, and the

finish was effected by a neat little ledge along the left wall, passing out just at the edge of the pitch. The hole through the cave is not so small as the first investigators imagined ; the trouble in passing through is due to its crookedness, but the name of the chimney is generally supposed to indicate with proper remoteness the garment that is here threatened with a complete inversion.

We hurried across the top of C gully and round the Horse and Man to the Pulpit rock. The D gully had a great deal of snow in it, and we indulged in sundry glissades. The snow was not too hard nor the angle too great, otherwise ice-axes would have been necessary. The upper pitch was passed on our left with perfect ease. Then further snow led to the lower pitch, a much more imposing sight. Two sharp-edged boulders of immense size formed a cave. On the side of the Pulpit rock there seemed to be no chance of passing it. The other side, though mossy, might easily be made to go. In our descent we kept a little further away, and came down ledge after ledge with excellent holds to the foot of the pitch. Then more glissading brought us down to the open fell again. We spent a quarter of an hour watching with much interest a party coming down Scawfell Pinnacle by Steep Ghyll, and having seen them safely into the lower part of the ghyll, where the steady click of the leader's axe intimated slow progress over ice-covered rocks, we turned our backs to the fell and moved leisurely homewards.

CHAPTER II

DEEP GHYLL. THE GREAT CHIMNEY AND PROFESSOR'S CHIMNEY

Deep Ghyll.—This will remain for long a favourite resort of climbers, partly because the two pitches are always interesting and may be turned in so many different ways, partly because the gully gathers annually a big snow drift, which can generally be relied upon between Christmas and Easter to afford some practice in the use of the ice-axe, and partly because the rock scenery is of the finest character throughout. The ghyll has been familiar to the visitors of Scawfell for many years. It was first ascended in March, 1886, by Messrs. Geoffrey Hastings and Slingsby, and an interesting account of the expedition appeared in the 'Alpine Journal.' It had been descended twice before, in 1882, by Messrs. Mumm and King, with heavy snow blocking the pitches, and in 1884 by Mr. Haskett Smith. The quickest way of reaching the foot of the ghyll is to walk up Brown Tongue till within a couple of hundred feet of the level of Hollow Stones. It is here unnecessary to keep straight over towards the centre of Mickledore, for a shallow depression to the right of Brown Tongue may be traversed

DEEP GHYLL—FIRST PITCH

obliquely upwards, and the scree struck close to the well-defined edge of the lower crags of Scawfell. Thence it is best to keep close under the cliffs, following an easy gradient up to the Lord's Rake. This is the large scree gully passing up to the right, under the main mass of Scawfell. The scree forms at the foot of the Lord's Rake the usual fan-shaped talus, which here stretches down towards Hollow Stones. In summer it may occasionally be worth while making directly up the centre of the scree.

Just opposite the corner round which one turns into the Lord's Rake a rather slightly marked gully starts up from the side of the rake. It becomes better defined a few yards higher, and leads directly into Steep Ghyll. Almost at the same spot a ledge is to be noticed passing round to the left of the huge wall fronting us at this corner. This is the start of the Rake's Progress, the happy name given to the well-known terrace leading to Mickledore. We shall have further occasion to allude to this ledge, but we now pass up the Lord's Rake till in a few feet we come to a magnificent gully on our left, recognizable under any conditions except the most snowy by the cave at its foot. A fine view of Deep Ghyll and its surroundings may be obtained by scrambling up to the low ridge that faces us as we look outwards from the cave. The ridge is somewhat broken up, and the terrible accident that caused the death of Professor Milnes Marshall at this spot must be a warning to any who wander up without thought of danger.

The orthodox route up the first pitch in Deep Ghyll is by the cave and chimney. It is the most interesting way, and probably in dry clean weather it is the easiest. When the chimney is cased with ice the route may become impossible. In that case a recess in the right wall (right, of course, when looking up at the climb) is often taken as a winter emergency exit; for although the holds are slight in summer, loose stones well bound up make it quite feasible in frosty weather.

The hardest way up the pitch is by the thin cleft between the big boulder and the left wall.

Passing up for about 150 feet we find a steep slope of rock occupying the left half of the gully. The scree in the other half leads up into a cave whose black rectangular aperture may have been observed from the Lord's Rake ridge. The cave is formed by the ubiquitous jammed boulder, and no through route can be effected. A thin chimney cuts between the rock slope and the huge vertical left wall that rises with scarcely a break to the Low Man on the Scawfell Pinnacle. This chimney constitutes the easiest and safest route over the second pitch. On the right face an irregular ledge leads to a larger chimney (Robinson's), which with some trouble can be followed till a level about twenty feet above the top of the cave pitch is reached. Thence a small terrace offers an easy promenade to the upper bed of the gully. A third way of taking the difficulty has been found; indeed, it is the most obvious way, though much the hardest. It is to climb the left wall of the cave entrance, and then wriggle up between the rock slope and the cave boulder.

There are many pleasant reminiscences of parties in Deep Ghyll. The hardest struggle I ever had with the first pitch was on Christmas Day, 1897. The rocks were badly glazed, and though we had no trouble in penetrating to the inmost recesses of the cave, we could find no easy way of getting higher. We were loth to try, seeing that one of our party had, with a mistaken philanthropy, loaded his rücksack with preserved fruit, prunes, and Carlsbad plums, and proceeded forthwith to dignify our primitive lunch with these unwonted luxuries. A halt called to consume a beef sandwich may be quickly terminated—and that, moreover, without a sense of sorrow, unless the beef is very bad—but those who know Carlsbad plums will realise how easily we were demoralised by their seductiveness, and how much we preferred to sit in our cave and argue on complicated topics with the plum-box open. But the owner was a man of some resolution, and heroically vowed that we should see no more of the plums till we reached a small recess at the top of Moss Ghyll, where we should ensconce ourselves after climbing the gully. So we made a start at once. The back way out of the cave promised well at first. It showed no trace of ice, but on emerging from the chimney (at the spot where the lower figure is shown in the view facing p. 12), and looking straight down

to the entrance of the cave, it was found that a
thin sheet of ice covered all the rocks. Generally
speaking it would be better to let the rocks alone on
such an occasion—in fact always, unless Carlsbad
plums are at stake. Then, perhaps, the second man
may be held firmly by the rope from behind while
he gives the leader a shoulder. This help is of no
use unless the leader can venture to trust the icy
handhold above him, by which he is to swing round
the awkward corner to the right. Some such scheme
our party devised, after many futile attempts to fix
an axe firmly as a foothold, and the leader dragged
himself up the glazed surface to the deep snow
above. In the ordinary state of things, be it
remembered that where the climber emerges from
the hole, he has first to stride round to a small ledge
on the right. He can use as a take-off the rough
surface of the boulder, and can reach a rigid
handhold of small dimensions but good shape.
Thence to the top of the pitch is easy scrambling,
though care is needed.

The snow in the gully was in grand condition
for kicking steps, and after the last man had been
brought up the pitch in safety we marched to the
upper cave and discussed the question of route over
the second pitch. The direct way was ruled out of
court at once, for its largest ledges are but half an
inch wide, and ice on these rendered them useless.
With a keen recollection of our trouble down below,
we thought of the Robinson Chimney on the right,

which is quitted by crossing on to a slabby rock that slopes down towards the centre of the gully. With ice on this an attempt to force the way up would more likely find us shooting over to the foot of the cave. Such a finish to our little day would no doubt exactly coincide with the anticipations of our more sanguine relatives and friends, but for the moment we had to consider each other's feelings and I suggested the easy way up. There was a smiling unanimity of agreement in the party which pleased me far, very far more than a hundred strictly impossible ascents. We descended the gully again to the foot of the rock slope, and rounded into the little chimney. Things went very well for a few feet. But as we rose the ice became more troublesome, until it was necessary to chip it away from each diminutive ledge, and to proceed upwards with the utmost caution. The first part finished with a little snow patch twenty feet above the top of the cave boulder and the bed of the ghyll. Some years before, when first I visited Deep Ghyll, we had found it impossible to climb directly upwards from this point, and a man was let down by the rope into the ghyll. He cut steps up until he had obtained a higher level than the others waiting, and then induced them to traverse out a bit and jump into the snow below. The process was possible only with a long rope. Here we could all rest and contemplate the rock slab opposite which finishes the Robinson Chimney. Forty or fifty feet higher we

could see, well marked out by the snow, the upper
traverse that enables a careful walker to pass up
Deep Ghyll without any hand-and-foot work.   It is
readily accessible from the Lord's Rake, a few feet
higher than the ordinary entrance to Deep Ghyll,
and leads at an easy angle to a point in the main
gully some hundred feet above the second pitch.

Looking up at the left wall of the Ghyll we could
see that our slender chimney was but the beginning
of a long crack that cut obliquely into the wall, and
curled upwards in a fine sweep of eighty feet
towards the summit of the Low Man.   The curtain
of rock that closed in the crack on its right hand
made our next few yards rather troublesome, for it
encroached on our ledge and rendered the work too
open.   Facework is always more trying than chimney
climbing, especially when ice is about.   But the
leader's recollection of the ease with which this part
could be overcome in summer time divested it of all
its fancied terrors and perhaps of some of its real
dangers, and he had therefore a better time of it than
his companions, whose extremities were somewhat
benumbed by their patient waiting in awkward
places, and whose activities were confined to their
vivid imaginations.   All actual danger was over
when a horizontal ledge was reached well above the
centre-level of the gully, which we followed with
ease to the broken rocks that almost form a third
pitch for Deep Ghyll.

Here the pleasantest way of finishing the day

was to cut steps in the snow up the central gully, the angle gradually steepening from 35° to 55° at the top. That way we therefore took, and were soon enjoying the plums. But a rise of a few feet will show the Professor's Chimney immediately to the left, cutting deeply into the rock between the Scawfell Pinnacle on the left and Pisgah on the right, and terminating at a fine-looking notch, 'The Jordan,' in the sky-line. Exactly opposite, on the right-hand side of the ghyll, is the Great Chimney, a black and formidable square-walled recess crowned by a jammed boulder. This was for a long time regarded as impossible and scarcely ever attacked, but at last it yielded to the combined ingenuity of Messrs. Blake and Southall, and has since shown itself to be very amenable when approached with due precaution.

First pitch, New route.—The Christmas Day of 1896 was very windy and cold. Our party had fought continually against the weather all the way to Deep Ghyll, and inasmuch as we had only the previous day arrived at Wastdale our limbs were scarcely fit for such a desperate grind. I had the pleasurable responsibility of guiding a lady, Mrs. H., who had been persuaded to accompany her husband on a winter excursion. We had a great deal of very soft snow to get through on our way up, and I was looking forward to a long halt in the lower cave, where we should at least be protected from the wind and snow. Great was our distress when we found the entrance completely blocked up by a huge

drift. It must have been fully twenty feet deep
in front of the cave, and the prospect was most dis-
heartening. In disgust I clambered up the wall
immediately to the right of the boulder, and at last
managed to reach the aperture leading into the cave
from above. It was festooned with huge icicles, and
at first the entrance looked effectually blocked.
Smashing down the ice with the energy of despair,
the tremendous clatter suggesting to my friends that
of a bull in a hardware shop, I discovered that the
chimney was only iced at its entrance, and that the
upper storey of the cave could be reached. Some
of the others quickly followed, and we found ourselves
in a spacious chamber into which the great heap of
snow had scarcely encroached. This was delightful.
We threw ourselves into the drift that blocked the
main entrance, and cut away at it with vigour till at
last we had tunnelled through to the daylight. The
biggest man of the party yet remained outside and we
persuaded him to insert his legs into the aperture.
Without giving him time to change his mind we seized
his boots and hauled hard. For one dread moment
we thought him jammed for ever, but immediately
afterwards we found ourselves lying on our backs
in the cave with a yawning opening in the snow-
drift, the while our massive friend measured his
diminished circumference with a loop of rope. The
others then came in and made themselves at home on
ropes, ice-axes, and other people's cameras. We were
a party of ten, large enough to be a merry one.

G. P. Abraham & Sons, Photos.

SCAWFELL PINNACLE AND THE PROFESSOR'S CHIMNEY

Keswick

(Face page 20)

Our surroundings were weird and savage, unlike the British notions for a Christmas Day, but I remember that we behaved like civilized people in perhaps one respect. We discussed the year's literature. Fancy Troglodytes discussing 'Trilby'! Then it occurred to us that our feet were very cold, and that we should not have much daylight for climbing if we waited longer. Our intention had been to climb Deep Ghyll in two separate parties, by the ordinary way. But the drift suggested a trial of the crack up the left-hand side of the first pitch. The snow would serve as a high take-off, and also a good cushion to soften the fall if the leader were destined to fail. The first difficulty was to get safely into the crack; then it was found that the holds were very scarce, and the recess somewhat too constricted to allow any bracing across from one side to the other.

Think of a foothold; double it. Put your whole weight on to it as you straighten out. Take away the hold you thought of, and you will find yourself wondering how you got there. In some such vague way are very bad bits climbed, and while gasping for breath at the top the climber usually feels that it was the worst place he has ever been in. Seriously, however, this route is severe at all times. In summer the drift is absent, but with rocks slightly wet, as they usually are in that corner, the effort of working upwards is extreme. It is probably best to keep one's back to the boulder all the way up.

My section of the party came up first. We were

very cold, and some fear that Mrs. H. would have
frost-bite prompted us to change our minds concerning Deep Ghyll, and to traverse away to the left
towards the foot of Steep Ghyll. The others came
up the pitch by our route, led in good style by
Mr. H. V. Reade. They expressed regret at our
untimely departure, and worked laboriously up the
ghyll. It was ungenerous of us that evening to gloat
over the fact that they had had a terribly cold time
of it higher up.

Our route out of the ghyll was known to Mr. Haskett Smith in 1882. It is not often used, and, indeed,
in winter it offers certain risks of its own. Starting
from the top of the pitch we bore directly down towards the entrance to Lord's Rake, and when within a
reasonable distance of the snow, jumped down to it,
sinking in up to our necks. Hurrying down to
Hollow Stones as fast as our limbs would carry us,
we endured the pangs of returning circulation in our
hands and feet, and finished the descent in exhilaration, and with a sense of having well earned our
share of the Christmas festivities.

Second pitch, Variety routes.—A description of
the direct way over the second pitch is scarcely
necessary. The leader must start just at the entrance to the cave, and work up the corner to the
recess between the jammed stone and the cave
boulder. The holds are minute, and the necessary
stress on the finger tips excessive. He should try it
first when there is snow below him, and with his

second arranged to pay out twenty feet of rope from the innermost corner of the cave. If the leader is destined to slip, it will take place at the point where the slope suddenly becomes easier, for then his fingers are fatigued, his centre of gravity wants for the first time an onward as well as an upward motion, and his foothold will fail him at the crisis. Therefore his centre of gravity will describe the ordinary parabola back into the snow, and the tremendous jerk on the rope will make the man wonder whether the remains of his centre of gravity are worth retaining. Supposing that he has safely rounded this awkward edge, the utmost caution is necessary for six feet till the scree is reached. Then comes the trouble of manipulating the rope without shaking down stones on the next man who is to pass up. If the leader wants the rope to be in actual tension on his account, he has a hard task in bracing himself firmly without dislodging the scree from under his feet. This trouble of course is minimised when good firm snow can be cut to supply him a footing.

On the whole this direct route over the second pitch may be regarded as too risky, except under the best possible circumstances—such, for example, as existed when Messrs. Robinson and Creak found the two pitches in Deep Ghyll entirely covered with snow, and an easy route available straight up the middle from bottom to top. Then there was no second pitch !

The chimney on the right is excellent, but is not a course open to beginners. It is in two parts. At

the two places where it must be quitted the route
lies up the buttress on the left.   I recall the remark
of an unenterprising follower as he looked up at the
vertical walls above him ; he had been in difficulty
down below and was inquiring my intentions.   His
patience had been all but exhausted, and he said so,
adding : 'It is not merely steep parts that so upset
me.   They can be borne, but I don't like this infernal
dangling.'   The discussion was diverted into a side
issue, as to whether the adjective was permissible, but
in justice to his memory—he never visited the Lakes
again—be it said that very few climbers like the
sensation of suspense.

The Great Chimney.—The position of this has
already been defined.   Its ascent affords the best
finish to the Deep Ghyll climb if snow is absent from
the gully and the screes are wearisome.   The aspect
of the chimney is most forbidding from below, and
there is probably but one way of vanquishing it.   I
had been told how the first party had proceeded
up it, and had also heard an account of their
defeat at a second attempt.   There is much likelihood of defeat even when one knows the way, by
reason of the awkwardness of the corner that needs
careful negotiation, and I am bound to admit that a
first ascent rapidly accomplished may help the climber
very little in his second attempt.   At the time of my
visit the rocks were warm and dry, our party of three
had just come up Collier's Climb, and were keen on
completing their knowledge of Scawfell by making

for the only chimney with which they were un-
acquainted. We all gathered together high up in the
recess, and then, when the rope had been satisfactorily
arranged for a long run out, I started working up the
right wall by some small but strong ledges till the
roof of the cavern was approached. Then it became
necessary to work out of the cave and round by the
jammed stone. Just outside was a ledge within
reach for the hands; but to work the body up the
corner so as to kneel on the ledge was very awkward,
the main trouble arising from the depressing effect of
the corner of the jammed stone which forced head
and shoulders almost to the level of one's feet. The
prayerful attitude realized, I could anchor myself a
little by looping the rope round a stone in the roof
and had then only to stand up and clamber between
the boulder and the living rock, trusting to footholds
on the latter. A few feet landed me in safety and the
others came up like smoke, carrying my cap that the
gymnastics round the corner had shaken down to them.
A short scree and a few easy rocks completed the
gully, which both in regard to the aspect from above
and to the form of its one great difficulty reminded us
of the Shamrock Gully over in Ennerdale. The main
differences in these two pitches are that the Shamrock
Gully pitch looks easier but proves to be harder, also
that it has less cave and more boulder. Neither
pitch is suitable for beginners.

By walking across to the foot of the lower part
of Professor's Chimney—a name, by the way, given

first to the easy exit on the right of Pisgah—a pitch
of some severity can be taken or left, as fancy
dictates. The platform above this pitch leads well
into the chimney and the climb again gets stiff. A
direct ascent of the pinnacle is probably feasible
from this level, but the first thirty feet will need
the utmost enterprise on the part of the daring
aspirant to fresh honours in this well-explored
region.

The Professor's Chimney. — This looks
almost as difficult as the Great Chimney opposite, but
is more a test of style than skill, the only trouble
being that of loose rocks. Though unworthy of
perfect confidence at all times, it may become most
friendly in times of frost; many loose stones occur
that can be safely *pressed* though dangerous to *pull*,
so that with a slight modification of style they are
rendered highly useful. Then of course two loose
stones may share one's weight when one cannot
take it.

The introduction of all this elementary practical
mountaineering is due to my recollection of a huge
stone that came away near the top of the Professor's
Chimney when my party were coming up it. I was
out of harm's way on the Jordan above, but in
wrestling with the last part of the chimney, a portion
that slightly overhangs, the second in the party pulled
away the rock. It bounded down, ricochetting from
side to side, and for a moment placed the startled
climbers in imminent peril.

G. P. Abraham & Sons, Photos.

Keswick

SCAWFELL CRAGS FROM THE PULPIT ROCK

(Face page 26)

In conclusion, just a word to pedestrians who have come out to climb only by telescope. The ascent of Scawfell from the Lord's Rake may be safely and rapidly accomplished by following its lead past the entrance to Deep Ghyll.

The best plan is to keep as straight a course on the scree as the up-and-down nature of the Rake will permit, with the steep rocks immediately on the left. A pinnacle is almost at once passed on the right that in former times was oft mistaken by the unlearned for the great Scawfell Pinnacle, more especially because a cairn had been erected on its crest as a decoy, by the wily discoverer of the true pinnacle. Then it becomes necessary to descend a little, taking care not to slither down to the right with the loose *debris*. After a few yards the slope again rises for a while, and an easy gully shortly discloses itself on the left, following which the tourist will find himself in a few minutes on the stony plateau that at an easy inclination travels away westward to Burnmoor. In clear weather he will see the huge cairn that crowns the top of Scawfell, at a slight elevation above the top of the gully, and can safely make a bee-line for it. Climbers often descend by this route in bad weather when the Broad Stand appears to elude their anxious search.

The quickest way down from Scawfell is to make for the head of this gully, and then, instead of descending, leave it on the right and follow the edge of cliff straight towards the head of Wastwater;

where the edge is deflected to the left, a scree-run
to the foot of Brown Tongue takes us over rough
but safe ground to the diminutive footpath that
starts at the stone wall.   It should be learnt first in
clear weather, if possible, as there is no royal road
to safety for the befogged novice on the fells.

CHAPTER III

THE RAKE'S PROGRESS AND CERTAIN SHORT CLIMBS NEAR IT

The Rake's Progress.—This happy title dates from about 1881. The Progress is an easy ledge leading from the lower end of the Lord's Rake to the point where the Mickledore ridge joins the main mass of Scawfell. It runs along the base of the vertical walls of this mountain, and though at a great elevation above the huge Mickledore hollow, is scarcely entitled to the thrilling adjective *vertigineuse* of the French climbing vocabulary. Yet it is capable of carrying one into the finest situations; and even the hardened expert, with his steady head and well-trained muscles, realises while on it that danger is hovering about him at every step, though it does not touch him. Years ago I read, in Freshfield's 'Italian Alps,' of the Pelmo traverse in the Ampezzo Dolomites, and memory seized on the Rake's Progress as the nearest approach to it that mountain experience had then afforded. Let there be no rise on the Mickledore; make the Progress thrice as long, and a little more rakish; change the rock from porphyry to magnesian limestone; let the drop below the ledge be a few hundred feet instead of a few score; make it necessary to crawl on all fours in one or two corners, and the resemblance will be perfect! In a few yards after the preliminary scramble on to the ledge, the crags are broken on our right by the short chimney entrances to Steep Ghyll and Moss Ghyll. These cannot be mistaken, inasmuch as they mark the last possible points of attack on these cliffs for one-half of the traverse.

Passing the entrance to Moss Ghyll, to which we must return for the ascent of this fine gully, a steep rise marks the accomplishment of one-third of the course. A little further a thin cleft cuts obliquely up the cliff towards the left. It is wonderfully straight, and the slabs of rock on either side are hopelessly smooth. The crack widens higher up, but until 1897 the terrific simplicity of its lower portion had warned off all who examined it with the view of storming this side of Scawfell. The upper half, reached by an ingenious zig-zag route on the face, is now well known as one of the safest and best climbs on Scawfell. Shortly afterwards we reach a rectangular recess looking as though it had been quarried for a gigantic monolith. Here again the great difficulty of starting up is manifested at a glance, though in the same direction up above the recess is so much more deeply cut and the sides so much nearer to each other that one's safety is assured for the second half of the climb. In this case also, the middle is reached by a slight detour on the left. A few yards further along the Progress are two thin cracks uniting at a height of twenty feet and leading to a platform ten feet higher. Thence a perfectly safe cleft passes

G. P. Abraham & Sons, Photos.

Keswick

The Ascent of the Broad Stand

(Face page 30)

directly up for another forty feet, till a grassy ledge, clearly visible only when marked by snow, takes one easily to the middle of the long chimney. To mount the chimney is an undertaking well within the powers of the average rock-climber, and with the additional merit of being perfectly safe for a party of three.

Such are the Keswick Brothers' Climb and Collier's Climb, two of the best conceived problems of the district and worthy of their discoverers. The lower half of the latter is undeniably severe; even the best have failed at it, and I propose in a separate section to describe an ascent in detail, to point out the method our party adopted to eliminate the risk that the climber is popularly supposed to accept as inevitable, and to indicate how the Keswick Brothers' route enables us to avoid the worst piece altogether.

The next halt we make close to the Mickledore, within thirty-five feet of the end of the Progress. Here a thin cleft, known as Petty's Rift for the last twenty years, leads to a square recess ten feet up, and marks the start of the North or Penrith Climb up the Scawfell crags. These are now only a few score feet above us. The illustration facing page 26 shows how the upper outline of the cliff and the Mickledore ridge approach to within a few feet of each other.

Having reached the Mickledore ridge it is well worth while walking along it to its furthest end, and then bearing to the left on to the Pulpit rock, for the sake of the fine view of the climbs we have just been enumerating. The Eskdale side of Scawfell is terminated by an abrupt vertical cliff that seemingly offers no sort of route for the cragsman. Half way down to the corner of this cliff, a gully cuts deeply into the mountain, and passes upwards at an apparent angle of 45° towards the tops of Moss Ghyll and Collier's Climb.

The gully—Scawfell Chimney or Mickledore Chimney, as it is sometimes distinctively called—has its own peculiar difficulties in wet or snowy weather, but when at its best it may be attacked by comparatively inexperienced men, if they are properly equipped and exercise ordinary precautions. On the other hand, the gully represents the drainage channel for a considerable area, and is usually wet.

Undoubtedly the easiest way from Mickledore up to the ridge facing us is by the Broad Stand. The start is made in the cleft half way between Mickledore and the foot of Scawfell Chimney. Three short pitches, each less than ten feet, take us on to an easy slope that can be followed to the upper part of the chimney. To keep up between the chimney on our left and the steep cliffs to our right is an easy matter in clear weather, till Pisgah appears on our right, the descent into Deep Ghyll straight in front of us, and the cairn-crowned summit of the mountain a hundred yards away towards the left.

This finishes the preliminary survey of the eastern face of Scawfell, during the perusal of which the reader is recommended to examine the diagram facing page 46.

The Broad Stand.

—My first climb in the Lake District was up the Broad Stand. Dr. S. and I had planned a week's walking tour over the Cumberland fells, guided by Baddeley and Jenkinson, and ignorant of the existence of any regular rock practice hereabouts. We walked up from Langdale one Sunday morning in heavy snow to the top of Rossett Ghyll, and then studied the guide book for information concerning the small tarn that lay a few feet beneath us. 'Deep and clear, and good for bathing,' we read; so we bathed. It was long ago, and neither of us has bathed during a snowstorm since. Our feet got benumbed standing on the snow while we were dressing ourselves, and we had much ado to restore circulation. Then as the day advanced and the air cleared a little, it seemed possible that we might find a way up Scawfell Pikes, which, we had read, was the highest point in England. With much ploughing through soft snow, loaded with heavy knapsacks, and supported by but one broken walking stick, we reached the topmost cairn in perfect safety and realised the height of that Easter ambition. Then it was that Dr. S. read aloud to me a thrilling description of the Mickledore chasm, which presented an almost impassable barrier between the Pikes and Scawfell, a terrific gap that only hardy cragsmen of the dales were able to traverse. The ice-cold bath on that Sabbath morn had done much to quench our spirit, but we had partially recovered ourselves, and a burning desire to scale the majestic peak opposite flamed up in each of us simultaneously, and drove us down towards the Pulpit rock that sentinels the Mickledore. The guide-book was not wanting in detail. There were three ways of attacking Scawfell from Mickledore; first the Chimney, then Broad Stand, and then the Lord's Rake. I believe we guessed the position of the chimney correctly, for after all there is something to show for the name; but we were hopelessly at sea with the other two. Dr. S. argued that Lord's Rake sounded so much worse than Broad Stand that we were bound to go for it wherever it might be and however easy its aspect. Nobody at home would believe us if we described a Broad Stand as a vertical wall hundreds of feet in height, glistening with ice, and guarded above by overhanging boulders ready to pulverise the bold invader. On the other hand, the Lord's Rake seemed remotely to suggest Jacob's Ladder, and offered the imagination a goodly choice of adjective and epithet. Where, then, was the Lord's Rake? We had little time to consider, and rapidly decided that the Broad Stand was away down in Eskdale on the left, and the Lord's Rake straight up from Mickledore. Wherein we were wrong, as the previous pages may show the reader. Then we tried to get up the wall just where the Mickledore ridge strikes the cliff, but the cold soon drove us to seek some easier start lower on the left. Thus it was that fate took us to the actual Broad

Stand, up which, inexperienced though we were, we could scarcely help finding the correct route. Place a man at the right starting point, and he will easily find the upward line of least resistance, though not so swiftly as he would trace out the downward line if he slipped.

Twelve yards down from the Mickledore we came to a deep recess in the mountain side, large enough to penetrate if one is not burdened with a knapsack. (A confirmation of the right spot is supplied by a thinner crack six feet lower down the screes.) Wriggling up into the recess and then out on to the slightly sloping platform above it was a matter of only a few seconds, and we then found facing us a wall of from eight to ten feet in height offering very little hand or foothold for a direct attack. But by descending the sloping grassy ledge at its foot we could see some iced ledges (clear rocks show the marks of many boots) that suggested the circumvention of the difficulty. To these we in turn trusted ourselves, and by passing round the somewhat awkward left-hand corner of the wall we found an easy though steep route to its flat top. Then a smaller wall of about seven feet barred the way. It was easier than the last, though in those days the frost had not scooped out the hollow on the edge, and by the help of my comrade's shoulders I reached the summit. The difficulties were obviously over; we could walk up by the right on to the snow slope, above which, as our early inspection from the Pulpit rock showed, there was an easy route to the top of Scawfell. Unfortunately my friend was not up the last step. I could not reciprocate his kindness and offer him my shoulders. We had no rope, and the rocks were all glazed. I had not intended to mention our ropeless condition, but the truth will out sooner or later; neither had we nails in our boots. But apparently we had sense enough to realize that an accident might happen if we tempted Providence any further, and with some sorrow we decided to descend again. We found our way down the Mickledore screes and Brown Tongue to Wastdale, and there learnt that we had tried conclusions with the Broad Stand at its worst. We also learnt that from the top of the third step which I had reached the route lay up the snow slope to the broken rocks, then slightly to the left until the easy part of the chimney could be looked into, then obliquely up to the right over rough ground to the small cairn overlooking Deep Ghyll. Many times since then, rattling down the Broad Stand when the rocks were dry and our party well acquainted with every inch of the ground, have we recalled that Easter Sunday and our first essay of the Broad Stand. There have also been many occasions to remember the golden rule in the descent of these crags. First find the top of the Scawfell Chimney; keep it on the right till its one pitch is just below. Then bear to the left down the grassy slope and hunt for the notch in the top step of the Broad Stand.

The usual thing in a fog is to find oneself down in Eskdale. I remember a photographic friend once leaving his camera at the foot of Deep Ghyll while he went for an hour's round of Lord's Rake, Scawfell Cairn, and the Broad Stand. The dense mountain mists gathered about him at the top, and rendered useless his efforts to steer the true course. That night he discovered himself at Boot, and three days elapsed before he found his camera, suffering from the effects of over-exposure as much as himself.

The North Climb.—This starts at Petty's Rift, already referred to on page 31, about twelve yards from Mickledore along the Rake's Progress. From a distance it looks as though the climb would necessarily include the funnel-shaped gully below the Progress, and the whole aspect of the work is somewhat forbidding. Nevertheless the difficulties are concentrated in the first six feet. When once the climber can get a foot on to the floor of the little square recess, his safety is assured. In the photograph facing page 40 the positions of the three members of the party indicate sufficiently well the course usually taken. The last man is taking off with his left foot, and has his right hand at the edge of the recess on to which he intends to climb. The face is very exposed in wintry weather, and several stories are told of parties who have suffered here from frostbite. It is not a safe place to descend when ice is about the rocks.

The following account of the North or Penrith Climb is taken from Mr. C. N. Williamson's article in

'All the Year Round.' Introducing, as it does, Mr. Seatree's original description, I make no apology for quoting it in full : 'There is yet another and a more direct way of climbing the Scawfell cliffs from Mickledore, which, for want of a better name, we may christen the "North Climb." The route is known to very few. It was discovered for himself in 1874 by Mr. George Seatree. . . . Major Cundill had already climbed it in 1869.

'From the ridge we traversed a ledge of grass-covered rock (the Rake's Progress) to the right until we reached a detached boulder, stepping upon which we were enabled to get handhold of a crevice six or seven feet from where we stood. To draw ourselves up so as to get our feet upon this was the difficulty. There is only one small foothold in that distance, and to have slipped here would have precipitated the climber many feet below. Having succeeded in gaining this foothold, we found ourselves in a small rectangular recess with barely room to turn round. From here it was necessary to draw ourselves carefully over two other ledges into a small rift in the rocks, and then traverse on our hands and knees another narrow ledge of almost eight feet to the left, which brought us nearly in a line with the Mickledore ridge. From here all was comparatively smooth sailing.

'The detached boulder may be identified with certainty by noticing that it is imbedded in the Rake's Progress close to the top of a funnel-shaped

grassy gully about ten or twelve yards from Mickledore. None but experienced climbers should
attempt the North Climb from the Mickledore.'

Scawfell Chimney.—A year after our first
sorry attempt on Broad Stand Dr. S. and I were being
shown the merits of Cust's gully on Great End as a
school for step-cutting, by an enthusiastic wielder of
the ice-axe, Mr. C. G. Monro. Neither of us knew
much about the subject, but it was pleasant to be well
instructed, and on reaching the summit of Great End
we wondered where we could cut steps next.
Monro suggested an adjournment for lunch at
Mickledore and a subsequent passage up the doubtless
snow-filled chimney : to which we all agreed.

On reaching the chimney, Monro took the lead
and hopefully ploughed through heavy wet snow as
a preliminary. Unfortunately, the snow became
softer and deeper as we advanced, until at last we
were up to our waists in slush, and wet through.
The pitch was not very far to seek. We saw long
dripping icicles barring our direct route onwards.
Both sides of the gully were heavily glazed with wet
ice, and we foresaw an anxious time of waiting while
the leader prospected. At the time we were not aware
that the usual exit was upon the right-hand side of
the pitch, by a couple of easy broad ledges. Nor
could we see that the pitch was in two parts, cave
upon cave, with a large resting-place between ; for
the icicles hung in an impenetrable curtain. Monro
attacked the icicles valiantly. Twice he succeeded

in working half way up between the centre and left
wall, but twice he was repulsed vigorously, and
found himself landed in the snow below.   I was
getting cold and impatient.   Monro was willing to
take a breathing space.   I unroped and made for
the left wall.   Cutting little steps for hands and feet
in the ice that covered the wall, and using the fingers
for all they were worth, in some ungainly fashion I
reached the level of the top of the pitch and
traversed on to the snow above.   The axe had been
used, I suspect, more like a croquet mallet than anything else, and introduced its own particular dangers.
But it was of no consequence, the pitch was climbed,
and the shivering pair below tried to fling up the
rope to me.   This was a matter of much difficulty,
placed as we were, but by approaching each other
as far as we dared, a happy fling brought the end of
the rope to my hand, and I responded by throwing
down, to their extreme peril, the ice-axe that they
needed to effect their ascent.   We managed the rest
badly.   My position was insecure in the upper snow
of the gully, or at any rate it seemed to be so.   The
others were benumbed with cold and wet, unable to
feel the holds or to rely on getting any help from me.
We certainly were not a strong party, and there was
no possibility of mutual aid.   The only consolation
was in the fact that all danger was absent; a fall
could only result in a plunge into ten feet of soft
snow, but we never afterwards spoke with pride of
that afternoon's work.   The other two decided to

G. P. Abraham & Sons, Photos.   Keswick

THE PENRITH CLIMB FROM THE MICKLEDORE

(Face page 40)

give it up, and go down to Mickledore again. My
own feelings were not consulted, but what matter?
The Broad Stand was somewhere about. I might
descend that way and shout when in trouble. We
joined again at Mickledore, and rather gloomily
glissaded to Hollow Stones.

That evening at Wastdale we hunted out Williamson's reference to the Scawfell Chimney. 'It is
impossible to get straight up the chimney, as the way
is blocked by an overhanging slab, and escape must
be effected either by the right-hand wall near the
top, where handhold is miserably inadequate, or by
the "corner," forty feet up the chimney. The passage
of the corner is a matter of stride and balance, as
there is no positive hold for the hands. There is a
bad drop into the chimney behind, and a slip in
rounding the corner would end in broken limbs, if
not a battered skull. A man essaying the corner
must apply himself like a plaister to an unpleasantly
projecting rock, and then by shifting the weight
from one foot to the other (for the legs are stretched
widely apart) he can creep round.'

The chimney has not often been climbed by that
variation of mine since then. In dry weather it is
perfectly safe to ascend or descend direct by the
pitch. In the ascent both sides of the gully may be
used at first; then comes an awkward crawl over the
first jammed boulder, into the secondary cave. Then,
taking care of a few loose stones, another jammed
boulder forming the roof is overcome—it is only a

few feet high—and a passage out on the right is made
possible. A long stretch of scree next fills the bed
of the gully, the right wall of which is here broken
away almost entirely, so that the climber generally
makes an exit, and passes straight up to the Deep
Ghyll cairn. But a pitch still remains to terminate
the scree, and must be climbed by him who would
assure himself of having explored the gully in its
entirety.

The Parson's Gully.—An easy way of descending to upper Eskdale other than by the Mickledore route was pointed out a few years ago by the
Rev. T. C. V. Bastow. It is by a short gully with
two pitches, due south of the summit cairn. When
drift snow lies about it, it is generally possible to
walk or glissade down the whole length of the gully
on to the screes below.

CHAPTER IV

*MOSS GHYLL, COLLIER'S CLIMB, AND
KESWICK BROTHERS' CLIMB*

Moss Ghyll.—There are accounts of explorations of this famous gully as far back as 1889. It was styled Sweep Ghyll by Mr. R. C. Gilson, partly for euphonious grouping with Deep Ghyll and Steep Ghyll, and partly as a suggestion of 'the probable profession of its future first climber.' In June, 1889, a strong set of four managed to penetrate upwards into its recesses a yard or two beyond Tennis Court ledge, 300 feet above the Rake's Progress, and almost exactly half way from start to finish. Here the explorers saw the great jammed boulders apparently barring all further progress, and decided to return the way they came. Then, a few days later, another party went round to the top of the gully and descended to the lower edge of the small scree that so quietly terminates the high and difficult last chimney. Here they firmly anchored themselves, and let down an adventurous member on 160 feet of rope. He descended in this way as far as the upper portion of the great obstacle in the middle of the gully, but saw no way whatever for an ascending party to circumvent or attack successfully the immense barrier. He apparently realized that the upper chimney could be fairly climbed, though of course it would tax the resources of the best of cragsmen; but the jammed boulders he judged to be insuperable, and returned to tell his companions the melancholy news. They left Moss Ghyll with the conviction that it would never be climbed, and until December, 1892, everyone else who came and saw turned back with much the same impression.

On the 27th of that month Messrs. Collie, Hastings, and Robinson made a determined attack on the ghyll. The winter was exceptionally fine and the rocks were clean and dry. They easily reached the Tennis Court ledge, and thence traversed into the gully. Penetrating the cave below the big pitch, Dr. Collie, who was leading, climbed up to the roof and out by a small window between the jammed boulders. Thence, by the ingenious expedient of hacking at a thin undercut plate of rock, he exposed a small foothold on the wall that enabled him to traverse out from the pitch and into a place of safety beyond. Thence to the top of the pitch was an easy matter, and the remaining members of the party quickly followed him. It has since been discovered that the hardest part of the gully was yet before them. They, however, had practically solved the main problem, and were contented to work out of the gully by steep 'mantelshelf' climbing up to the left. The honour of the first strict ascent of Moss Ghyll fell to Dr. Collier a few

days later, who climbed the ghyll from beginning to
end under the impression that the previous party
had done the same. Dr. Collier was accompanied
by four others, and was emphatic in his opinion that
the final chimney represented the hardest part of
the climb. Two days later he took up Professors
Marshall and Dixon, and from the former I obtained
sufficient information to start off one morning on my
own account to learn for the first time what Moss
Ghyll was like.

It was distinctly a day of adventure, and I learnt
a great deal concerning the ghyll. The passage
across the Collie step appeared to me the most difficult, but the loose slabs over which one has to walk
adroitly were then covered with fresh snow. The
famous step was invisible, and I had to stoop and
scrape in order to determine its exact shape and
position. At the first attempt on the traverse I
slipped, and fell into the snow-bed of the gully below.
The result was scarcely surprising, though eminently uncomfortable. But the falling was, under
the circumstances, almost part of the programme,
and a rope had been fixed in the interior of the
cavern, passed out through the 'window,' and then
attached to my waist, to eliminate the danger of
plunging some 400 feet down to the foot of the
gully. The second attempt was successful, though I
confess to a feeling of lively apprehension as the
critical point was being passed.

Thence to the parting of the ways was easy

travelling, and an exit was made by the left-hand route. I returned two days after to fetch axe and rope, that had been left at the big pitch, but it was not until the Whitsuntide of 1896 that a suitable opportunity occurred of visiting Moss Ghyll at its best, for the purposes of comparison and of explora-tion of the direct finish. During that interval the climb had been repeated many times, and Moss Ghyll was by way of becoming 'an easy day for a lady.' Hot-headed youths would arrive fresh at Wastdale, inquire for the hardest thing about, and at the mention of Moss Ghyll would straightway fling themselves into the breach and by hook or crook wriggle themselves up and out in triumph. Others were unsuccessful, and it was always amusing to learn where the stupendous difficulty had arisen, where no mortal man could have gone further. The personal equation was always in evidence, both in the actual climbing and in the history thereof.

My companions at Whitsuntide were Messrs. W. Brigg and Greenwood. Neither of them had been in the ghyll before, but both were very keen to make its acquaintance, though so far as reading could take them the smallest details of the climb were perfectly well known. We separated off from a larger party on the Rake's Progress, and at the entrance to the gully, which I have already defined in position, we roped up and began the rock climbing at once. There are a few small and stiff pitches that may be taken as they come in the first fifty feet of ascent from the Progress ;

SCAWFELL FROM THE PULPIT ROCK (p. 26).

The height of Pisgah above the Lord's Rake is about 520 feet.

a Scawfell Chimney.
b Broad Stand (p. 30).
c Penrith or North Climb (p. 40).
d Collier's Climb.
e Keswick Brothers' Climb.
f Moss Ghyll.
g Dr. Collie's Variation-exit.
h Steep Ghyll.
j Pinnacle Climb from Lord's Rake.
k Low Man.

l Scawfell Pinnacle (pp. 69 and 76).
m Pisgah.
n North Ridge of Pinnacle (p. 83).
p Lord's Rake.
q Easy Terrace into Deep Ghyll.

r Great Chimney.
s Entrance to Deep Ghyll (p. 12).
t Rake's Progress.

v Mickledore Screes.
w Mickledore.
x West Wall Climb (App.).

but we were quiet willing to make the usual divergence
to the right from the entrance to the first cave. This
led us up easy grass and rock close to the gully,
which soon dwindled into utter insignificance by
reason of its right wall being almost entirely cut
away. Keeping out in the open until the slope
suddenly steepened, we made a traverse into the
gully, and walked up the screes until stopped by a
long and awkward-looking grass-crowned chimney.
Then we were hemmed in on both sides, and my friends
were invited to define the nature of the next move.
They knew something of the locality; we had to
climb up the right-hand wall on to a level platform
some eighteen feet higher, and then work back into
the ghyll by a slightly upward traverse. The platform
was the well-known Tennis Court ledge, and its
vertical wall was one of the chief difficulties of former
days. When in 1893 I had first occasion to climb
the wall, there was much ice about and it was easiest
to work some way up the chimney before stepping
out on to the wall. The second attempt, two days
later, was in worse circumstances, and I preferred
working directly upwards to a still higher level before
diverging. On that occasion it seemed as though
the simplest plan would have been to avoid the
Tennis Court ledge altogether and keep to the
chimney. But Mr. Kempson has since pointed out
that the grass holds at the top are unreliable except
when frost holds the earth together. With Brigg
and Greenwood I should have been loth to leave the

Tennis Court unvisited. So we clambered directly up to it. The holds in the lower part of the wall were slight but very firm. The surface was rough and reliable. Two-thirds of the way up we found a little spike of rock that offered an admirable hold, sufficient to belay the rope safely while rounding the top edge of the wall and drawing up on to the platform. The others then came up with ease, and we halted a moment to look at the view.

The ledge is scarcely large enough for tennis, it might be eight feet long and two or three feet wide; the name is just the overflow of the pretty wit of some early explorer. Above us rose threateningly the vertical rampart that separates Moss Ghyll and Steep Ghyll. We could see the jammed boulders a little higher up in our ghyll. They appear small from Hollow Stones, but from our ledge each looked almost as large as a church. Wastdale Church we had in mind. The opposite wall of the ghyll looked hopelessly inaccessible, and we were little surprised that so many before us had been content to look and return. The traverse into the ghyll again was not so easy. If the leader slipped it would require clever management of the rope on the part of the others to avoid an unwilling follow on, though I believe a party was once tested here in that manner—and survived the test.

It was necessary to pass round a small buttress on to the scree bed of the gully. The first two steps were upwards, with just a steadying hold above for the hands. It was not desirable to keep too high, an unnecessary lengthening of the *mauvais pas* that some climbers recommend. The footholds are not perfect; they are large, but slope the wrong way. When dry, the friction is ample to prevent slipping. Where the rocks are glazed, as I have good occasion to remember, the passage is distinctly dangerous, especially the return from the gully to the Tennis Court ledge.

Thence, when all had rounded the corner safely, we walked up scree into the large cavern formed by the two jammed boulders. The one would of itself have formed a bridge across the gully, with a recess between it and the steep bed of the gully; the other, which is much larger, has fallen on to the first and roofed over the recess. When well within the cave we could see the 'window' high up between the two boulders, the one weak point by which the pitch could be attacked. I clambered up the interior of the cave and on to the window-sill. One of the others followed me, the third staying below to anchor the rope more firmly. From the window we could see the smooth steep wall on our right by which we were to traverse outwards. A couple of feet below our level we could observe that the rock formed a sharp horizontal edge six feet long, below which it overhung considerably. Just along this edge we were preparing to walk, using two steps that were sufficiently large for our needs. The first was the step cut by Dr. Collie. The second was at the further end of the short promenade, and was just

capable of holding the toes of both boots.   Starting
with the right foot on the first step, the further end
of the second step was taken in a long stride with the
left. The right was then brought up to it, and the left
reached round the corner at the end on to a respectable and satisfying foothold.   The trick of balancing
was not very difficult, providing of course that the
body was kept as nearly as possible vertical. A tumble
when no snow was about would be painful even with
a rope to limit its freedom, so we moved with deliberation and with a due sense of the difficulties of the
place.   After passing the dreaded *pas-de-deux*, I
reached in about ten feet of ascent a satisfactory
recess, where a 'belaying pin' was to be found.   It
is an excellent projection of rock, sometimes overlooked by climbers, behind which the rope can be
slipped, and held with firmness in the event of a fall.
It is a little awkward for the leader to pass directly
up into the ghyll again before the second man moves
away from the window.   Such a course would require
a long rope.   Using the belaying pin we found that
a sixty-feet length of rope was ample for the party
of three, and no time was lost in unroping or re-
adjusting.   When our second man reached the pin
I quitted the recess to make room for him, and
mounted into the gully while he played up the last
man.   A few feet of easy scree brought us into the
large open portion of the ravine which marks the only
spot where it is possible to break away to the left
from the gully. The final crags in front rose abruptly

G. P. Abraham & Sons, Photos. Keswick

COLLIER'S CHIMNEY, MOSS GHYLL

up for another 200 feet, and were deeply cut by the
vertical Collier's Chimney, which starts almost at
once from our level. The skyline trended downwards
by the left, so that the open route to the top was
not so long in point of distance as the other.

It certainly was easier to work up the wall to the
left. It rose at a steep angle, and was columnar in
structure, with long, porphyritic slabs crowned by
small levels of tufted grass. The leader would often
be unable to help his followers with the rope, but the
successive ledges could be so chosen that no great
distance would exist between the resting-places.
Such open work is often more trying for the nerves
than harder chimney climbing, but it is always
admirable practice when the ledges are reliable.

I had quitted the gully by this variation three
years before, and wanted both on my own account
and that of my friends to work out the alternative
route. I started up the right wall, at first steadied
by the left, but soon found myself too far out of
the chimney to feel at all comfortable. Thirty feet
up was a jammed stone blocking the narrow way,
apparently very effectually. But we had heard of a
possible wriggle behind the jammed stone, and with
a reprehensible lack of daring I made a traverse to
the chimney again, and began working up it with
back and knee in the orthodox manner. The
situation was safe enough, but the effort of lifting
oneself inch by inch was supremely fatiguing, and
when I discovered the hole behind the boulder to be

about half my minimum sectional area I began to
regret the scheme. But it was too late to return, and
with a dread fear of closing up the 'through' route
for ever, I straightened out one arm above my head
and thrust it through the hole. Fortunately I had
no camera sack to hold me back, a frequent source of
annoyance in a tight place. Here we were all travelling light, and I had nothing to thrust through the
aperture but a limp body that was at every moment
lessening its rigidity. As soon as both shoulders were
well in, the rest followed more easily by vigorous
prisings with the elbows, which are so useful in
upward thrusting. Dragging myself into a standing
position on the jammed boulder, I called on the
others to follow. They chose the outside course,
making two little détours out and back on the
vertical wall, probably the exact plan adopted by
Dr. Collier in the first ascent. My position in this
little 'sentry-box' was secure, and the rope could be
manipulated with all necessary care till the three
of us were gathered close together in the tiny recess.
Then we had a somewhat easier scramble up the
next vertical portion of the chimney, to pass some
small jammed stones twenty feet higher. We used
the same wall and found the footholds in it more
obviously arranged for our convenience. The first
climber had surely a bad time of it on this wall,
seeing that it was all moss-covered, and required an
immense amount of preliminary clearing before the
holds could be discerned. But moss has had no

chance of growing there for the last four years, and we had none to trouble us. A couple of minutes carried us from the sentry-box to the top of the next pitch. The slope of the ghyll suddenly became easier, scree led to a short and easy rock pitch, somewhat spoilt by loose stones, and then a walk to the top brought us in contact with friends and the commissariat.

The Pisgah Buttress.—In the second chapter mention was made of the small pinnacle of Pisgah that flanked the Professor's Chimney. Viewing the crags from Mickledore, it will be seen that this pinnacle is the culminating point of the ridge between Moss Ghyll and Steep Ghyll. It is convenient to introduce here a brief account of the first ascent of this ridge directly from the 'Tennis Court.' Messrs. G. and A. Abraham had repeatedly assured me that their inspection from neighbouring points of view had been favourable, but it was not until April 22, 1898, when ascending Scawfell Pinnacle by the Low Man, that I examined the Pisgah ridge with the object of attacking it. The same afternoon these two friends awaited my arrival on the 'Tennis Court.' I came along the Mickledore towards the Pulpit Rock to enjoy a rest and the society of a party of friends, but was disappointed of both by a call from the Ledge. In ten minutes from the Mickledore I joined them, and while recovering breath, was interested to hear of their attempts to reach the Ledge by other ways than Moss Ghyll. Then, disposing the rope properly, we went to the extreme right corner and started the real business. I had a vertical crack about twelve feet high to surmount. It led to a small platform similar to the one from which we began our climb, and presented the usual difficulties—no hand or foothold. A shoulder was given me, then probably a head, then a steadying hand for my struggling feet, the left arm being thrust well into the crack and the right doing as best it could on the wall, until it could reach the grassy edge of the platform above. Once on this the prospect was pleasing, and we dubbed the spot a 'Fives Court.' Thence a steep chimney rose directly towards the ridge. I mounted some twenty feet and debated whether the others might safely come up and help. There seemed to be a fair chance of entering an overhanging chimney away up to my left, or of following the direct route to the ridge. The first course attracted me a yard or two along a narrow ledge, until the way was barred by an immense poised block. It trembled as I touched the horrible thing; so did my friends down below, and they besought me to play the straight game, and aim for the arête instead of aiming at them. They were perfectly just in their choice, and it is as well that their advice was followed, for we should have had a terrible time working the overhanging chimney. Ten or fifteen feet of rather careful scrambling brought me to the edge of the buttress, at a point where I could descend a little on the Steep Ghyll side and belay the others with absolute security while they mounted.

The point we had reached was on a level with the top of the Slingsby's Chimney on the Pinnacle. Another party of climbers were operating over there, and gave us some useful information as to the work we had above us. Our rock was not altogether firm and reliable, so that the next bit of vertical ridge in front was discarded in favour of a slight détour on the left face. Belayed as he was by the others, the leader ran very little risk, and employing a succession of moderately firm, tufted ledges, he dragged himself steadily up for another twenty feet before his companions quitted their belay and joined him. Then we unroped and walked up the remaining hundred feet with no trouble whatever, astonished to find that our difficulties had been so few and so rapidly overcome. In an hour from the 'Tennis Court' we were swinging down the Broad Stand ledges.

Collier's Climb.—For many years it was currently supposed that any attempt to scale the precipice between the North Climb at Mickledore and Steep Ghyll round by the Pinnacle, ranked the daring enthusiast as one *quem Deus vult perdere*, and, moreover, that the gods would not give him the chance to finish his undertaking. But with the advent of a greater number of experienced climbers, coming to Wastdale with recollections of the stupendous rocks in the Swiss Alps or the Austrian

Dolomites, a reaction gradually set in.   To many nothing seemed impossible with a party of three and an Alpine rope.   But a line must be drawn somewhere to separate the possible from the impossible, and some try to draw it by their own experience. These constitute what is called the ultra-gymnastic school of climbing.   Its members are generally young and irresponsible.   With years will come a desire to depart this life in one piece, after the common joys are realized that life is able to offer.   The quick-burning fever for wild adventure dies away with the approach of workable theories of life.   Whatever the mental phenomenon may be, I am convinced that the physical is vestigial—a trace of our former savagery, a suggestion of the lively past, when the struggle for existence involved more muscle than mind.

Wherefore let live the ultra-gymnasts, if indeed they can pass through their March-madness without coming to grief; nor should we attempt to inoculate them with some harmless sport, for the result is to render the sport dangerous.

To return to the separating line that suggested this digression.   Those who have sought to define it theoretically have been of the foolish ones, for it has no absolute position for mankind.   Each individual possesses a line of his own, and at first in looking for it he causes it to re-arrange itself.   What was once impossible for him becomes easy.   But his search is more rapid than its advance, and a time comes when he realizes that he is perilously near; and in wisdom he vows evermore to keep at so many feet or centimetres (according to his choice of units) from its nearest point. The nearer he habituates himself to approach, the oftener does he discover some obvious retreat of his line. Those who live far from it find that it can narrow its limits. Which things are an allegory, for this line is a closed curve and limits us in all directions, only one of which leads to rock-climbing.

Our walk along the foot of the Scawfell wall by the Rake's Progress showed three breaks in the cliff after we left Steep Ghyll. The first marked Moss Ghyll, the second Keswick Brothers' Climb, the third Collier's Climb. The history of Moss Ghyll and its gradual yielding to the persistent attacks of active parties has been recorded in the first section. The news of its ascent came as a surprise to all who knew the place, so great a surprise that no room was left for wonderment when Dr. Collier a few months later proved the practicability of his route. But whereas Moss Ghyll became popular in a week by reason of the writing-up it immediately received, Collier's Climb was almost untouched for three years. The unknown is always the most terrible, and the brief note in the Wastdale climbing book recording its first ascent left much to an anxious imagination. Queer tales were told round at the inn of men who were flung back over the Rake's Progress after rising only ten feet. Even Dr. Collier was reported to have said he never wished to see the place again. Report was inaccurate, but that made no difference. I candidly admit that there seemed little chance of ever getting up such an awful wall. It was not till I found myself twenty feet up the crack that the attack seemed in the least degree hopeful.

It was just after Easter in 1896 (April 22), and my party had been climbing well on the Screes and in Deep Ghyll. The rocks were in marvellously good condition, perfectly dry and warm to the touch. G. and A. were with me, their last day before returning home. I thought it imprudent to take their votes, and announced that we were going to look at the first part of Collier's Climb, and to ascertain where its difficulty lay. Fortunately they were both sanguine, and placed their heads and shoulders at my disposal as footholds. We made straight for the right spot in an hour and a half of easy going from Wastdale. There could be no possible doubt of the place. A thin crack rose direct from the Progress, overhanging for the first ten feet, then leaning back a trifle towards the left. A yard or two to the left of this a square corner led directly up so as to join the crack just below a thin chimney, that started some twenty feet above our heads. To get to this chimney was the difficulty. Either the cleft or the corner should be taken. Which was the easier?

I first tried the cleft, but it overhung so seriously that I dared not venture further. Equally futile was the attempt up the corner. Was it possible that we had mistaken the right take-off? To gain time and recover our spirits we walked over to the other side of Mickledore and prospected the climb. There could be no doubt that I had actually started on the correct way. Thirty feet up we could plainly distinguish a grassy platform that promised us temporary safety. If we could get as high as that we had Dr. Collier's authority that the remainder of our chimney offered no such difficulties as those we had overcome. Even if it had, we could as a last resource fix an axe in the chimney and descend on a doubled rope in the usual Alpine fashion. In this manner, assuring ourselves that we had the worst immediately before us, we returned with some little courage to the attack. This time we decided to take the corner. A. was to stand on a small ledge about a foot above the Progress, and brace himself firmly enough to hold my weight. G. acted as a sort of flying buttress for his brother, and paid out my rope with extreme care. From A.'s shoulders I could just reach a high handhold with the left. But one grip at that height was useless, as the body had to be lifted up on to the rib of rock separating the two clefts. A. then padded his head with a handkerchief beneath his cap, and begged me to stand on it. However steady a young man may be, there are times when his friends think him weak in the head. Such a time was this, and I anxiously asked him if he could hold it perfectly still while I used it. 'You may do anything except

waltz on it,' was the encouraging rejoinder, and I
promptly placed my left foot on his parietal. 'That's
all right,' the tough young head called out, 'you may
stay there all day if you like.' This was reassuring,
but I had come out to climb and meant to move on.
Yet for the life of me I could not see what to do
next. The left foot required a lift before the high
handhold could be employed, and there was nothing
for it to rest against except the square corner of the
recess. Two or three times I tried hard to grip the
corner with the toe of my boot, but ineffectually.
Then A., seeing my trouble, reached up a hand and
held my boot on an infinitesimal ledge. It felt firm,
and I trusted to it. With the first movement
upwards my right hand felt a charmingly secure
depression in the rib above, and swinging clear from
A.'s head I dragged up on to the buttress and felt that
the game was half won already. The rib was easy
to ascend for a foot or two, till indeed it terminated
at the small chimney above. But caution was the
instinct uppermost in my mind, and the climb to the
grassy platform above might, in spite of appearances,
prove nasty. Casting around for some means of
anchoring on my own rope, I saw that in the crack
to my right a bunch of small stones were firmly
jammed, and that daylight could be seen behind them
down a hole that pointed through to the Progress,
fifteen feet below. Here was a chance that, if we had
known of it at first, might have been used to con-
serve our strength and nerve from the start. The

others were as yet unroped. Calling to them to let go the rope, I drew up the free end by my teeth and my 'unemployed' hand, and let it fall straight down the hole to them. If a fall occurred now in trying the next few feet I could only tumble three or four yards, and should not pass over my friends' heads and the Rake's Progress. But the chimney into which a few moves brought me was of no high order of difficulty; the situation was certainly a trying one, for a downward gaze could only take in the rib of rock immediately below and the distant screes 200 feet beyond. I flung some loose stones far out into space, and could only just hear a faint clatter as they touched the scree. Now was the time to appreciate the joy of climbing, in perfect health, with perfect weather, and in a difficult place without danger, and I secretly laughed as I called to the others that the outlook was terribly bad and that our enterprise must be given up. But they also laughed, and told me to go higher and change my mind, for they knew by the tone that my temper was unruffled. A few feet more and I drew up to the platform. It was about a yard wide and three yards in length, reminding us strongly of the Tennis Court ledge, a similar formation half way up Moss Ghyll. Between the ledge and the wall rising above it a fissure cut down into the mountain. It still held some old winter snow, and its depths were cold as a refrigerator. Shouting to the others to rope up at a distance of thirty feet apart, I sat down on the

grass with my legs dangling in the frigid fissure,
bracing myself to stand any jerks that might be
given to the rope by a sudden slip of the second man
at the rounding of the rib. G. came up second, using
his brother's shoulders and head much as I had used
them.   When he reached the ledge he helped me to
haul his brother.   A. was unable to stand on his
own head as we had done, though we reminded him
of Dent's famous climber's dream, and he hung on to
the rope with both hands while we pulled.   It must
have been rather an unpleasant sensation that of
swinging away from the rocks, but he bore it like a
philosopher, and caught cleverly on to the rib and
so up to us.   I am afraid our satisfaction was now
somewhat premature, but we were certain of a safe
descent whatever the remainder of our climb might
involve.   But there was no sign of failure in store.
The chimneys above us looked steep, but they were
deeply carved and therefore safe.   Also, they cut
obliquely up the vertical wall, and were not likely to
involve any inch-by-inch wrestling against gravity.
These surmises all proved correct, though we were
astonished at the ease with which the remaining
difficulties were overcome.   It was now two o'clock
in the afternoon, and we had been half an hour
getting up the first thirty feet.   The remainder only
took us an equal time, though five times the height,
and consisting of genuine rock-climbing all the way,
as the following notes testify.

After a short lunch and a few minutes spent in

erecting a diminutive cairn, we moved on. Dr. Collier had climbed into the upper part of the next chimney by a traverse of some difficulty from the right. I started the same course, but A. had descended a little to look up the direct route, and called out that it was safer, though perhaps awkward. Therefore we all descended and entered the chimney, which is practically a continuation of the crack up which our climb had started. It sloped slightly to the left, and offered just a sufficiency of holds, without demoralizing us with a superfluity. In fifteen feet its difficulties were over, and a few yards higher we reached another grassy ledge, more protected than the former but giving an equally grand view of the neighbouring precipices. There then followed a vertical pitch of twelve feet, simple enough with the help of a shoulder— or without it, for that matter—and an easy step from the top towards the right led to the beginning of the upward grassy traverse that so strikingly marks the break in the continuity of direction of Collier's Climb. Many people have expressed doubts as to the safety of this traverse; on the other hand, these many have not all been there to see. The route is perfectly safe; there are corners on the Rake's Progress that are intrinsically as hard, though perhaps the sublime situation may have its effect on some susceptible organisations. Possibly in wintry weather the traverse may have its difficulties, but if ever it were dangerous the first pitch would be impossible.

We found the first part of the final chimney slightly moist. Probably it is very rarely dry. As the diagram facing page 46 indicates, it slopes up towards the left and is very deeply cut. The first piece was practically a walk up a steep incline, using tiny ledges that were disposed along the slope in the most suitable places. It ended with a magnificent pull up with the arms over a projecting edge on the left.

Then came the pleasantest part of the whole, the negotiation of twenty-five feet of smooth, slabby rock by faith in friction and occasional reference to the overhanging side of the gully. Collier had rightly made special mention of this part, but to his account I should like to add that with dry rock and rough garments all will go well. Even a slip on the part of the leader will not be serious if he is carefully watched and fielded at the bottom of his slide.

At the finish of this exciting portion we saw the sky-line a few feet in front of us, and with a spurt we ran up and reached the summit breathless.

Since that time I have descended by the same route with a different party. We had just come up Moss Ghyll, and my two friends were well contented with their day's work; for Moss Ghyll had been the limit of their ambition, and they were willing to rest contentedly on their laurels. To tackle Collier's Climb had never entered their heads before—like the death-dealing pebble for poor Goliath—and they shyly suggested that we had climbed enough for one

day. But with the sense of possession of a trump
card up my sleeve—that handy rope-hold at the
bottom pitch—I succeeded in rousing their enthusiasm sufficiently, and we started downwards. They
were perfectly safe men to accompany; this had been
proved in Moss Ghyll, and it was perhaps not so
very wrong to indulge in a harmless exaggeration of
the excitement that the finish had in store for them.
But they climbed extremely well in spite of fore-
bodings, and gratified me immensely by agreeing that
for beauty of surroundings Collier's Climb has no
equal in all the gullies of the Lake District. The
descent was rather easier than the ascent—a state of
things so often experienced in difficult climbing work
—and we reached the lowest grassy platform in half
an hour. There we found the little cairn I had erected
a few months before, and were cheered to see a couple
of friends approaching from Mickledore to give us
any aid necessary near the finish. I let down the
first man by the rope; he went well till within ten
feet of the Progress, and then, slipping away from the
hold, was left for an uncomfortable moment dangling
in mid-air. Lowered a yard or so his legs were seized
by the men below and he was pulled to their level in
safety. There he unroped, and thus also descended
the second man. But he came on the middle of the
rope, and before reaching the spot where he was
destined to quit the rocks he was instructed to slip
the lower end of the rope through the safety-hole.
On reaching the Progress he also unroped, and with

the united strength of the party holding me through the jammed stone I also was willing, when my turn came to let myself hang and be lowered gently down like a bale of goods into a ship's hold.

To descend alone, without adventitious aid of this kind, it would be better to take to the crack.

Keswick Brothers' Climb.—This occupies a position between the two chief routes already described in this chapter, but chronologically it comes last, and on that account we find it best to treat of it after the others. The brothers Abraham and I had independently arrived at the conclusion that the Scawfell face offered a feasible route between Collier's Climb and Moss Ghyll, of which only the lower half required any elaborate planning. In the summer of 1897, before I had a suitable opportunity of trying my fortune there, came the news that my two friends had succeeded with their design, considerable assistance having been given them by the preliminary scrambling of Mr. J. W. Puttrell at the lower end of the course.

On Christmas Day, 1897, I was one of a large party exploring the new route and its environs. An attempt to work directly up the long crack marked by the top *e* in Plate II. was thwarted at a height of forty feet or so above the Rake's Progress by the smoothness of the rocks, and by the presence of ice in the crack. It will probably go some day when conditions are more favourable. I managed to traverse to the edge of the buttress on my left, but the prospect round

G. P. Abraham & Sons, Photos.   Keswick

THE KESWICK BROTHERS' CLIMB

(Face page 66)

the corner was not a bit more attractive. A descent was therefore effected and the ordinary route tackled forthwith. It was interesting and remarkably safe. We started close to the foot of Collier's Climb, and, working along a nearly horizontal cleft, arrived without trouble at the corner of the rectangular recess of which mention was made on page 30.

Thence we had a steep bit of edgework for thirty feet before the leader could ask his second to advance from the Progress. This part admits of a little variation, but the main fact to be grasped is that the long chimney in which Collier's Climb finishes is retained close on our right for fully ten yards, until it suddenly narrows, and a grass platform extends away to the left with ample accommodation for a score of people. This platform, in fact, is part of the same grassy ledge that forms the first resting place after the troublesome introduction to Collier's Climb ; and since that date I have frequently taken friends up and down the latter course by this variation. The expedition is one that can be strongly recommended for moderately good parties, both for its beauty and its sustained interest throughout. That day, however, our course was ordered differently. We had first to follow the original line of ascent for fifteen feet up an awkward chimney with its best hold insecure. Then on reaching an upper grass corner there came an open movement across the face of rock to our right, working gradually upwards and aiming for a narrow cleft that partially separated a small pinnacle from the face. The view of this pinnacle from the middle of Collier's Climb is simply exquisite, well worth showing to an enterprising camera.

From the pinnacle a slight descent gave an inspiring view downwards of the long smooth corner that I had unsuccessfully attacked a short time previously. At our level the crack had expanded into a respectable chimney, that could be easily entered twenty feet higher after a brief clamber on the buttress. It was disappointing to find then that something very like a scree gully, with only moderately interesting scrambling, was to finish our work in the great cleft. Rather than close the operations so quietly the majority voted for an attempt on the slightly-indicated branch exit thirty feet to the right; and their enterprise was rewarded by the conquest of a particularly neat pitch at the top.

ATTITUDES ON SCAWFELL PINNACLE

(Face page 69)

CHAPTER V

SCAWFELL PINNACLE

Ordinary Route.—This magnificent pinnacle offers the finest bit of rock scenery in the Scawfell *massif*. It rises up some 600 feet from the foot of Lord's Rake in steep and almost unclimbable slabs of smooth rock, forming the left-hand boundary of Deep Ghyll and the right of Steep Ghyll. The latter, and the Professor's Chimney springing up out of Deep Ghyll, cut it away to some extent from the main mountain mass, from which it is separated by a narrow *col* or gap familiarly known as the 'Jordan.' Unfortunately this gap is too high, and the top of the pinnacle is reached therefrom by a couple of minutes' scrambling. If only the gap were impossible to reach from above, the climb of Scawfell Pinnacle would necessarily involve some splendid work, and it could almost claim the suggested name of the Little Dru of the Lake District.

From a higher point of view Mr. Williamson's comparison is very apt. 'The most conspicuous object at the upper part of Deep Ghyll is a pinnacle rock with some slight resemblance, from certain points of view, to the celebrated Pieter Botte, in

Mauritius, except that the stone on the top is much smaller than the knob which forms the summit of the Mauritius mountain. The Deep Ghyll Pinnacle is perhaps best named the Scawfell Pillar, for on examination it will be found to have several features in common with the Ennerdale Pillar. Both have a Pisgah rock and a Jordan gap, both have a High and a Low Man, and both have a slanting slab in similar positions. So inaccessible does the Scawfell Pillar appear, that it is probable no one ever thought of making an attempt upon it till Mr. W. P. Haskett Smith, whose climbs on the Ennerdale Pillar were referred to in a previous article, looking at the rock with the eye of a genius for climbing, thought he could see a way to the top. He made the attempt alone in September of this year [1884] and successfully reached the top, being the first man to set foot on the summit of this 'forbidden peak.'

But the gap can be reached easily from the summit of Scawfell. If we walk over to the top of Deep Ghyll we may look across to the pinnacle on the right 'and notice the black cut made by the Professor's Chimney that separates it from us. The knob of rock to the right of the Jordan gap is appropriately called 'Pisgah'; it is almost exactly of the same height as the cairn on the pinnacle, and is barely thirty feet away from it. By rounding Pisgah to the right, and carefully skirting the head of Moss Ghyll, we reach the Jordan, and find ourselves on a narrow ridge with extremely steep

plunges on either side.   The short climb that faces
us begins in an awkward way, for we have to get up
a few feet of overhanging rock before the slope
eases off, and a slip backwards of an unroped man
would inevitably result in a fall down the Professor's
Chimney or down Steep Ghyll.   The firmest rope
anchorage for the leader is at the top of Pisgah, but
with more to follow him the usual plan is to descend
to the gap and loop the rope over a large boulder
that lies on the crest of the *col*.   He need not worry
about the danger of the pitch if the rocks are in
good condition.   When Mr. Haskett Smith first
found this way up on September 3rd, 1884, a few
days before he reached the top by way of Steep
Ghyll, large quantities of moss had to be removed,
and the finger-holds cleared of earth before they
could be estimated and safely utilized.   Not a
particle of moss remains here now ; nay, more, a
decade of gymnasts have removed much rock by
dint of scraping with their nailed boots, and have
made obvious the safest route to the summit.

It starts a yard or two to the right of the gap,
where a sloping foothold in the overhanging wall
shows traces of considerable wear and tear.   The
hands can find a sufficient bearing pressure near
the edge of rock above, but it is unwise to place
them too high up on the sloping slab.   Then,
straightening out on the foothold for a moment, the
left hand can find a thin crack good enough for a
hold while the body is being levered up over the

awkward edge. Then the crack can be followed up the slab to the left till it ends near a little chimney, up which a scramble of six feet brings the climber within touch of the cairn. Formerly a small tin box held many visiting cards, and an ancient pocket-book with the names of the early climbers of the pinnacle. It was almost a breach of etiquette to pay a call here without leaving a card, but the polite old days are past, and men come and go now without this ceremony. A year ago I hunted in vain for the box and fancied that some curiosity-monger had feloniously appropriated it, but since then I believe it has again been seen there. It may easily slip down between the loose stones.

This little climb is dangerous in icy weather, and should not then be undertaken. For there is no particular fun in it when the rocks are glazed, when bare fingers are necessary for the diminished holds, and the slow going inevitably involving benumbed hands.

The long routes up are impossible except when conditions are favourable.

The first long way up the pinnacle was climbed on September 20th, 1884, by Messrs. Haskett Smith and John Robinson. They made the ascent of Steep Ghyll, and then, emerging on the right, climbed up a steep *arête* to the pinnacle, where they left their names in a glass bottle. Descending again to the upper portion of Steep Ghyll, they passed over to the Jordan and so on to the mountain. With but

SCAWFELL PINNACLE AND DEEP GHYLL—WINTER

(Face page 75)

slight variations, these were the only ways known
until 1888.   In July of that year a party led by Mr.
W. Cecil Slingsby succeeded in climbing out from
the lower part of Steep Ghyll on to the north-east
face of the pinnacle.   By a long and difficult chimney
in this wall they reached the Low Man, as the nearly
horizontal crest of the first huge buttress is called.
Thence a sharp ridge took them direct to the final
rocks, which were sufficiently broken to make the
finish easy.   This route at once commended itself to
the better climbers at Wastdale as being safe and
sound.   The rocks throughout are excellent, and
indeed enthusiasts like to compare the finish with
the famous ridge of the Rothhorn from Zinal.   The
chief objection to be urged against the climb is the
exposure to wind and cold.   I remember once
starting up with Mr. Robinson one wet day in
August.   He led as far as the foot of the difficult
Slingsby Chimney, and then resolutely refused to
budge an inch further because of the wind, which he
asseverated would blow us away to Hollow Stones.
I am inclined to believe him now, but at the time
we wrangled all the way down to the Lord's Rake,
where some damp but enterprising tourist, pointing
up to the vertical crags down which we had been
dodging our way, inquired in a feeble tenor voice:
' Is there a road up there ? '

It was not until December 31, 1893, that I made
my first complete ascent by this route, accompanied
by M. and C., the latter leading all the way up.   We

crossed the foot of Lord's Rake, and made for the
slight suggestion of a gully that serves to mark the
beginning of the ordinary Steep Ghyll Climb. It
was quite easy to follow, and rapidly deepened as we
rose. In a hundred feet we were in view of the
enormous cleft of the ghyll, with its black and
glistening walls apparently almost meeting each
other a hundred feet over our heads. None of us
were attracted by that climb, which is never quite
free from hazard, and we looked about for the spot
where our route diverged to the right. Here the
side of the ghyll was very steep for thirty or forty
feet up, but was cut about by ledges and clefts quite
good enough for us to mount the wall safely. Then
we bore up a little towards the left, so as to approach
the smooth outer face of the Low Man. Advance
was only possible in one direction, our course taking
us out on a nose or pinnacle of rock separated from
the main mass by a deep fissure.

The position was very exposed. It could only
be approached from one direction, that of Steep
Ghyll. A glance down the fissure beneath us
revealed the lower half of the tremendous wall to
which we were clinging, and though we had plenty
of room to sit down and rest ourselves, there was a
sense of coming peril in the next move. The illustration facing page 73, taken off the wall from the Lord's
Rake ridge, shows the pinnacle and the fissure that
partially separates it from the face. Standing on the
highest available point, C. had next to draw himself

up on to the little shelf by means of the smallest of
holds and the use of his knees.   We were able to
guard against his slipping back, and were glad to see
him clamber up easily to the beginning of the Slingsby
Chimney.   This begins very awkwardly ; it would be
proof of unusual agility and nerve for the leader here
to manage the first six feet without assistance from
below.   But an unaided ascent is not impossible, and
careful examination will generally cause the climber
to discount much of the terror that he is pretty sure
to have invested in the spot after reading the early
literature of the subject.   We hoisted C. up on our
shoulders ; without hesitation he crept well into the
crack vertically above our heads, and wriggled his
way out of sight.   When we had paid out forty feet
of rope, he shouted out to M. to advance, and I was
left to speculate on a possible variation of the ascent
by the left of the chimney.   In due course M. was
firmly fixed, and my turn came.   The steepness of
the first fifteen feet was rather appalling, but it was
so simple a matter to wedge firmly into the chimney
that there was no sense of insecurity.   After the
vertical bit, the chimney sloped back at an easier
angle, and though some distance had to be climbed
before a man might be of much help to those behind
he would be perfectly capable of looking after himself.   When we reached this level the aspect of
the remaining rocks was very much less threatening.
It was still a matter of hand-and-foot work, but we
could all forge ahead together instead of moving one at

a time. The slope eased off again when we reached
the Low Man, and by preference we kept to the
ridge on the right as much as we could. This was
for the sensational view down into Deep Ghyll,
though that day we saw little but the rolling mist
above and below us. The rock was firm and rough
to the touch, and we could well appreciate the comparison with the best parts of the Zinal Rothhorn.
Leslie Stephen's frontispiece in the 'Playground of
Europe' might have been drawn on our ridge. There
was a sense of perfect security out there as we sat
astride the sharp ridge or clasped the huge blocks
with a fraternal embrace. My only regret was that
the *arête* was all too short—we arrived at the
pinnacle much too soon. I proposed to descend to
the Jordan and down by the Professor's Chimney,
but my companions pointed out that the latter
would be damp and rickety, and such a change from
our recent sport that we could get little fun out
of it. I reluctantly yielded to the vote of the
majority and went off to a halting-place in the
hollow at the head of the Moss Ghyll variation
exit.

Scawfell Pinnacle, Deep Ghyll route.—

In October, 1887, a strong party led by the brothers
Hopkinson found a way down the outside face of the
Scawfell Pinnacle, to a point on the ridge within a
hundred feet of the first pitch in Deep Ghyll. There
they built what is now known as the Hopkinsons'
cairn. In April, 1893, Messrs. C. Hopkinson and

G. P. Abraham & Sons, Photos.   Keswick

THE LAST HUNDRED FEET ON THE SCAWFELL PINNACLE

(Face page 76)

Tribe worked up the left wall of the ghyll from the second pitch, and reached the main north *arête* about sixty feet above the cairn. They were apparently unable to force a way directly up the ridge, and managed instead to descend it for a few yards and then to climb up the face of the **Low Man** by the 1887 route on the east side of the *arête.*

They thus succeeded in reaching the summit of the pinnacle from Deep Ghyll, and an examination of the illustration facing page 83 of the great wall that they climbed will prove that the performance was an unusually brilliant one. (The photograph shows the north ridge twenty feet to the left of the leader, who is about forty feet above the second man.)

Very little was generally known of that day's work, the note in the Wastdale climbing book being of the briefest description ; and it cannot be counted unto me for originality that in a climb made in 1896 that was intended as a repetition of the above our party left the older route at a point eighty feet up the Deep Ghyll wall, and reached the Low Man by a new line of advance.

We were a party of three. Messrs. George and Ashley Abraham were very keen on trying the new route, and equally anxious to get some good photographs of the great wall. We climbed up the first pitch in Deep Ghyll by the crack on the left, and took the second in the ordinary way. Just where the traverse commences fifteen feet above the top of the central obstacle, a crack starts up the left wall, with a prominent jammed block guarding its entrance. Traversing over a leaf of rock on to the jammed stone, I was steadied for the first twenty feet of ascent by the rope, and could not have come to much harm in the event of a slip.   But there was scanty room for a second, and I was compelled to rise with an ever lengthening rope below me.   The crack was followed closely, though it soon became so thin and so erect that there was nothing to do but keep on the face of the mountain just to its left, every now and then gripping its sharp edge for handhold.   It seemed to be a virgin climb, though this part had really been visited two or three times before. Stones had to be flung down, and grit scraped from the tiny ledges.   But on the whole that first sixty feet was not very difficult, though markedly sensational, and I went on slowly to a little niche in the wall.

The eighty-feet length of rope just reached to the crack from which the start was made, and getting George to tie himself on at the lower extremity, I mounted to a higher and larger niche while he cautiously climbed up the crack.   The situation was very novel.   Some may remember the *firma loca* in Mr. Sanger Davies' account of the Croda da Lago. This grass-floored hermitage of mine was truly a *firma loca*, and sitting down comfortably in it I took out a biscuit from my pocket and tried to realize all the view.

It was every bit as appalling as a Dolomite climb. Direct progress upwards seemed quite impossible; a feasible traverse over some badly-sloping moss-covered ledges to the right led to the sky-line at a spot where the *arête* made a vertical spring upwards for forty feet. A descent would have been seriously difficult, but it was the one thing we did not want. I could hear another climbing party finishing an ascent of the pinnacle by the ordinary route, their voices echoing down the ghyll and cheering me with a sense of neighbourliness. My companions were holding an animated discussion below on the subject of photography. The light was excellent, and our positions most artistic.' The cameras were left in the cave at the foot of the ghyll. Ashley was afraid I meant to go up without him ; but his professional instinct got the better of his desire to climb, and, shouting out to us to stay where we were for five minutes, he ran round to the high-level traverse on the other side of the ghyll, and down the Lord's Rake to the cavern.

George had the tripod screw and could not hand it to his brother ; so, asking me to hold him firmly with the rope, he practised throwing stones across the gully to the traverse. Then, tying the screw to a stone, he managed to project this over successfully. We composed our limbs to a photographic quiescence. Ashley had a splendid wide-angle lens, which, from his elevated position on the traverse opposite, could take in 400 feet of the cliff, showing the entire route to the summit. It was his turn to take the lead. 'Mr. Jones! I can't see you, your clothes are so dark.' I apologized. 'Will you step out a foot or two from that hole?' I was in a cheerful mood and ready to oblige a friend, but the platform was scarcely two feet square, and to acquiesce was to step out a few hundred feet into Deep Ghyll. For this I had not made adequate preparation and told him so. 'Well, will you take off your coat?' That I could do with pleasure, and for a while his instructions were levelled at George.

He was in an awkward place and was much cramped in ensuring safety, but Ashley was dissatisfied and insisted on his lifting the left leg. This gave him no foothold to speak of, but in the cause of photography he had been trained to manage without such ordinary aids. He grumbled a little at the inconvenience but obeyed, resolving that if he were living when the next slide was to be exposed he himself would be the manipulator and his brother the centre of the picture. The ghyll had become rather gloomy and we had a lengthy exposure. I was glad to slip on my jacket again and draw in the rope for George's ascent. When he reached the smaller platform just below me, we tried the traverse over the slabs to the north ridge, and found that it went well enough. We were delighted to find traces of the previous party on the rocks at the corner. They were made by the Hopkinsons three years before (April 2, 1893) in their attempt to mount by the ridge. Their cairn was fifty feet further down, and we now had the satisfaction of seeing for ourselves how to connect the Hopkinson cairn directly with Deep Ghyll.

Then came the question of getting our third man up. We tried to throw the rope-end to him, but it persisted in clinging to the face vertically below us and would not be caught. I had to return to the *firma loca* and throw the rope from there. Ashley now reached it safely, tied himself on, and hastened up to our level, having left his camera on the traverse below. In this way we found ourselves together again, on the corner of the *arête*. The others fixed themselves to a little belaying-pin while I attempted to swarm up the vertical corner. A couple of feet above their heads I found that the only available holds were sloping the wrong way. They could be easily reached, but were unsafe for hauling, and after clinging for some minutes without advancing an inch I was compelled to descend and reconsider the problem. I thought of Andrea del Sarto :

> Ah ! but a man's reach should exceed his grasp
> Or what's a Heaven for ?

and wondered whether Browning meant this to apply to the crests of climbing-pitches as well as to other objects in life.

At the time we did not know the exact history of the early attempts on the *arête*. As far as we could judge our corner might be inaccessible except with the help of a rope fixed above us. Certainly the scoring of bootnails on the face was scanty. The earlier party three years before might have planned to avoid the bad bit. With doubts like these, I craved permission to look up a chimney on the Deep Ghyll side of the ridge. The other party of climbers had now reached the top of the ghyll, and were watching our manœuvres with interest. Seeing my hesitation they called out to inquire whether we should like a rope from the Low Man. We were grateful for the suggestion, but there was no peril in our position, and we asked them to wait for awhile at the top of the gully, and see the issue of our next attempt upwards. Then, traversing over a buttress, I looked up and down the chimney.

It was what is generally called hopeless. To speak definitely, it was much worse than the *aréte*, and seeing no alternative I returned to the corner and prepared for another attempt. This time Ashley gave me a shoulder at a slightly lower level on the ghyll side of the ridge. A trying drag upwards with very scanty fingerholds brought my knees on to a satisfying hollow in a little ledge, and steadied by the two side faces of the sloping slab I stepped up and on to it. The cheers of the observing party told us that our *mauvais pas* was practically overcome. The other two men came up with a little assistance from the rope, and we cleared away the loose stones from our platform. It shelved badly downwards and offered no guarantee of safety in case I fell from the next vertical bit. But George sturdily rammed his brother close against the wall and intimated that the two would accept the responsibility of fielding me if

G. P. Abraham & Sons, Photos.   Keswick

ASCENT OF SCAWFELL PINNACLE FROM DEEP GHYLL

(Face page 83)

necessary. I mounted their shoulders, and reached up at arm's length to a sharp and firm edge of rock. A preliminary grind of my boot into a shoulder-blade and then a clear swing out on the arms, a desperate pull-up with knees and toes vainly seeking support, and at last the upper shelf was mounted. But we were all breathless.

The lower edge of the broken crest of rock that marks the Low Man was now close at hand. Close by was the fine cairn built when the pinnacle was first climbed from Lord's Rake. A few yards off to the east the edge of the cliff was cut by the top of Slingsby's Chimney, and before us remained the magnificent ridge up to the summit.

Boot scratches were now numerous, both along the ridge and by the left. We took the finish hand over hand, and reached the pinnacle cairn in five minutes. Our time up from Lord's Rake had been slow—something like four hours—but much had been spent with photography and in reconnoitring. Another day, two years later, I managed it in less than half the time.

A party of three should have 150 feet of rope, or else our awkward tactics in letting the rope down to the ghyll would have to be repeated. Perhaps the long run out for the leader will prevent this route ever becoming popular. It is a great pity that there is no resting-place half way up the wall. With icy conditions it would be criminal to attempt the open face. Yet the climb is one of the very best in the

district, and I shall always look back with pleasure
to my first introduction to this side of Scawfell
Pinnacle.

We hurried down Deep Ghyll by the traverse
above both pitches. One of us rushed down too
jubilantly, and ill repaid the kindly attention of the
other party, now below us, by a profuse shower of
stones. With thoughts of all the possible consequences of this indiscretion, we picked up our
cameras and strode more sedately down to the others
and to Wastdale.

Scawfell Pinnacle from Lord's Rake.—A
very fine expedition was undertaken in December,
1887, by Messrs. C. Hopkinson, Holder, H. Woolley,
and Bury. Their note on the day's sport is quoted
almost in full: ' Three of the party, led by Hopkinson,
made an attempt on the Deep Ghyll Pinnacle from
the entrance to Lord's Rake. They succeeded in
climbing 150 to 200 feet, but were stopped by a
steep slab of rock coated with ice. From this point,
however, a good traverse was made to the first gully,
or chimney, on the left. They forced their way up
this gully to the top of the chimney. At the top
there was a trough of ice about 30 feet long, surmounted by steep rocks glazed with ice, which
brought the party to a stop. They descended the
chimney again and returned to Wastdale, unani-
mously of opinion that the day's excursion had
afforded one of the finest climbs the party had ever
accomplished.'

So we may well think, and it is a great pity that the icy conditions of the rock prevented their direct ascent into Slingsby's chimney. The gully they entered and almost completely ascended, is marked plainly in the general view of the Scawfell Crags from the Pulpit, and at first sight appears to run up continuously to Slingsby's chimney. Actually, however, it finishes on the side of the nose or pinnacle of rock a few feet lower down, and I believe this pinnacle could be ascended from it by either side. What this earlier party found impossible in the winter of 1887, Mr. G. T. Walker and I in April, 1898, favoured by the best of conditions, were just able to overcome. We had spent a long and exciting day in the neighbourhood, and were descending Slingsby's chimney late in the afternoon, when we were suddenly struck with the idea of descending the fissure behind the nose and prospecting the face of rock between it and Deep Ghyll. A rough inspection of the first fifty feet below us proving satisfactory, we hastened down Steep Ghyll and traversed across to the top of the first pitch in Deep Ghyll. In spite of the late hour I could not refrain from a trial trip on the edge of the great Low Man buttress. At the point where the earlier party found the direct ascent barred by smooth ice on the wall, and decided to traverse off to the gully on the left, we had a council of war. It resulted in my throwing down my boots to Walker, and then crawling up fifty feet of, perhaps, the steepest and

smoothest slabs to which I have ever trusted myself.
This brought me to a tiny corner where I essayed to
haul in the rope attached to my companion. But he
also had to remove his boots and traverse to a point
vertically below me before he could follow up in safety.
We were now some distance to the left of the edge of
Deep Ghyll, and straight up above us we could
distinguish the crack where our new route was to
terminate. Getting Walker to lodge firmly in a
notch somewhat larger than mine, six feet away on
the Steep Ghyll side, I went off again up another
forty feet of smooth rock, aided by a zig-zagging
crack an inch or so in width, that supplied sufficient
lodgment for the toes, and a moderate grip for the
finger-tips. After both had arrived thus far, we
were able, with extreme care, to reach the side wall
of the nose itself, and at a point, perhaps, fifty feet
from its crest we turned round its main outside
buttress and found ourselves in a spacious chamber
with a flat floor and a considerable roof, the first and
only genuine resting-place worthy the name that we
found along our route. We could look straight
down Hopkinson's gully, and would gladly have
descended into it and 'passed the time of day' with
a little speculative scrambling thereabouts. But
darkness was coming on apace, and we had yet a
most awkward corner to negotiate before finishing
our appointed business. Standing on Walker's
shoulders I screwed myself out at the right-hand
top corner of our waiting-room, and started along a

traverse across the right face of the nose. The toes
of the feet were in a horizontal crack, the heels had
no support, and the hands no grip. It was only by
pressing the body close to the wall, which was
fortunately a few degrees away from the perpendicular,
and by sliding the feet along almost inch by inch,
that the operation could be effected. It was with
no small sense of relief that the end was reached in
a few yards, and a narrow vertical fissure entered
that gave easy access to the top of the nose. Then
we put on our boots again and hurried.

It is thus possible to reach the summit of the
Scawfell Pinnacle by a route up the buttress quite
independent of either of the great ghylls that flank it.
A good variation that has yet to be performed in its
entirety, though I believe that every section has been
independently climbed, is that of the Hopkinson's
chimney, the nose, and Slingsby's chimney. Further,
that evening's climb has convinced me that we could
have safely reached Hopkinson's cairn on the edge of
Deep Ghyll, and that there is in consequence a most
thrilling piece of work possible in the direct ascent
of the buttress, the whole way up to the High Man
from its base. Slight divergences are, probably,
unavoidable in the lower half of the climb, but
permitting these there now remain only about forty
feet of rock hitherto unascended. It is worth while
inspecting the view on page 73. The top of the
nose is there plainly seen in profile $4\frac{3}{8}$ inches from
the bottom; our climb was roughly speaking up to

the nose, by a vertical line drawn an inch from the left edge of the picture—somewhat less as it approached completion.

Upper Deep Ghyll Route.—Three days after the ascent recorded in the last section, I found that the sharp ridge between the Low Man and the summit of the pinnacle could be reached from the foot of the lowest pitch of the Professor's Chimney. The suggestion is due to Dr. Collier, who told me some years ago that the only real difficulties are concentrated in the first thirty feet of the ascent. The climb is almost in a straight line, running obliquely up the Deep Ghyll face of the Pinnacle, and is best inspected from the west wall traverse. The first part overhangs considerably, and the holds are of the same character as those on the long slabs of the Low Man buttress, with a sort of absent look about them. But the rocks were dry and warm, in the best possible condition, and two minutes of deliberate movement led me out of danger. There is great variety just here, but the simplest course was to make for a slight chimney in the sharp ridge above my head. In twenty minutes the High Man had been crossed, and the starting-point reached by way of the Professor's Chimney, but if a companion and a long rope had been vouchsafed on that occasion it would have been a pleasing undertaking to have tried the traverse along the wall to the *firma loca* of the second section in this chapter.

CHAPTER VI

GREAT END AND ITS GULLIES

As we walk up towards the Styhead Pass from Wastdale we may see well in front of us the long ridge of the Pikes monopolizing a goodly portion of the sky-line. The high dependence at the head of the valley we are skirting is Great End, a reasonable enough name for the north-east head of the range. It sends down a buttress towards the Styhead Pass that, at a closer view, is shown to be well separated from the main mass by a deep gully of some architectural merit. This is Skew Ghyll. It twists its way up to the ridge, and offers a pleasant variation route over to Sprinkling Tarn, whence a steep rise brings the tourist to the Esk Hause, the lowest point between Great End and Bowfell. The climber's interest will be concentrated in the view of the long northern face of Great End, well seen from Sprinkling Tarn, and his experienced eye will notice at once that the face is marked by various gullies that invite approach. The whole ground has been thoroughly well examined from time to time, with the result that several gullies which from below or above appear to promise continuous climbing have proved to be deceptive in this respect. Yet there

remain two that are always interesting, and a third
that is at any rate popular as a winter course.

Seen from the tarn there are two gullies that cut
the full height of the precipice from top to bottom.
The lines of fresh scree that trail down from their
lower ends show up plainly on the older *débris*
that marks the decay of this mountain wall. They
both slope downwards towards the left when seen
from this point, and are both obviously provided
with variation exits at their upper extremities That
to the left was formerly called Robinson's Gully, but
is now generally known as the South-east Gully.
There has always been a lack of originality in the
nomenclature of such places, and with several routes
on the same mountain the christener's wits seem
driven to all points of the compass. The second
gully is a hundred yards to the right of the first,
and has long been known as the Great End Central
Gully. It divides half way up into two well-
marked portions, the right-hand route constituting
the main bed of the gully, and terminating at a
huge notch in the sky-line. The left-hand branch
as seen from below appears to terminate blindly in
the face, but actually it leads to a deep and narrow
chimney cutting into the top wall within a hundred
feet of the main gully.

Far away to the right, where the cliff has shrunk
to but one-third of its full height at the Central
Gully, a black cleft may be descried that leads from
scree to sky-line. This is Cust's Gully, indifferent

G. P. Abraham & Sons, Photos.   Keswick

THE GREAT END GULLIES SEEN FROM SPRINKLING TARN

(Face page 90)

as a summer climb, but always beautiful in the richness of its rock scenery, and especially interesting in
winter, when drift snow offers a royal road to the
top. Every one has a kind word for Cust's Gully.
It is only called the Cussed gully by ignorant
novices who inquire whether Skew of Skew Ghyll
fame was a member of the Alpine Club. When it
is marked out by snow we can from the path just
distinguish the great rock bridge or natural arch
across the upper part of the cleft.

Great End Central Gully.—This wonderful
ravine offers some special feature every winter. Its
individuality changes so completely under the mask
of snow, or ice, or rain, that an attempt to describe
the gully by an account of any one expedition must
of necessity be only partially successful.

One fine winter morning a year or so ago we had
a large party at Wastdale, and for once in a way
were all of the same mind as to our day's plans.
The walk up towards the Styhead Pass—the Schwein-
hauskopfjoch of the Swiss travellers among us—
would just suit our conversationally-minded fraternity, to whom Brown Tongue or the Pillar Fell
or the Gable-end offered gradients too steep for
words. We sallied forth from the inn with many
axes and great lengths of rope, and lazily worked
our way along the valley. The lower path, entirely
obliterated by the snow, took us across the stream
to the right on to the low slopes of Lingmell.
Piers Ghyll stream was crossed without notice, for

here the gorge is not at all in evidence and requires
closer examination to reveal its magnificence.   Then,
rising a few feet, we crossed the hollow of Grainy
Ghyll and made towards Spout Head and Skew Ghyll.
The snow gave us some glorious effects on the hills
around.   The Mosedale amphitheatre of noble mountains towered above Wastdale, and mutely questioned
us as to the accuracy of the surveyors who could
give them not even three thousand feet of elevation
above us.   Nowadays theodolites are taken to the
mountains and misused with great effect ; why should
not the Pillar and Red Pike benefit similarly to the
extent of a thousand feet or so ?   There above us on
our left was Great Gable, a white pyramid cutting
into a dark sky, at least ten thousand feet of mountain
beauty between us and its snowy crest.   Who could
believe that the summit was only 2,900 feet above
sea level ?   But the engineer among us calmly
reminded me of an interesting aneroid observation I
had once taken of the top of Moss Ghyll on Scawfell,
making it a hundred feet higher than Scawfell itself.
Was I to rank myself as a truthful scientist and be
contented with the ordnance survey records, or as
an artist who should represent heights, shapes, and
colours as his imperfect senses make them ?   We
closed the discussion in favour of the artist and then
sloped (without slang) up to Skew Ghyll.

   This was in splendid condition ; the snow was
deep and hard, and out of sheer pleasure in step-
cutting, three or four enthusiasts carved their own

staircases up through the 'narrows' and away
towards the little pass above us. It was to be noticed
that the steps gradually converged to one line as
the leaders felt their muscles wearying, and they were
willing to fall in with the caravan now trailing up
in single file like the elements of a kite's tail. At the
top of our little pass we could see straight down
Borrowdale. Skiddaw and Blencathara formed the
distant background. Derwent-water reflected a dark
sky, and by contrast with its snowy shores looked of
an inky blackness. Styhead Tarn was not very beautiful ; ice had formed on it a week before, but had
since been broken up by the wind, and the great
flakes of crystal unevenly crusted with drift snow
gave a sense of roughness and of incompleteness out
of keeping with the finished beauty of the surroundings.

We stayed up here for a few minutes, and then
contoured along the side of Great End in the direction
of Esk Hause. The ground was rough ; here and
there the snow required cutting. But no difficulties
were met with until the narrow entrance to the Central Gully suddenly disclosed itself in the precipitous
wall on our right. The gully points down towards
the eastern corner of Sprinkling Tarn. It begins
where the cliff stands nearest to the Esk Hause path,
and is not to be mistaken for the South-east Gully
that points directly towards the sharp bend in the
little stream rattling down to Borrowdale.

At the entrance to our climb we stopped to

consider the question of roping up. 'Union is strength' only within certain narrow limits, when the bond of union is an Alpine rope. It often involves loss of time.

> Down to Gehenna or up to the Throne,
> He travels the fastest who travels alone,

and his speed is inversely proportional to the number of his followers. We decided to split up into three equal parties of four, my men to lead up the main gully, the engineer to convey the second set up the middle course, and the more substantial residue to bear to the left, up a slighter branch that contains a very creditable cave pitch half-way towards the summit ridge.

Our work was easy at the outset. The gully was narrow and steep, but the snow was good, and small ledges on either side were utilized whenever the little icicle-clad pitches were too slippery for direct attack. Where the gully widened a little we could see the first serious obstacle in front of us—a vertical wall with a ragged ice-curtain flung over it in a most artistic way. It would perhaps have been possible to cut directly upwards, but the crowd of eager climbers behind could not be expected to fight against frostbite for an hour or so while the leader amused himself, and the obvious method of circumventing the difficulty had its own merits. The right wall slightly overhung; close below was a glazed rib of rock leading up at an easy angle to the top of the pitch.

PLATE III.

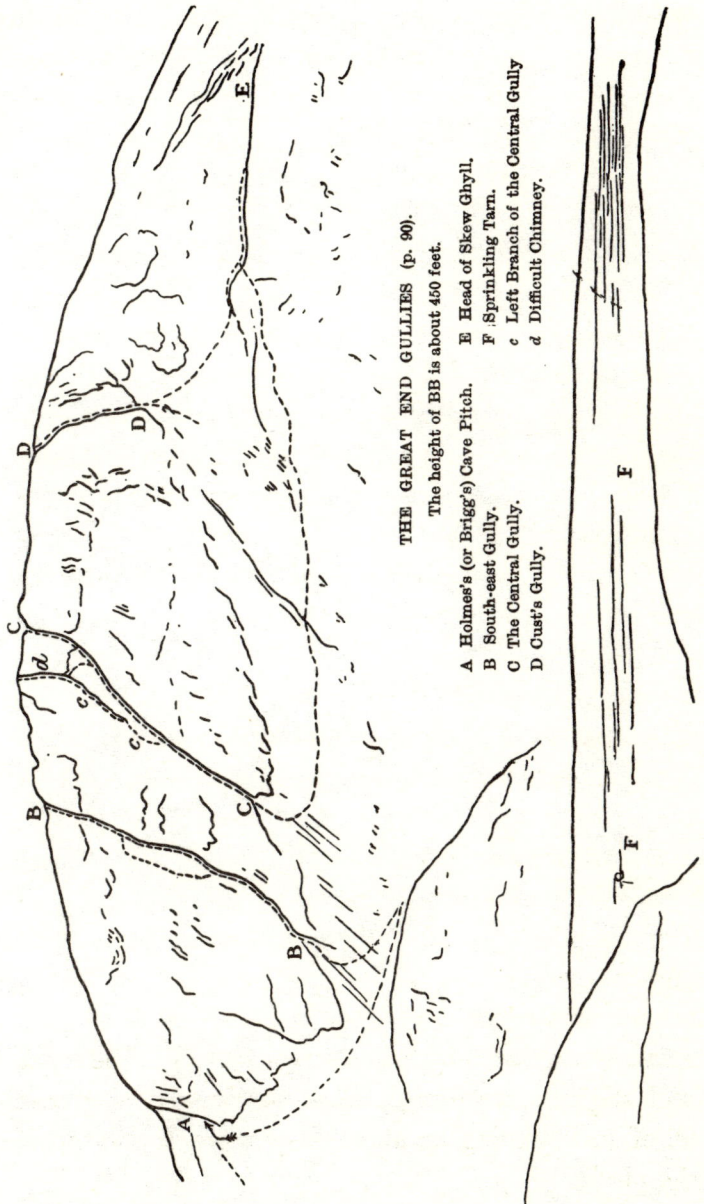

THE GREAT END GULLIES (p. 90).

The height of BB is about 450 feet.

A Holmes's (or Brigg's) Cave Pitch.
B South-east Gully.
C The Central Gully.
D Cust's Gully.
E Head of Skew Ghyll.
F Sprinkling Tarn.
c Left Branch of the Central Gully.
d Difficult Chimney.

Steadying myself against the wall, I started cutting slight steps up the thin ice on the rock, keeping as near to the corner as possible. Now and again the foothold felt insecure, but for the most part the ascent was safe, with slight probability of a slip into the snow below. The second man followed close up, and steadied my feet occasionally with an ice-axe. Then came a more gentle snow-slope, up which we could kick steps without effort; and while the second party were busy with the difficulties that we had just overcome, we reached the second pitch and hastened to leave it behind us. This was rather a harder task than we had yet undertaken. The gully was more open and its ice covering less extensive, but the pitch was higher and involved our climbing up to the centre from the right-hand wall, so as to reach the base of the big boulder that crowns the pitch. All this would have been easy with the rocks clear and dry, but we had to make our footholds on the flimsiest rags of ice, and the traverse to the middle demanded some long stepping with scarcely a hand to steady. On reaching the boulder I was compelled to crawl on all-fours round its front to the slope on the left-hand side of the gully, and then by cutting a dozen steps or so in the hard snow found myself in the wide part of the gully at the foot of the great divide. The others of my party followed on rapidly, and we shouted adieu to our companions beneath.

Here we had the finest view of the climb. Below, the beauties of the two pitches were greatly increased by our own elevation. They looked very difficult, and the picture offered its living element in the cautiously advancing parties now just in the interesting part of the climb. Above us rose the huge buttress that divides the gully, and on either side the most fantastic drapery of ice well-nigh frightened us with its appearance of impregnability. We advanced carefully up to the right, congratulating ourselves on having taken the lead, for our friends were not pleased with the battery of hard chips of snow that our step-cutting gave them. The buttress was rounded, and we gained a full view of the troubles in store for us. Immediately on our left a smooth rock-shoot led straight up to the top of the buttress. Between the vertical pillar on the right of this shoot and the opposite side of the gully rose a sheer wall of ice, like a frozen waterfall twenty-five feet in height. So far as we could see at first, there was no chance of forcing a quick way up this obstacle, and it was obvious that slowness would introduce the risk of frostbite. During the previous summer my fingers had been rather badly frostbitten in the Alps, and there was some chance of their still manifesting a susceptibility to cold. We almost turned back to follow our friends up another way; we could trust each other to exaggerate the terrors of this bit, which honestly enough was a trifle too stiff for a cold winter day. But while mentally framing an excuse for the return, I had advanced up to the left-hand edge of the ' ice fall,' and started the

ascent of its spiky edging of rock. From below the
spikes had appeared fragile and untrustworthy.
Actually they were too well frozen into place to
become detached with one's cautious drag. This
discovery altered the prospect for us all, and the
chilly watchers below warmed up with the returning
enthusiasm. In fact they needed reminding that I
might yet come down suddenly to their level and
sweep them off their feet unless they were prepared
to receive me. When ten feet up, the axe was called
into requisition to cut a few steps in the fall itself.
These were useful just so long as the left hand could
utilise the rocks, but they tended to carry me away
from my comparatively safe corner, and I soon
decided to keep away from the fall as far as possible.
The corner where the gully sloped back was very
exciting, for implicit trust was reposed in the
benumbed left hand that had been thrust, well gloved,
into a thin and icy crack in the wall, and held there
by frost and friction. It offered no sensation either
of security or of danger, but it could not very well
slip out, and we hoped for the best. A few moments'
struggling landed me safely on the steep slope above
the pitch, and a vigorous handling of the ice-axe on
the bed of the gully fully restored circulation to my
hands. Then followed my cold companions, who had
been shivering spectators for a long twenty minutes.
They were thus handicapped from the outset, and
found the pitch very severe, notwithstanding the
gentle suggestion of safety that the rope offered.

We had some careful work still before us. The bed of the gully led steeply up to another large and slightly overhanging boulder that blocked the direct route, and our only possible method of getting above it was to cut steps away on the right, trusting to sundry very insecure grass holds. But these were much better than usual by reason of the frost. In fact the whole climb is perfectly sound in winter, though rendered very difficult. In summer it is often easy but dangerous.

From the steep right-hand side of the gully we could traverse with care to the main bed again, just above the boulder; whence to the top of the gully, looking from here like an Alpine pass, was a broad stretch of unspotted snow. There we joined the second party, who had come by the steep grass ledges of the central route. Their labours had been great—or else, indeed, they would easily have managed to get ahead of us—but not so much from the intrinsic difficulty of their route as from the need of continual caution in the more open portions of the climb. They had reached a ledge that overlooked the right branch, and were proposing to descend to our snow slope and cut steps up with us. We were nothing loth to give them a chance of showing their skill with the axe, and for a while halted to enjoy the grand prospect behind us, looking straight away towards Sprinkling Tarn and Borrowdale. Bnt we found ourselves frequently buffeted by strong gusts of wind that swept

G. P. Abraham & Sons, Photos.

Keswick

GREAT GABLE FROM SPRINKLING TARN (WINTER)

furiously down the gully. The whirling snow at the little *col*, now so near, warned us of an approaching *tourmente* on the ridge. Our section soon decided to start again, and just below a small cornice that crowned the gully we forged ahead, and plunged through the powdery fringe of overhanging snow. We sank in up to our waists, and had to wrestle mightily against the hurricane to find a firm footing on the wind-swept rocks beyond. It was no joke standing about there with the sharp, cold, drift snow from the Pikes blowing into our smarting faces. We could not hear ourselves speak, it was almost impossible to see the correct course ; but there were two or three among us well acquainted with this ridge in its bitterest moods, and to these the others trusted. We floundered down to the right towards Esk Hause across the wilderness of blocks strewn over the great plateau, and in a hundred yards came to a boulder large enough to possess a lee side of its own. Here we halted for a chilly half-hour, waiting for the third section to arrive. I possessed their luncheon in my knapsack, a most regrettable circumstance from our point of view, inasmuch as it tied us to Great End so long as it pleased them to amuse themselves down there on the leeside of the mountain. We quickly demolished our own share of the provisions, and with an unselfishness rarely present in the great latterday mountaineering expeditions, decided to leave them a few sandwiches and to cloy the hungry edge of our remaining appetites with tobacco. We were not all smokers, but everybody present assisted in lighting the first pipe, such a labour was it to keep a match burning. We waited there in a close bundle until our feet were half frozen and our faces stiff with icicles. Then we became rather nervous about our missing friends, and debated whether they meant to reach the top that day, or whether they had turned their backs to the lunch and made for Sprinkling Tarn. The latter course seemed at once the most expedient for them and the most convenient for us, and gladly we acted on this assumption. It was just as well we did so, for the frost had sharply nipped some of us, and it was long before my heels gave me any sensation but that of a pair of snowballs in my boots. We slung round the Esk Hause, and had some fine glissading to the hollow of the hill below the crags.

When well opposite our climb at the point whence we had started some five hours earlier, our united shouting brought back an answering call from the gully. Soon we could see the burly form of their greatest member slowly descending the crags at about the same spot where we had long before left him. Having distinguished him as a preliminary landmark easy of recognition, the three others were one by one made out. We were relieved to observe that they were all coming down in a normal condition ; no broken limb or sprained ankle had occurred to spoil their pleasure and stop their climbing. After a few minutes' waiting we learnt their story. The left-hand route had begun in a vertical ice-sheet twenty feet high that took them two hours to surmount. Then, when with sighs of relief, or hyperbolic language, or eloquent silence, that marked each individual's satisfaction at the happy completion of a difficult pitch, they had cut their way over the edge of this wall and rounded the traverse that dominated it, they were aghast to meet a wall of ice in every respect similar to the first, but magnified! This was heart-breaking, but they made a bold bid for success, and started afresh on the new task. But the daylight was already within an hour of vanishing, and a night on those rocks would have been too much for even the sturdiest of them.

So with a wisdom not often met with in such cases where an element of competition enters into the day's work, they resolved to retire and join us below. There we met again, and they received their lunch. I was censured to a slight extent, but blame is pretty sure to be the portion of him who carries the provisions. He that shoulders the bag is a responsible individual, and the condition of good training that it induces is moral as well as physical.

Then let me insist on the value of such physical training. The photographer who takes his camera to the High Alps is often too fond of his apparatus to give it up to a guide or porter; he frequently decides hurriedly to take a shot, and soon learns that it is best to carry all for himself. Economy may often preach the same precept. Now to lift his own weight is a labour he at first fancies will tax all his strength, but a little practice in carrying a well constructed and well packed rücksack on small expeditions will teach him something different. The weight of the whole equipment for half-plate photography—camera, three lenses, tripod, and other accessories—is so small a fraction of his own weight that its mere lift is a negligible consideration. His pace will be diminished and his back often uncomfortably heated. But supposing the burden well arranged, many a climber could habituate himself to it. One of our greatest Alpine climbers is said to train in Cumberland by carrying a rücksack filled with stones. Without attempting to persuade any one but a geologist so to burden himself on principle, I strongly advise the man who hopes ultimately to climb without guides to get early into the habit of carrying loads on smaller ascents. It will always be a joy to travel free when occasional opportunity offers, and then he will assuredly improve his pace. On a really stiff pitch the sack may have to be raised independently by the rope, a cause of serious delay when the rope is rigid with frost and the party inexperienced in tying knots or reliable loops. It should be remembered that the sack has more than once protected the climber from serious injury by falling stones, and that a pound or two of extra luggage carried up to an Alpine hut may mean all the difference between a night of misery and a comfortable rest before an arduous expedition.

I have mentioned that the middle route up the Central Gully leads by easy stages to the upper portion of the right-hand branch. Some three years ago a strong party effected an ascent of the chimney that points directly up to the top of the cliff from the high ledge between the two routes. We found the main difficulty was in traversing over an open slab on the right of the foot of the chimney. The slab was split by a narrow fissure, but the handholds were slight and rather insecure. To have trusted to one alone would have been dangerous, and I recall with amusement the spread-eagle attitude of the leader as he endeavoured to distribute his weight equally on four rickety points of support. The position was good enough in itself, but to move involved a dangerous increase in the stress on one of the supports. Fortunately the second on the rope was able to offer an axe-head as additional security, and the passage to the left was effected in safety. The chimney was narrow and its sides smooth, but with the exception of a loose stone near the finish, which rattled down and tended to disturb our wedging, nothing seriously interfered with our advance.

But there was one amongst us who, in expectation of falling stones, had thrust his head and shoulders into the little cave at the foot of the chimney. When the leader shouted to him he did not hear, and the accompanying pull on the rope resulted in the hitching of his shoulders firmly in the cleft and the elevation of his legs only. The previous evening we had been having a heated discussion as to the futility of naming the sides of a gully or cave after the manner of the banks of a river—*i.e.* of calling the 'true' right side of a gully its left and *vice-versâ*. Professor M., who was with us now, had been a listener to the discussion. Looking down from the top of the chimney and observing the unusual method of our friend's ascent, he called out, 'It's all right, Jones, he is coming up well enough—the " true up." '

South-east Gully.—This in summer time can often be accomplished in half an hour if the climbers are few and in a hurry. Before December, 1896, I had not made a winter ascent; moreover, I had forgotten much of the detail. Thinking of climbing notes, I persuaded a small Christmas party to join me in exploring the gully under these new conditions.

We were only a band of three ultimately, though at Kern Knotts, which we visited *en route*, our number was considerably larger. The other two were both experienced Alpine climbers, one a very tall man, the other very short. I was anxious to determine the advantages and disadvantages of size and weight, and to that end took the lead myself and placed the tall man second on the rope. We had but little wind, and the temperature was slightly above freezing-point.

The climbing began almost at once, for in five minutes from the foot the gully walls were close together and were encrusted with thawing ice. The narrow bed was broken up into easy pitches, but to avoid the stream of water that came down beneath the soft covering of snow it was necessary to use small ledges on either side, and span the gully like diminutive colossi—here I am referring only to myself and the little one. Now and again we would plunge up the gully for a short distance in loose snow. Occasionally the crystals became more compact, and two of us could manage to creep over its surface without slipping through. Rarely was this the case with our middle man—a sixteen-stone Teuton with a scientific training. If snow could be crushed he crushed it. He became so indifferent in the matter after awhile, that he made no attempt to distribute his weight evenly over the surface according to the rules laid down by Badminton. The little one, coming last, naturally suffered by this indifference, and was plaintive over what he called the 'fallacy of the undistributed middle.'

The first pitch of any size occurred within 200 feet of the foot of the gully, a perfectly vertical rise of twenty feet in the bed level with a slender waterfall interfering with our direct progress. The retaining walls were the least bit too far apart for the utilization of both simultaneously, and the right side commended itself to us as the easier to attack. Our only trouble again was the glaze on the rocks, a black, shiny veneer too thin for axe operations, too thick to be trifled with. Such ice always interferes more with the hands than with the feet, for sharp boot nails can roughen the surface of an ice ledge

enough for a foothold, whereas the hands can make
no impression. If the ice is very cold, gloves must
be worn as a protection against the frost. They
have the merit of adhering slightly to the ice when
pressed, and often in that way give the climber
a safe-enough grip. With wet ice such regelation
will not occur, and if the work is hazardous I prefer
to climb with free hands, trusting to friction to
restore circulation wherever an ' easy ' may be
called.

Making slowly up this wall to a snowy ledge at
the top level of the pitch, I called on the others to
follow, and then worked back into the gully. Here
we found ourselves facing the 'divide,' a high and
narrow rib of rock that cut down into the gully and
gave us a choice of routes. Our way lay up to the
right, which a distant view from Sprinkling Tarn
had shown us to be really the main line. The other
branch ends somewhat abruptly out on the face, and
involves a traverse into the main again. A few
yards further up, and a very imposing pitch rose
before us. It was in three portions, the gap between
the second and the third blocked by a huge stone
that bridged the gully. As on the lower fall, so
here the water kept us off the centre-line of the
ravine, and drove us to seek diversion on the right.
On the first part we had the difficulty of snow and
wet ice. Without comment I noticed the little one
carefully wipe out a handhold with his handkerchief
when it was his turn to mount. By the same

manœuvre he had some three years before shown me how to scramble up a small boulder in the Engelberg valley that I was forced to admit I could not climb. It was interesting to observe how little space he needed for his fingers. On a wall with diminutive ledges that might easily pass unnoticed, he could show us all what 'walking up' a face of rock really meant, though his short reach naturally handicapped him now and again very seriously. I believe a short man generally does best on rocks. His hands are as a rule stronger in proportion to his weight. The long climber can reach further but is often unable to utilize the distant grip to which he has stretched, if it is small or badly rounded. Moreover, he often finds himself in the attitude of a looping caterpillar, a pose that demands a firmer handgrip and that rapidly exhausts the muscles.

We all reached the first ledge safely. Then came the passage of the bridge. If we passed under it we should get terribly wet and cold, though there would be no particular difficulty in getting through to the final chimney. Every inch of the boulder was glazed, and it offered very few excrescences to hang upon. But it had the making of an edge at its crest, and I gradually worked up the outside till I could reach this and pull up. There is one advantage of a glaze— possibly its only one—it offers no friction to one's body in an arm-pull.

Thence it was an easy step over to the final chimney. A small spout of water as thick as one's wrist was jetting from the top against the right wall, and we were inevitably in for a wetting in spite of the circumvention of the bridge. I essayed to finish the pitch before the others started from their ledge twenty feet below. A fairly good lodgment for the right foot was utilized and passed. The body had to be jammed across the chimney, the fingers seeking for a crevice high up on the right wall. When a slab is streaming with water and handholds can be found within easy reach, it is a good plan to keep 'thumbs down' as much as possible ; for then the water will drain off by the thumbs, and run clear of the coat-sleeves. The strain is too great to operate in this way with arms at full length above the head. That was manifest in my trouble on the wall. The ice-cold water trickled down my arms and body, making me wet through in a few moments. But the horror of it came with the realization that I was unable to move backwards or forwards. The situation was almost critical, but not an unusual one for winter climbing in Cumberland. I could at any rate give it my cool consideration, and decide whether to call up the big one to help me or to try an independent descent. The men below saw me in trouble and made a move upwards towards the pitch. Then it occurred to me that the big one would not be able to force a way under the bridge, and that he might be a long time working over it, longer than I could manage to hold out. That decided me, and I started wriggling downwards.

Luckily the hands were not yet benumbed, and by entire disregard of the main water-supply down the central line of flow, which now included the back of my neck, I managed to reach the platform again. Until my second came up it was useless to make another attempt, and indeed it was now eminently desirable that everybody should get wet. I am not an advocate for monopoly in such cases. With some slight inducement suggested by the rope, the big one pulled himself over the bridge and came up to the platform. Here he was invited to hold himself firmly against the wall, and give me his shoulders and head for elevating purposes. He was immediately drenched before I had effected a start up his mighty back, but there was a sense of perfect security now ; it would be impossible to fall past him. As for the effect of cold and wet on him, we could neglect so small a consideration. In any case he would not feel it till the trouble was over. I thought of the old dynamics problem beginning : ' Let a fly of mass m be crawling up the trunk of an elephant, whose mass may be neglected,' and realized for the first time that there was some sense in the quaint hypothesis. Once on his shoulders I reached up to a dry ledge, dragged myself on to it, and thence strode across to the top of the pitch.

The third man had managed to reach the platform during these operations, and now nobly offered his little all as a foothold for the giant. My heart sank when I heard it graciously accepted, but it rested with me to share the responsibility and let the rope take up some of the stress. The big one came up grandly with these small aids, and we hurried the little one to send along my camera sack and then himself. This pitch was the hardest part of the day's work, and showed itself to vary much with existing circumstances. I can just remember enough of a former expedition to add that it needs care in summer time, though it cannot, rightly speaking, be called difficult.

We then went upwards again over snow at a gentle angle till the third pitch was reached. This was of a simple design, just a cave formed by a fallen boulder, and no doubt it could be taken in many ways. We climbed up a six-feet wall on the right from the entrance to the cave, and scrambled easily into the snow-bed beyond. Thence to the top was a matter of only ten minutes, the single hindrance being a pile of boulders that were climbed by an easy tunnel that led to the crest of the left-hand wall of the gully. We walked out at the top just as twilight set in, after some two hours' gentle excitement. We were naturally still damp, and felt no inclination to stay about on the ridge, so hurrying round towards Esk Hause we glissaded rapidly to the path and walked home.

The left-hand variation in the gully is often taken, but is scarcely as interesting. Just after passing the divide we find another buttress of rock cutting the gully into two sections. Here the buttress is not much thicker than an ordinary brick wall; it is sometimes called the 'curtain.' There are pitches on each side of it, that on the right being more definite and more interesting. It leads up a steep chimney to the crest of the curtain, which is crossed to the left. The climber is then in the left-hand branch, and has no difficulty in ascending the gully till it dwindles down to nothing, and he finds himself looking into the main south-east gully just above the third pitch. It will be best, then, to climb down and finish by the usual route.

Cust's Gully.—The climbing in this is of the slightest character in summer time, there being but one short pitch beneath the natural arch, and very little in that. But with hard snow about there is scarcely a pleasanter way of playing at Alpine climbing above the snow-line than by taking Great End *viâ* Skew Ghyll and Cust's Gully. The snow slope will alter in inclination from about 30° at the bottom to 70° at the top. If the pitch is but thinly covered, there is the fun of tackling a pitfall, and of bringing to bear on the safe crossing all the science that glacier crevasses may have taught us in Switzerland. Nor let any think that it is all make-believe and that of difficulty there is none. I have had grand times in Cust's Gully, where we were actually tired out with the labour of cutting steps. The snow when fresh is soft and yielding. Give it a week or two to settle down, and it will bind together so as to offer firm support on scraped footholds.

But let cold rain fall on hard snow and the temperature then fall below freezing-point, the surface will become icy and every step will require careful making. Then should the picturesque attitudes of step-cutting depicted in Badminton be imitated in all seriousness, and the axe wielded with the scientific swing. It has happened more than once that a bad axe has proved its worthlessness when tested on the Cumbrian fells in a winter expedition—a much less dangerous discovery than if it were taken new to the Alps and there found wanting. The difficulty in the latter case is that our axes are so rarely used for hard work, if we are led up the great peaks by competent guides. They delight in removing every obstacle in our way, and it may be that long usage of the axe has really been but a test of the *bâton*, not at all of the pick. Then comes a time when the leading weapon is broken, or carelessly dropped, or still more carelessly pitched up to a ledge of only suppositious safety. Do not imagine that these things never happen, for each has been within my own experience during the last three years; and woe to the party if the untested axe is a weakling when emergency calls on it!

The upper part of Cust's Gully when the snow is at its hardest may almost be regarded as a test of nerve for the novice. I once was starting to cut down the gully in such a state, with a young man of limited Alpine knowledge, who diffidently suggested that step-cutting was rather slow and that he would prefer a glissade if I did not mind. I shuddered at the vision his naïve suggestion conjured up, of a species of chain-shot shooting viciously down the tremendously steep slope, ricochetting from wall to wall of the gully, and scraped very bare by the sharp-toothed icy surface. That novice had no nerves, and my remarks are not intended for him. The contention is that an amateur party cutting up the steepening slope, and forging a way through an incipient cornice of overhanging frost crystals at the top, will learn much of the genuine safety of an ice-slope, and will see how to divest it of its imaginary dangers. There are many Alpine climbers positively afraid of harmless slopes, that are not nearly so bad as they appear, and still less formidable than they show up in photographs. Such men have never led up steep snow.

Near the foot of Cust's Gully a branch passes up to the right, of less altitude and gentler inclination ; its rock scenery is not so fine, and the place is rarely visited.

CHAPTER VII

GREAT GABLE.   THE ENNERDALE FACE AND
THE OBLIQUE CHIMNEY.

GREAT GABLE takes high rank among the hills
of Britain for grace of form and for the beauty of
the views it offers to the climber.   It is a square
pyramid in shape, and shows nearly its full height
(2,949 feet) from the Wastdale level.   It stands at
the head of the valley, and when seen from the
shores of the lake appears completely to shut off the
valley from all approach by the north end.   Its four
main ridges offer fairly easy walking to the summit.
The north - east ridge runs down towards Green
Gable, Brandreth, Grey Knotts, and the Honister
pass, a little *col* marking the lowest point (2,400 feet)
between the peak and Green Gable.   A moderate
path leads the pedestrian from Borrowdale up by
way of Aaron Slack towards this little pass, which is
known as Wind Gap, and then bears up towards
Great Gable.   The pass may be crossed into Ennerdale
and a rough descent taken to the Liza stream.

The north-west ridge leads down towards Kirkfell.   The broad depression between the two
mountains is known as Beckhead (2,000 feet).   It is
often marshy in the neighbourhood of the diminutive

G. P. Abraham & Sons, Photos.

Keswick

WASTDALE AND GREAT GABLE

(Face page 114)

Beckhead Tarn. A wire fence that adorns the summit-ridge from Kirkfell can be followed for some distance up Gable. Thence to the summit is somewhat craggy, but not difficult for pedestrians.

The south-west ridge is called the Gavel Neese (Gable Nose), showing from Wastdale Head as a rounded grassy shoulder leading directly towards the peak. Up this shoulder we may make the shortest ascent of Gable from Wastdale, avoiding the easy crags of White Napes that face us where the upper limit of the grass is passed, by skirting round the screes on the left. An ancient path with the strange name of Moses' Sledgate leads up Gavel Neese till the level of Beckhead is nearly reached, and then bears away on a traverse over the screes round to the middle of the Ennerdale side of the mountain, there to lose itself in the wilderness of stones that are bestrewn all over that desolate region.

The remaining ridge to the south-east is scarcely definite enough to be worthy the name, though from Wastdale it seems to be at least as well marked as Gavel Neese. It leads towards the Styhead pass (1,579 feet) and offers a quick route to the top. Mr. Haskett Smith suggests 'half an hour's rough walking,' but that pace is too severe for most walkers.

Of the four faces of the pyramid the north and south are precipitous, the west offers very little scope for the cragsman's skill, and the east absolutely none. The north or Ennerdale face is practically a single, exposed section of some 400 feet of rock, seamed with traverses and split with numerous gullies and chimneys. The south face is of a complicated design. Springing up from the 2,000-feet level, the Great Napes appears in the centre of the south face as a great rock screen belonging to the main mass of Gable. In reality it is well separated off by deep hollows cutting behind it to right and left. The highest point of the Napes is connected with the upper crags of Gable by the crest separating these two hollows, either of which may be followed down in safety by benighted wanderers who are past all wish to avoid screes, and whose one desire is to reach a low level in some inhabited valley.

Let us more happily suppose for the present that we are upward bound and desirous of circumventing Great Napes. We can observe from Wastdale Head the line of lighter scree that comes down either side of the Napes. That to the left leads through a beautiful natural gateway between White Napes and Great Napes, and thence trends to the right up to the summit ridge connecting the latter to the final crags of Gable. The streak of reddish scree to the east leads up through larger portals into the very heart of the mountain, penetrating round to the back of the Napes, and thence up by the left to the same summit ridge. This hollow is floored with small red scree that glows with a marvellous richness of colour in the sunlight.

The passage between the foot of the Napes and

a rock pinnacle at the entrance to the hollow is called Hell Gate. Philologists may be led to connect the name with the colour of the scree, for the primitive mind of the namer would have naturally associated redness with an infernal intensity of heat. The White Napes offers a little scrambling, but the Great Napes precipice gives us the best climbing to be had on the Gable; and if, after reaching the crest of this wall, we bear slightly downwards across the upper part of Hell Gate screes, we can finish our climbing by some excellent rocks that lead to the large Westmorland cairn close to the highest point of the mountain. These Westmorland crags, as we presently find it convenient to name them, are irregularly continued away towards the south-east and the Styhead pass, by Tom Blue, Raven Crag, and Kern Knotts. The last named are in two tiers, the lower being close to the Styhead path, and only some 1,200 feet above Wastdale Head. The upper Kern Knotts offer climbing of great interest and perhaps exceptional severity, and are rapidly becoming popular among the climbing fraternity.

The Ennerdale Face.—Looking first to the north side of Gable it is a matter of regret that no satisfactory inclusive view may be obtained of the whole width of this mountain wall. Seen from the slopes of Kirkfell the face recedes in such a way that very little of its climbing can be prospected. From the ridge between Scarth Gap and Brandreth we have a front view of the crags, but they are much dwarfed by distance, and their northern aspect is unsuitable for long range photography.

From Kirkfell we can readily mark the Oblique Chimney which cuts deeply into the upper half of the centre of the face, and terminates at a right-angled notch in the sky-line. Some distance to the right we may with a good light identify the Great Central Gully that cuts the face from top to bottom. To the immediate right of this is an easy scree leading the whole way to the top of the crags. Near the foot of this on the right there used to be a slab pinnacle some fifteen feet in height that has since been completely disintegrated by rain and frost. A year or two ago the freshly exposed rock that bore witness of the recent departure of the pinnacle could be clearly recognised by contrast with the older face. This climb is now reported to have been exceedingly difficult ; such will probably be the future reputation of the fast disappearing Stirrup Crag on Yewbarrow. A little higher up this scree slope, on a small plat-form out to the left, the remains of an old stone-walled enclosure could once be distinguished. It may have been the haunt of whisky smugglers or the hiding place of some miserable outlaw. It is to be regretted that the remains are now in too bad a state of repair to be recognised as artificial. Between the Oblique Chimney and the Central Gully lies the easy route or natural passage by which a mountain sheep of ordinary powers 'might ascend' ; though it not in-frequently occurs that the perplexed climber roundly declares that the mountain sheep of average mental capacity is not so foolish as to venture into such a bewildering region of small grass traverses, steep stony slopes, and ledgeless walls.

Immediately to the left of the Oblique Chimney is the climb that leads past the Bottle-shaped Pinnacle and up the huge retaining buttress of the chimney. Further towards Wind Gap the sky-line suddenly drops at the upper level of Stony Gully—an easy, though rough, passage up broken boulders and loose scree, by which the crags can be outflanked. The wire fence that leads over Wind Gap to Green Gable and Brandreth begins here, and is a useful landmark in misty weather. Mr. Haskett Smith found in 1882 a ' high level route ' across the face at about two-thirds of the way up. It is an excellent ramble, and full of strange surprises, passing along exposed ledges, in between towers of rock and the great upper wall, offering a peep into the black recess of the Oblique Chimney, and an easy digression up to the Bottle-shaped Pinnacle. It finishes close to the foot of Stony Gully, and can be recommended for a preliminary survey of the more difficult routes up the Ennerdale face.

Oblique Chimney.—From a few notes added to a sketch of the known routes up the Ennerdale face, which Mr. John Robinson inserted in the Wastdale Climbing Book, April, 1890, I derived my first impressions of the Oblique Chimney : ' This has, I believe, not yet been climbed and is not very safe, owing to the jammed stones in it being loose, and the clean-cut walls on each side making these stones of consequence.' This description was realistic though brief, but I thought little of the place till the Christmas vacation of 1892-3, when I learnt that Mr. R. C. Gilson had proposed to attack the chimney one fine day, but was forestalled by Dr. Collier's party. These latter took the precautionary measure of partly descending the chimney, so as to clear away the *débris* and loose stones that hovered over the edge of each pitch; they then returned to the foot of the chimney and forced a way directly up to the top. The important jammed stones required for the middle portion were quite firm enough for safe holding, and the party returned with a fuller praise of the beauties of the chimney than any one had anticipated. I was given an account of the expedition a day or two later, and was glad enough to get the opportunity of trying conclusions with the crags on that side of Gable, which till then was unexplored country for me.

My companion that Christmas was a learned classic, weary of brain work, whom I had induced to take a little climbing in Cumberland as a tonic. Some people cannot take quinine, others apparently cannot benefit by rock-climbing. This latter I found to be the case with my friend, whose struggle with the *confracti rudera mundi* made him despondent instead of inducing a healthy exhilaration. The sore limbs and torn clothing he never seemed able to forget, far less to enjoy. Yet the ruling passion of phrase-making was strong even *in extremis*, and he longed to put his sufferings into words. Sometimes on the rocks I might casually turn to see that he was coming up well. His eyes would be gazing at nothing and his lips moving as if in prayer. But it was not prayer, it was a Greek or Latin quotation, preferably the former because of its rich vocabulary for description of scenery. On the whole he was enjoying the new experiences hugely in his own melancholy way, and I felt no compunction in insisting on his joining K. and A. when we planned our excursion up Gable by way of the Oblique Chimney. The day was rather cloudy and snow threatened, but we took plenty of provisions, and K. carried a pocket compass. We started somewhat late in the morning, and walked leisurely up Gavel Neese and round the Beckhead by way of Moses' Sledgate. But on reaching the wire fence we found that the mist completely enveloped the Gable crags and gave us no chance of identifying our climb from below. Then we skirted along the base in the vain hope of a momentary disclosure of the chimney by a parting of the mist, but no such chance offered, and we reached Stony Gully without making a start up. Here we saw the 'rake' or traverse that has been described as passing along the face about two-thirds of the way up. It was an obvious course to take, inasmuch as it led to within a few feet of the foot of the Oblique Chimney—so near that even the dense mist could scarcely prevent our striking it.   Here the classic assured us that he would much prefer ascending by Stony Gully to the top of Gable, and that it would give him extreme pleasure to carry our lunch up to the cairn and wait for us there.   We let him go, and promised that we should join him again by three o'clock in the afternoon. Thus did we lose our lunch, not to find it again for another week.   There was much ice and fresh snow plastering the rocks, and the so-called 'easy' traverse wanted all our care.   K. was an expert Alpine climber, his friend A. a plucky young Harrovian with plenty of nerve and endurance in him, but at that time with next to nothing in the way of experience of the mountains.   He came along well enough, but our pace was necessarily very slow.   Three o'clock found us still working westwards on the traverse, but without a sight of the Oblique Chimney. I think in one place we must have descended too much. At any rate, we found ourselves in difficulties on a sloping slab of glazed rock that gave me serious pause. A. slipped on this, and started slithering away rapidly.   Luckily he held his axe tightly, and was brought up by the rope with a jerk. Shortly after this, he pointed to some blood on the rocks, and solicitously asked me whether I had cut myself very badly.   It turned out, after a hasty glance at my hands, that he himself was the wounded one. My little complaint was a slight frostbite in the finger-tips, my gloves having been worn threadbare by much scraping with the hands.

At last we reached a pinnacle that promised us variety. We tried to climb up it by the outside edge, but found the ice too troublesome. Then, when resting on the shoulder half way up, we saw a deep and narrow cavern in the mountain wall behind the pinnacle. Surely that must be the object of our quest and our pinnacle the redoubtable ' bottle-shaped.' Eagerly we scrambled over the shoulder and down a slight gully on to the scree that issues from the mouth of the cavern. It was getting dark, and we were very hungry. My jacket pocket still held the crumbs of a pulverized biscuit that I had taken up Snowdon the week before. These and a fragment of chocolate we scrupulously shared, and then began the attack in earnest. The conditions had much changed since Dr. Collier had effected his ascent, and though the gully overhangs too much to permit any drift snow to settle in it, the smooth walls of the gully were black and shiny with ice, and the damp cold of this dark hole tried our endurance to the utmost. It must be admitted that my ascent of the first part was slow and ungraceful. I had started with my back resting against the left wall, bracing my feet as firmly as the ice would permit against the diminutive knobs on the opposite side. Now in this position the back cannot be worked up an overhanging wall unless the hands have something definite to thrust against. The process went on fairly well for about twenty-five feet, working outwards as well as upwards, but then the two sides of the chimney became perilously far apart and the smooth left wall commenced to overhang.

Then ensued a few moments of awkward suspense, an uncertainty as to the best method of transferring one's weight to certain small ledges against which the feet were now pressing.

The process of 'backing up' is excessively fatiguing, the thrust necessary to hold oneself firmly *in situ* being as a rule much greater than the equivalent of one's weight, and the whole of this thrust being at every slight lift transmitted through the arms. He who fails to realize the attitude I am describing may easily perform an experiment that illustrates the mechanical principles involved, by sitting down across a doorway or narrow passage, and attempting to work upwards by pressure of the feet against one side and back against the other. If, when some three feet from the ground, he waits a minute or two and then attempts to move again, either up or down, he will perceive that the simple holding in place has tired his muscles and made advance or retreat equally difficult.

Our doorway had already extended up for twenty-five feet and yet another five remained before a comfortable halting-place could be reached. The cleft forming the chimney was so much undercut that the view vertically downwards included the scree some distance below the entrance to the cavern, and anything that I might have let fall, myself for instance, would have dropped some feet further out than the two men waiting below. The halt was a mistake; there was only one course open, and that should have been taken at first. It was to work inwards until the doubtful jammed stones could be reached with the left hand, and then, trusting mainly to the footholds, hoist the body over to that side of the gully and thrust the hand into the recesses between the stones. K. shouted up some suggestion to this effect from below. How he managed to discern the proper place through the dim twilight I never was able to ascertain. But I resolved to try it, and in some strange way the cramped muscles that had appeared incapable of further effort were in a second or two relieved by the change of attitude, and the pull over to the right side that I had dreaded as the severest tax on my strength proved to be easy enough. With fists in two convenient little holes clenched to prevent the hands slipping out, I was able to take a momentary survey of the slightly rickety ladder of jammed stones that led to safety. The passage of these few feet was not at all pleasant. Had ours been the first climb of the chimney we might have reasonably decided to brave the perils of descent and return again by daylight, rather than fumble about in the dusk pawing at wabbly boulders that threatened to fall out with us at even a caress, much more promptly at a cross word.

But the knowledge that others had tried them, and had learnt the futility of these threats, gave me some degree of courage, and, taking heart of grace, I, walked up the ladder and out of the first great difficulty. A. came up next, and as the hour was late and we were all a little anxious to finish, he did not scorn to use the rope at the bad corner just below the ladder. K. came up remarkably well, and I felt that if he had led us we should have mastered the pitch earlier.

We were now able to walk towards the roof of the upper portion of the gully, which was as completely closed in as the cave below. The left wall everywhere overhung so much that there was no chance of climbing out by its aid. The right wall was nearly parallel to the left and showed a few more possibilities.

Looking backwards we could see the two walls projecting several yards out, apparently a little nearer together at their extreme edges than they were in our upper chamber, which was now much too wide for any opportunity of backing up. But we knew that the second pitch was not so bad as the first, and started prospecting. I crept up as high into the cave as possible, and then felt round the edge of the roof for a firm hold. This came to hand almost at once, and with a step out on to the sloping wall, and probably a steadying hand from below, I worked up between the roof-stone and the right side. This led to a steep little snow-slope, evidently covering loose stones that might prove excitable in dry weather, and thence a few yards of broken rock extended to the summit of the crags.

G. P. Abraham & Sons, Photos.

THE ENNERDALE FACE OF GREAT GABLE

Keswick

(Face page 187)

In five minutes we had assembled there, and decided that we were still distressingly hungry. I felt in my pocket for more crumbs, but only brought out stones. We hurried up to the cairn at the highest point of the mountain. It looked a picture of Alpine solitude. Not a trace of the classic, no hope of our lunch. Fresh snow had fallen during the last hour or two, and had obliterated all signs of his visit. Nay, worse, we had not that implicit confidence in his knowledge of the district to feel certain that he had found his way safely down to Wastdale, for he had never been on the mountain before; nor was he quite so familiar with the mountain mists as we proud climbers of the Oblique Chimney. But he had the laugh of us that night! We expressed sorrow for the poor man, and then with a sigh turned to consider our own position. It was a trifle unpleasant to be on the summit of Great Gable after six p.m. on a snowy winter's night, with something of a wind blowing through us and very little to obstruct its free passage. But for all that we were happy enough, and arranged elaborately to steer by compass direct for White Napes and Gavel Neese. South-west by west was our direction. K. was positive of that fact, and offered to lead. Some twenty yards behind him came young A., still going well; then I followed at an equal distance behind him, just able by the reflected light from the snow to distinguish the leader and keep him in the straight line he was marking out for us.

By the light of a match that we kept flaming for a sufficient time in an improvised tent of coats, he examined the pocket compass he carried, and was confident that ten minutes' good going would carry us down to the grassy shoulder below the White Napes. On we went steadily downwards, and I wondered whether, if we took to running when the boulders were passed, we might get down in time to start dinner at the usual hour. Happy thoughts in this connection kept me from attending particularly to our route and its details, but when we got to a thicker mist I looked about for a landmark. Nothing could be recognised. The ground sloped rapidly down on the right; the left seemed to rise most oddly to a sort of ridge. But the strange thing was that there seemed to be another mountain fronting us. K. was at a complete loss, and took out his compass again. We erected the tent once more, and all crowded over the instrument to determine our fate. Alas, we had been travelling towards the north! K. had mistaken the two poles of the magnet. The mountain mass looming ahead was the Green Gable, and we were within a few feet of the Wind Gap. Our dinner was at least two hours further away than ever, and we were still hungry. There was nothing to be done but walk round the mountain by way of the Styhead tarn and pass. We had no lantern, and it would have been a legbreaking business to attempt to skirt the Ennerdale face and strike off the Moses' Sledgate in the dark. The snow was soft all the way down

Aaron Slack.   I have often come down in daylight since and wondered what we could have found to tumble over that night ; we were always slipping through snow pitfalls into water, or tripping over boulders and on to our heads in snowdrifts.   Now and again we would find ourselves sitting side by side in the stream, the leader's tumbling having been too sudden to permit of any warning to the others. Such occasions we generally seized on as suitable opportunities for halting, only to be ended by sleepy realization that the water was both damp and cold. And all the time the inexperienced classic was enjoying his dinner and his phrase-making in princely luxury and comfort at the inn.

At last we reached the shores of the frozen tarn and turned wearily up to the right.   The path was in a shocking state, and on arriving at the cairn at the top of the pass we found a continuous glaze of ice along our route.   So, at any rate, it seemed to be that night—my first experience of crossing the Styhead in the dark.   It was nothing less than actual hand-and-foot work in many an awkward corner. Subsequent opportunities of climbing down the path in the dark have often been given me, but that first night was the worst.   How we managed to avoid broken limbs has ever been a mystery.   We would suddenly slip over on the ice, and slide furiously down the path and into some obstruction below.   We had tried to smoke, but pipes were too dangerous to hold between the teeth during these

unpremeditated rushes. But time ends all things. By
ten o'clock we were anointed with vaseline and
massaged with Elliman, with the prospect of substantial fare to follow. The classic slippered into the
dining-room to report himself. He had waited on
Gable cairn till half-past three, and then had returned by the way he had come. Our lunch he had
left under a stone, and as a guide to our finding it
had stamped the snow down and drawn with his
finger several arrows or asterisks or other marks
of reference in the snow. It was very clever,
but the fresh fall thwarted his ingenuity only too
effectually.

The Oblique Chimney rapidly became popular,
and has since been visited by many climbers. But
it can never be regarded as an easy ascent.

Some time during the summer following I looked
down it to see how a descent might be managed.
The loose stones at the top were most uncomfortably unstable, and the clamber down towards the
entrance of the upper cave required great care,
without being exactly perilous. A friend was with
me who counselled waiting till we should find ourselves up there again with a rope, and ultimately
his advice prevailed. Some eighteen months later,
in January, 1895, a large party of Wastdale Christmas
revellers made for the Oblique Chimney top.
The crags were approached from the scree below,
a few feet to the north of the entrance to the
Central Gully. We took to a little chimney at once,

and then up a grassy slope to another chimney that brought us to steep grass and scree with frequent outcrops of rock.

Thence we made up towards the entrance to the Oblique Chimney then visible, and before reaching it clambered up an incipient gully on the left wall that bounds the scree just there.   It led over the sharp crest of the buttress that supports the bottle-shaped pinnacle, and thence we had a steep but fairly easy descent of ten or twelve feet to a ledge that led round to the other side.   The rocks were dry and very free from snow, so that each member of our party found himself able to pull up easily from ledge to ledge in the little gully till the notch between the pinnacle and the main wall was reached.

Thence the leader turned up to the left, and recommenced a similar series of ledge-climbing operations, of which only the first from the notch could be called in any sense difficult.   We had a magnificent view down the face, which is particularly steep just here, and the frequent halts rendered necessary by the size of our party afforded plenty of time to admire the huge slabs that separated the 'sheep walk' from us. A small stone-man marked our point of arrival at the summit of the crags, and after adding a block or two as our contribution to the cairn we turned right, and in a few yards had reached the rectangular entrance to the Oblique Chimney.

The main difficulty in the descent was to prevent stones sliding on to the heads of men lower down,

who were in the direct line of fire and rarely able
to raise a protecting arm for themselves. The upper
ones were continually cautioned by those in peril to
keep an eye to the rope, and prevent its dragging
over the bed of the gully. All passed down safely,
but I remember making a mistake when descending
the great overhanging pitch at the bottom, in
assuming that it was an easy matter to climb down
with a camera sack on my back. I had descended
part of the 'ladder,' but then found the need of a
back pressure, and hesitated about crushing in the
contents of my sack. The rope is of no use to the
last man in a place of that kind, and I therefore was
permitted to untie the knot round my waist and fix
on the sack instead, letting it down gently to the
others by the left hand. The right was needed to
hold on firmly to the ladder, so that the teeth were in
requisition for the tying. The descent offers another
instance of the ease with which a chimney that is
exceptionally severe in the ascent may be traversed
in the reverse direction. Where gravity helps the
motion we have only to consider the best means of
opposing it. During an ascent much strength is
spent in the mere lift, to say nothing of the extra
force needed to prevent slipping.

At the foot we joined up again and traversed
round to the 'sheep walk.' This was easy to discover but hard to describe. The route bore obliquely
upwards towards the right, always well out in the
open, giving us pleasant hand-and-foot work the

whole way. We reached the top in safety, and then proceeded homewards by way of White Napes.

Mr. Haskett Smith says that the top of the easy passage bears 23° east of north when viewed by prismatic compass from the highest point of Great Gable. It probably means magnetic north, and the fact is of value to benighted climbers who know which end of the compass is the north pole.

On April 3, 1896, a new variation route was found into the upper cave of the Oblique Chimney by Messrs. C. and A. Hopkinson and H. Campbell, who worked up a slightly marked gully in the great wall to the left of the sheep walk, and then, after an ascent of fifty feet, traversed round by the left into the chimney.

CHAPTER VIII

THE ENNERDALE CENTRAL GULLY AND TWO LITTLE CHIMNEYS

THERE is no royal road to learning, and the converse proposition is equally true. There is no learning along a royal road. Some years ago I went up the Central Gully of the Gable behind an experienced climber, when conditions were at their best. It was a royal road to me, and I came away with but a vague notion of its difficulties, without having learnt anything. It is the leader that can give the truest description of an easy climb. Where the one man can do all the work, his followers go up without a thought beyond their rope's length. When difficulties are shared discussion is necessary, and the memory is assisted by subsequent references to faulty moves or to troubles that all were instrumental in overcoming. It is astonishing how few men can recall the details of a rock climb to the extent of recapitulating the successive pitches in, say, two hours of gully work. And yet the faculty is well worth cultivating, inasmuch as it accentuates the pleasures of retrospection and may be called into active service by the inquiries of others wishing to follow. Indeed the best introduction to guideless

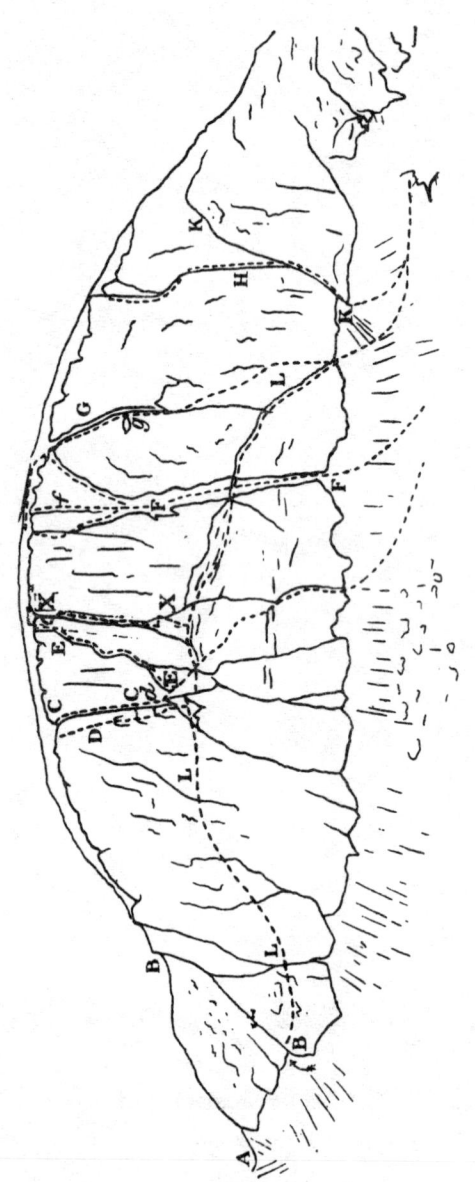

PLATE IV.

THE ENNERDALE FACE OF GREAT GABLE,

Showing about 400 feet of Cliff.

A Wind Gap.
B Stony Gully.
C The Oblique Chimney.
D The Bottle-shaped Pinnacle Ridge.
E The Sheep Walk.

F The Ennerdale Central Gully.
G Scree Gully.
H The Doctor's Chimney.
K An Easy Scree Gully.
L Gable Crag Traverse.

X Engineer's Chimney.
d The Bottle-shaped Pinnacle.
f Chimney Finish of F.
g Smuggler's Retreat.

climbing is to ascend rock peaks that we have afore-time accomplished with guides in front of us, where we shall find our memories taxed now and again in the effort to recall the route taken previously. To lie in bed and remember every foothold on the Matterhorn may require more ascents than one ; but however wicked it is for a Zermatt guide to indulge in such a pastime, the average amateur may well envy him his accomplishment.

Quite recently I had the opportunity of joining a party up the Central Gully. We had come over to Gable Crag after an hour or two on the Eagle's Nest *arête* and the neighbouring rocks. Our plan was to get up the chief pitches in the gully, and then, instead of bearing up to the right at the foot of the final wall, to take to the narrow vertical chimney that passes up its centre and leads to the highest point of the crags—to treat it as an old friend with a new face.

But before taking to the gully there was another little chimney to visit, that had been recently 'invented' by Dr. Simpson and Mr. Patchell, on their way to the Great Central. It is a singular thing that this remarkably interesting way up Gable Crag should have so long remained undiscovered. The reference in the Wastdale book is as follows : 'A walk of a hundred feet along a grass ledge from the point where the wire fence from Beckhead touches the rocks of the Gable, followed by a hundred feet of scrambling up a wild and much broken gully, leads to a small cairn which marks the foot of a chimney on the left. This runs up in a direction parallel to the face of the cliff, and so is not clearly seen except at close quarters. It is very straight and narrow, especially in the middle pitch, and makes an interesting climb of about eighty feet.'

We worked round the scree and broken rock from the top of the Napes to Gable Crag. Then by keeping fairly low down we arrived at the end of the wire fence from Beckhead, and were in a position to profit by the description already supplied. The fence ends abruptly on the face of a crag that is somewhat separated from the main mass of Gable. Between the two a scree gully runs downwards in the direction of Brandreth, and the Doctor's Chimney is found to spring from a point a hundred feet up from the foot of this gully. The crag interferes with the view of the chimney from the neighbourhood of Beckhead, though from the nearer slopes of Kirkfell the little climb is almost as well marked as the Oblique Chimney.

The hand-and-foot work begins on the right side of the recess, and the climber makes directly up to a little pinnacle about thirty feet above him. There is no need to back up the chimney at first. The pinnacle offers comfortable standing-room for one only, but the leader can manipulate the rope for the second until the latter is within a foot or two of the platform. Then by passing a few coils of rope round the top of the pinnacle he can make the second safe while he effects the rather awkward passage back into the crack. Both hands seize an excellent hold on the opposite wall, perfectly safe but a trifle remote for a man with a short reach, and then the foothold is quitted and the body dragged into a good jamming position. The crack is very narrow, and extensive slipping is almost an impossibility. It now becomes necessary to wriggle up inch by inch with slight hold for the extremities and too much for intermediate excrescences. A few feet higher and the chimney is at its narrowest. Here follows an uncomfortable rearrangement of the system. The handholds have hitherto been best on the left wall, and the climber has accordingly faced that way. But now the holds dwindle down to nothing on that side and others appear on the right. We may either climb out of the crack and on to the buttress, or preferably effect a half-turn of the body and so get to face the right wall. This is most safely accomplished by working outwards a bit before twisting. A small stone is half jammed in the crack and may be used for a foothold, though too insecure for any hauling purposes. The struggling now becomes a little less irregular. The ledges are excellent for the hands, and in a few feet we reach the level of the floor of a little cave roofed in by a couple of overhanging blocks. This place again is only large enough for one cave-dweller to inhabit, and the leader has his choice of procedure—either to run out another twelve feet before the second man comes up, or to wait till his follower reaches the narrowest part of the crack. To avoid the trouble of re-arranging the rope, the latter plan is better, though it involves a little risk of peppering the crack man with small stones that are only too willing to lower their present level at the roof of the cave.

The last move is moderately easy. By pulling up on to the horizontal ledge on the left buttress the loose stones are almost avoided, and then some easy steps land the leader in safety a few yards from the upper edge of the crags. When all are up, a traverse of about fifty yards to the right discloses a rough but quick route down to the scree gully and the wire fence, or the same traverse continued along the contour-line leads to the Westmorland crags and the beginning of the ordinary scree descent towards Gavel Neese.

The Doctor's Chimney deserves to be popular. It is a perfectly safe climb, and offers excellent practice for the arms. On the whole it is probably a little easier than the Oblique Chimney, especially when descended, for it is so narrow that there is little need to seek footholds until the level of the pinnacle is reached. It has the advantage over its more famous rival of being easily hit off in misty weather; for a scree gully is then less mistakable than a rocky sheep walk, and a wire fence than a ' bottle-shaped ' pinnacle.

Such, then, was our digression before making for the foot of the Central Gully. Another party of friends had comfortably ensconced themselves in various corners on the small crag opposite the chimney, and were interested observers of our performance. They smoked cigarettes and offered advice freely; their day's work was done, and to watch others still hard at it was perfect luxury. When we emerged panting from the top they threw away their cigarette ends and strolled down to Wastdale for tea. It required much moral strength to refrain from joining them, but there was the Great Central still on hand, and that other little chimney to prospect. If it were as difficult as report said, then we were bound to stay and climb it. So we worked round to the end of the wire fence and looked for our gully. Its name perhaps suggests a great gap in the mountain side, visible for miles round, and as unavoidable by the wanderer on this side of Gable as the Edgware Road is said to be by the Frenchman in London. But if this be so the name is misleading. Many people fail to find the gully in bad weather. Its entrance from below is narrow and its exit above is ill defined. A short distance to the east of the Doctor's Chimney the scree-walk up the crag, that leads past the relics of the smuggler's inclosure, insures a safe passage to the top of the cliff. This scree gully faces Kirkfell, and but for the usually poor light on this north face of the mountain it might be easily recognized from that side. Scarcely a hundred yards away from the end of the fence the narrow opening of the Central Gully may be found; from Beckhead it appears in

profile, and is not always manifest.　Walking eastwards along the scree beneath the crags, it is the
first really obvious passage into the heart of the
mountain after leaving the Doctor's Chimney; the
easy scree walk is not much impressed in the face,
and in a mist it has often been entirely overlooked.
Even in cloudy weather the first pitch of our gully
can be discerned a few feet above us, and identified
by the buttress that partially divides it, the chock-
stone in its right branch, and the fine-looking
'jammed-stone pinnacle' that shows up a little
higher on the left.

The first clear account of the gully appeared in
the Wastdale book : 'In the great gully are found
two pitches near the bottom.　The top part may be
varied by crossing a grass slope and joining the easy
scree route, or the climb may be continued by going
straight forward.　This looks very hard, but on close
inspection the difficulty entirely disappears; for the
climber is able to pass behind a square tower of rock,
and in this way to enter on the final bit of grass and
rock that brings him out at the top.'

We were a party of three, and managed comfortably with eighty feet of rope.　The first pitch was
easy, what with dry rocks and warm weather.　Our
guide started up the buttress that divides the gully,
and at a convenient opportunity stepped back on to
the loose stones in the bed.　A few feet brought us
to the second pitch, a trifle harder than the first.
Again the leader worked up a buttress on the left of

the gully, but this time well in the hollow. Near the top of the obstruction the left leg had to take the place of the right, a good handhold above serving to insure the safe transfer, and then a ledge could be reached by the right foot. The body was next swung over to that side, and so to the crest of the pitch.

Here the gully looked very attractive. On the left rose the jammed-stone pinnacle, an easy chimney leading up to the cleft that separates it from the mountain. Two big boulders bridge the cleft near the crest of the little passage, the higher one offering a safe way to the summit of the pinnacle. It is from here that the progress or 'rake' can be made out across to the foot of the Oblique Chimney and on towards Stony Gully at the east end of Gable Crag.

Just above us a third pitch barred the way. The gully was much wider here, and greater diversity of method was now possible. The guide counselled the direct attack of the short crack in front. The philosopher prudently suggested that time was an object and the crack a hard nut; we ought to take the easy corner on the left. The friend that completed our trio gave the casting vote in favour of overtime and ten hours' work per day during holidays. The crack was certainly awkward. It was at first easiest to face towards the right and work up nine or ten feet. Then when the foothold was of the fanciest of orders it became desirable to effect a half-turn of the body so that the other side of the crack might be faced. Once the turn was accomplished, a fine hand-hold made the rest easy ; we could pull up the corner and walk out at the top, some twenty-five feet above the foot of the pitch. Our friend was thinking evidently of his casting vote when he followed the guide ; for at the turning-point a slip cast him on to the rope and gave him an extra turn that he scarcely appreciated. But the leader was safely ensconced above, and the poor fellow hastened up to assure himself that the rope really had been held tightly. The philosopher eschewed the cause of this momentary retrogression, and came quietly up the grass and rock corner well to the left of the gully.

We were now almost out on the face of the mountain. Very little remained of the gully as such. The ordinary walk away towards the right was perfectly plain. Mr. Robinson's route upwards, described in the extract just quoted, was a little to the left, but not at all easy to locate, for the square tower of rock blocked the direct view of the climb. Straight up above us we saw a wall of about a hundred feet of apparently sheer rock, down the centre of which passed the crack or chimney that we were to take for our finish.

Loose earthy steps led to the foot of the wall, and for a moment we thought with some apprehension that the first part was going to be seriously troublesome. At a height of twenty-five feet or so some narrow splintered boulders completely filled up the crack and overhung considerably. Just below them the climbing was obviously awkward, by reason of the footholds that were not there, if the ancient Hibernianism may be tolerated, and the necessary leverage on the boulders when we were using them for all they were worth would imperil their stability and our own. But after mounting the first twelve feet with, perhaps, more ease than we had anticipated, a narrow ledge showed up on the right wall for about ten feet, and we noticed with relief that at its further extremity another traverse led back to the crack in a slanting direction to a point just above the critical spot. This diversion we promptly accepted, and found it altogether satisfactory. The lower ledge was just wide enough for the feet, and handholds just good enough for the balance of the body during the transfer. At the further end it was easy scrambling to the upper ledge, which showed itself as a broad and safe path to a little niche where the crack was somewhat enlarged. The floor of the niche was formed of loose stones supported on the larger jammed blocks that had affrighted us below, and was sufficiently commodious for all the party to place themselves securely thereon. Probably the next part of the climb was the hardest. That, at any rate, was the opinion of those who had recommended the route to us, and after their kindly advice we were gratefully prepared to accept anything from them in the way of opinion. The chimney was vertical and its two walls almost holdless.

Direct progress seemed barred by three thick plates of rock wedged into the crack and projecting outwards some three or four feet. Over these we had to make our way, and if their edges proved to be unsatisfactory for the fingers to grip or the arms to clasp, then we should have to return with the ignominy of defeat. On the one hand appearances were against us; the pitch looked impossible. But on the other we knew it had been climbed once or twice before, and assuredly under no better conditions than were vouchsafed to ourselves. Far away down at the foot of the gully we noticed a couple of men who had been walking Wastdale-wards after a hard day, but were gazing up at us in some curiosity to know how we were going to tackle our problem. It would never do to go back now.

And thus, after sacrificing such time and small reflections to the reputed difficulty of the place as its admirers would have claimed of us, we turned our gaze upwards and climbed the pitch. It went off pleasantly enough. An easy clamber led to a second platform immediately below the jammed plates. A foot or two higher, and a ledge on the left could be used for the one hand, the edge of the lowest overhanging block with the other, while the left leg was swung up on to a shelf. The attitude was awkward just for the moment, but with both arms clasping the plate of rock, which was perfectly trustworthy, there could be no thought of falling for the leader, who had only to thrust himself forward into an upper recess and wriggle into safety.

Here he discovered another level platform, neatly turfed and obviously constructed as a climber's resting place. It would have been easy to stay there and negotiate the rope for the other men below, but the next pitch was only ten feet higher up, and led to a still better corner. Therefore he went on by straightforward hand-and-foot work, and climbed the pitch by its left-hand branch. The chimney is here about eight feet wide, divided into two by a long and narrow boulder.

The right-hand branch is just possible, but the sense of insecurity at one spot almost demands help from below. On the left a deep recess is floored with splintered blocks that threaten to break away but cannot easily manage it. The boulder offered enough assistance in the way of holds, especially a sharp edge at the top, and when overcome showed itself to be the last genuine obstacle in our course. We were soon all gathered together at the little notch that marks the top of the chimney, and after adding a stone to the cairn that stands there, we marched up some thirty feet of solid buttress and broke at a plunge through the thick cornice of old snow that yet remained as a token of the hard winter that had come and gone.

The easy finish to the right of the last vertical wall passes up scree from the top of the third pitch, and takes us on to a ridge of rock above the Smuggler's Retreat. Here it joins the Scree Gully, and we have a small piece of hand-and-foot work before it narrows, then curves away to the left, and finally ends on a ledge of broken rock close to the highest point.

CHAPTER IX

IT has already been explained that the Great Napes rises like a huge screen out of the southern slopes of Gable. Its crest runs from north-west to south-east. It is possible to travel along the whole length of the ridge from Hell's Gate (called Deep Gill on the Ordnance map) to the White Napes scree at Little Hell Gate, and this route, religiously followed without divergence on to either face, will be found to offer many interesting pitches. The outside face of the Napes is cut by the Needle Gully, the Eagle's Nest Gully, and the Arrowhead Gully, taken in order from east to west.

The Needle Gully has two separate branches leading to the crest of the Napes, neither of them particularly difficult or interesting. The Eagle's Nest Gully is in summer time little more than a scree walk. So likewise is the main Arrowhead Gully, which, however, has a branch up to the left leading to a fine-looking chimney and out on to the open face two-thirds of the way up towards the ridge. To the west of the Arrowhead Gully the Napes is much less imposing, and though small gullies cut it up considerably they are too indefinite to particularize.

G. P. Abraham & Sons, Photos.

Keswick

GREAT GABLE FROM LINGMELL

(Face page 146)

The chief *arêtes* on the face are, taking them in order from east to west, the Needle ridge immediately to the right of the Needle Gully; the Eagle's Nest ridge between the Eagle's Nest Gully and the Needle Gully; and the Arrowhead ridge between the Eagle's Nest Gully and the Arrowhead Gully. All these *arêtes* offer most enjoyable climbs. The Gable Needle (or Napes Needle) is a sharp pinnacle rising vertically from the lower part of the Needle ridge. It is a climb for experts only, with steady heads. The Bear rock is a smaller pinnacle a few yards to the west of the foot of Arrowhead Gully. Its ascent is a simple problem in rock-climbing—a pull up with the arms from the notch at the back—but it is worth visiting on account of its singular aspect.

The Arrowhead Gully is almost entirely devoid of interest. It has not often been visited, for the reason that its material is loose, its one pitch is easy, and the neighbourhood is very rich in more inviting climbs. A large party went up it last April and were exceedingly unhappy so long as a single member remained in it. Our interest had been concentrated on the Eagle's Nest ridge, and after some considerable time had been spent about the crags, we found ourselves at the foot of the Arrowhead Gully, afflicted with the unanimous desire to reach the summit of the Napes by a way that none of us had attempted before. There remained to us this gully and its branch up by the left. It soon

became manifest that we should have to divide, for
the place was too small to hold us, and too narrow
to permit free passage of loose stones that the higher
members almost immediately began to dislodge. We
lunched a few feet up the left branch, and were
decidedly uncomfortable during our hasty meal.
The ledges that we had chosen were so uncertain
and the scree below so steep that all were glad when
the sandwiches were finished and preparations commenced for roping-up. My own section of the party
elected to follow the branch to its abrupt ending
out on the face. The others kept to the main gully,
and were busy chimney-sweeping most of their time.
Their one pitch was straightforward, but loose blocks
abounded and required careful treatment so long as
their fall might endanger the safety of any one.
Over would go a boulder as soon as the last man had
passed it, smashing from side to side, and we in our
gully vaguely wondered, at each successive bombardment of the Arrowhead, whether it would not be fair
to give the next comers the credit of trying a new
climb; the old gully was rapidly altering, and the
change in its ancient landmarks testifying to the
influence of man as a geological agent. But in spite
of their extensive quarrying operations they reached
their destination before us. We found that our
variation involved some good climbing, spoilt, however, by a plentiful supply of dangerous *débris* on all
its available ledges. I was leading, and therefore
safe from bombardment; but those below me were

now and again peppered, and my feelings hurt by their objurgations. Those who read this book as a literary production will, no doubt, sympathise with the writer in his difficulties with so limited a vocabulary as climbing affords. That words of primary importance are few is a fact patent to all students of the "Alpine Journal." But in moments of excitement the climber is urged to expand his limits, and to call on other sciences (notably the theological) for suitable expressions that will relieve his feelings.

We started by working up on the right to a ledge at the foot of the big pitch. Then followed a traverse across to a short chimney on the other side. This chimney was obviously a possible route, but for greater safety and in order to avoid a lengthening of the rope between the second man and myself, I worked up for a few feet and then rounded the buttress into the central portion of the gully, where a second crack started upwards. Six feet higher this crack terminated at the same level as the left-hand chimney, and some dangerously loose grass holds helped me to drag up into a small cave where moderate anchorage could be obtained. Unfortunately a block as large as my fist managed to escape past me and to attack deliberately the unlucky member of our party. He, poor man! has the reputation of never being missed by a vagrant stone, and on this occasion he was hit rather badly on the head. It was no use hurrying, but we feared a faint, and when two of us were squeezed well into the cave, the wounded man was engineered up to our level.   He was a bit dazed, but on the whole seemed moderately jubilant at this latest proof of his case-hardened condition.   When reassured as to his welfare we wriggled clumsily out of the narrow cave, feet foremost, and made our way easily by the left wall to the roof of the cave and the top of the pitch.   The rest of the gully was little more than mere walking, and a few minutes later we joined our friends on the crest of the Napes.

The Needle Gully has rather a bad reputation. My personal experience of it has not been altogether pleasant.   I tried it in January, 1893, with the enterprising classic referred to in my account of the Oblique Chimney, and found the soft snow so troublesome in its steepness and want of tenacity that we decided to leave the gully for some more auspicious occasion.   The opportunity came in the following August, after an ascent of the Needle, and with it came the conviction that in dry weather the gully possesses no interest to the climber pure and simple, if such an anomaly exists, but that it should be visited by those who take pleasure in rock scenery. The Eagle's Nest ridge is a marvellously fine sweep of clean-cut rock bounding the western wall of the gully.   The jagged outline of the Needle ridge on the eastern side is scarcely inferior in grandeur.

We found two easy pitches to begin with, taking us to about the level of the Needle summit.   Then a vertical wall interposed itself directly in our way. We scrambled in or near a slight cleft on our right, using rather treacherous grass-covered ledges, and distributing our weight over as many points of support as possible. That portion of the pitch was only about three feet high, and then came a momentary 'easy' before another steep little bit of eight feet. The resting place is just large enough for one man. At the top of the second piece a ledge led round by the left past an awkward corner that seemed to alarm our more substantial members by its narrowness, and then two or three steep grass steps had to be taken directly upwards. There we found a projecting knob forming a convenient saddle for each to anchor as he manipulated the rope for the man below, a deep crack offering itself in the right position for belaying the rope. A foot or two higher, and we were able to traverse back into the bed of the gully, and thence find an easy way up screes and short rock slopes to the top. The climb along the ridge itself to the highest point of the Napes was pleasantly varied. We could readily distinguish the points of articulation of the chief buttresses, for the general angle was too steep to disguise the contours. When close to the connecting ridge between Napes and the Westmorland crags we bore down on to Hell's Gate screes and crossed over to the opposite rocks to hunt out the little climb up to the Westmorland cairn. This was not so easy to find, and we wasted much time in attempting an attack by some smooth slabs too high up the scree. At last we found that the climb began in a small gully some distance down, which bore upwards a little to the right till a short pinnacle was reached. Then from the neck behind the pinnacle we traversed across the face to the left for a few yards, before climbing hand over hand to the summit ridge. It came as a surprise that the ascent had such neatness; and we were all at the end willing enough to indorse the favourable opinions expressed in the climbing book. Be it remembered that the cairn at the top was built by the brothers Westmorland of Penrith, not for the purpose of indicating the finish of a climb, but to mark the coign of vantage for one of the finest mountain views in the country. Remember also that proposition of a well-known mountaineer that the view from a summit is much the same whatever be the route taken to get there; and apply it by visiting Westmorland cairn to look at the Napes, even if the expedition involves no troublesome climbing.

THE RIDGES OF THE GREAT NAPES

(Face page 153)

CHAPTER X

THE RIDGES OF THE GREAT NAPES

The Needle Ridge is usually taken from the foot of the Needle itself. It was explored first in 1834 by Mr. Haskett Smith, who then made a general survey without actually completing the climb. Two years later he effected a descent of the whole route; and in 1887 Mr. Slingsby's party made the first strict ascent, and were emphatic in their praise of its fine character.

The introductory few feet from the notch behind the Needle are difficult, the problem being to climb up a steep slab of six feet or so to the foot of a slight grass chimney that slopes upwards to the right. Three fingers of the right hand can be inserted in a curious pocket in the slab; rather poor foothold is all that can be found for steadying purposes, and for the rest just enough will manifest itself to enable the climber to cautiously drag himself up to a small ledge, and thence to the foot of the chimney.

This takes him easily to about the level of the top of the Needle. There a poised block is passed on the left, that used to give trouble. I once saw my leader attempt to climb directly over it. When in the very act of pulling himself on to its upper surface it slowly swung round, as if pivoted at each extremity. Fortunately he was not tempted to let go, and it readjusted itself in a firmer position without quitting its niche. My friend led no more that day, and we afterwards solemnly warned folks against the boulder variation. The stone is yet there and is still insecure, but climbers pass round by the right and then work back on to the edge of the *arête* and up to the foot of the vertical wall that begins the second part of the climb. It is not unusual for the first part to take so long a time in severe weather as to convince a prudent party that it is expedient to utilize a grass traverse into the Needle Gully that here discloses itself on the left. This ledge takes them safely to a point in the bed of the gully above the chief pitch, and within a few minutes' easy scrambling of the top.

The first part of the Needle Ridge may be neatly varied by climbing the buttress up from the gully, or by working across to the same buttress from the Needle notch. These variations are a little harder than the usual climb, but both are safe in dry weather.

As illustrating the way not to use a rope, an amusing story is told of the first difficulty on the Needle ridge. Two young fellows had walked up to the foot of the gully with another party of climbers, and had lazily discussed their lunch and their plans for the day while the others were busy on the Needle. After deciding that they knew the Needle

too well to learn anything by climbing it, they went
on to examine critically, from a distance, the Eagle's
Nest opposite and to point out the way that they
would insure their own safety in an attack on it.
They scoffed at its reputed severity, and would
really have then and there shown the neatest method
of vanquishing it. On the other hand, it was a
warm day, and they felt a little slack. Perhaps the
Needle Ridge would tickle their jaded appetites a
bit. Yes! they would walk up the ridge and get
some fresh air 400 feet higher. Then they tossed
up for leadership, and tied on their forty feet rope—
one man at each end. Away went the leader from
the notch, over the slab and up the chimney. When
at the end of his rope it occurred to him to look
back and see what his companion was doing. The
poor fellow had stuck at the slab, and was in imminent danger of falling backwards. 'Good gracious,
man, what are you thinking of?' shouted the
indignant leader. 'I am not going to be pulled
down for any one!' and promptly began to unrope
himself. Then the man who tells the story hurried
up from below, and fortunately arrived in time to
prevent a catastrophe. Such an aspect of the utility
of the rope need scarcely be commented upon, but I
was not surprised a day or two after hearing the
story to be characterized by a non-climbing acquaintance in town as a desperate venturesome individual,
one who went about climbing mountains *with a rope*.
By non-climbers a rope must indeed be regarded as
a source of danger.

The plainest view of the upper platform of the Needle and the awkward corner that rises from it is to be had at the expense of a few minutes' digression from the ridge. It is best to climb from the top of the grass chimney over to the right, and then down a steep and loose recess to a grass platform. A photograph of the Needle from this point of view has been published, and is an interesting one to study.

The second part of the Needle Ridge begins with a vertical wall of rock that from below appears very formidable. With ice about it is certainly difficult, and the traverse to the gully on the left is the wisest course to pursue under such conditions. But on close inspection a square corner discloses itself in the wall, and the fifteen feet of scrambling in the cleft are perfectly straightforward. At the top of the wall the ridge is broken up in a wonderful way, and huge blocks are distributed along the route in great profusion. The climbing becomes very easy, though retaining its interest to the finish at the top of the Napes; and the whole ascent may be disposed of summarily in half an hour from the Needle notch.

The Eagle's Nest Ridge was climbed on April 15, 1892, by a strong party of cragsmen. They were led by Mr. G. A. Solly, who was well backed up by Mr. Cecil Slingsby. They left a record of the expedition in the Wastdale book, and let the climbing fraternity decide for themselves as to whether the ascent was worth repeating. No excep-

THE UPPER PART OF THE NEEDLE RIDGE

(Face page 156)

tion can be taken to the rocks, which are perfectly sound and reliable, but an inspection of the ridge from the Needle shows how little hold there is for hands or feet.   Moreover, the hardest part is so situated that a safe descent from it is well-nigh impossible for the unlucky leader who finds his strength or skill inadequate to cope with it.   Nevertheless, I have recently discovered that with an exact knowledge of the available holds, and with the best conditions of the rocks, a man may safely tackle the ascent if well supported by a sturdy second.   The situation is terribly exposed for the first 140 feet, and will try the nerves of even experienced mountaineers.   Dependence is often placed on small footholds that slope slightly to the climber's disadvantage; and on such ledges good nailed boots and perfect confidence are essential.   The fact is that the ridge is not to be recommended; and its virtue is that there is no deception about it.   The clean sweep of the sharp nose of rock from the green platform at the foot up to the patch of grass where the slanting chimney begins scares everybody away, tyros and experts alike.   That almost vertical buttress looks impossible, and to nearly everybody it is so.

It was a felicitous discovery of Mr. Solly's, a day later, that the worst part of the *arête* could be avoided by taking to a chimney a few feet away to the left.   Looking up at the ridge from the grass platform at its foot, the appearance presented is that of a vertical face of rock cut by two chimneys each about a hundred feet long. The right of these is shallow and open, with tufts of grass interspersed with smooth slabs. Whether it can be climbed or not I have never ascertained. But the left chimney or gully is deeply cut into the wall. Its aspect is ferocious, but its disposition gentle. It can be easily reached and comfortably climbed. Solly's original route was up the strict *arête* to the right of both chimneys. The *arête* to the left of both was investigated at Easter, 1895, and manifested an inclination to yield to the attack of a party. But the party has not yet preferred the attack, and the suggestion may be taken at its worth. Our gully is rather earthy for the first forty feet, and care must be taken by the leader to avoid dislodging stones on those below him. Then the rockholds change in character just above an outstanding pinnacle on the left, and there is an interesting passage into a niche at the back of the gully, a sloping and well-worn hold for the right foot offering the safest support as the body is dragged over into the corner. Hence the route is up the crack for a few feet and across a long slab to the right-hand wall, care being taken with a loose splinter that is generally seized as the handiest grip available. The rest of the gully is of grass and small scree, and at the top a view may be obtained down into the Arrowhead Gully. But for the ridge climb a divergence is made to the right almost immediately after the chimney pitch is passed.

A split is noticed in the *arête*, forming a small and sharp pinnacle, just below which the shallow, grass-tufted chimney finishes in sorry fashion. The climber passes through the cleft, utilizing a large block that is not quite fixed. On the other side he finds the junction with the original ridge route, ten feet below the finish of the curdling part. His next move is awkward, over a smooth rock with unsatisfactory sloping footholds, but there is no real danger with the second man at the cleft, and the leader reaches the grassy recess where, in the words of the first explorers, the difficulties moderated. It is large enough for two men to brace themselves firmly, and manipulate 150 feet of rope for an enterprising third man who may wish to come up by way of the outside edge.

This route to the recess we shall now briefly describe, suggesting at the same time that no man should attempt to lead up it who has not already explored the ground with the safeguard of a rope from above. From the horizontal grass platform at the foot of the climb a narrow cleft runs up to the ridge in such a way as to separate off the first fifteen feet from the main mass. The cleft is mounted with facility by aid of numerous holds of first-rate quality. At the top we find ourselves on the strict ridge, but after mounting ten feet the holds disappear entirely, and the verticalness of the next seven or eight feet makes a slight divergence absolutely necessary. On the face of the ridge that bounds the Needle Gully below us two parallel cracks run up steeply about a yard apart. They are so closed, and they run so obliquely up the wall, that good foothold is impossible in either, and handhold of even moderate quality requires much seeking. Nevertheless, they are both of immense importance, and are capable of giving all the required aid. The leader should here be joined by the second, and should belay himself to the highest effective part of the broken rock below him. His companion should be belayed independently. Then his next move is to work up for three feet on to the right-hand crack, with his fingers gripping the other, until the latter is felt to be good enough for a pull towards the ridge. The transfer of the right foot into the crack on the left is critical. I prefer to effect the passage without boots, as the toes can feel so much better where the crack is deepest. Then the outside edge a yard away to the left is within reach of the hand, and the leader, cut off from further assistance below, must manage very carefully to climb on to the ridge.

His holds are obvious; the difficulty is not so much in finding the way as in keeping to it. Fortunately a little flat platform is now reached, on which he can sit in comfort and recover his strength before attacking the next part. It is at about the level of the top of the Gable Needle, and Mr. Slingsby tells me it is the spot that the first climbers named the Eagle's Nest. It is just visible against the sky in the view facing page 153, $3\frac{1}{2}$ inches from the foot of the illustration. The awkward

PLATE V.

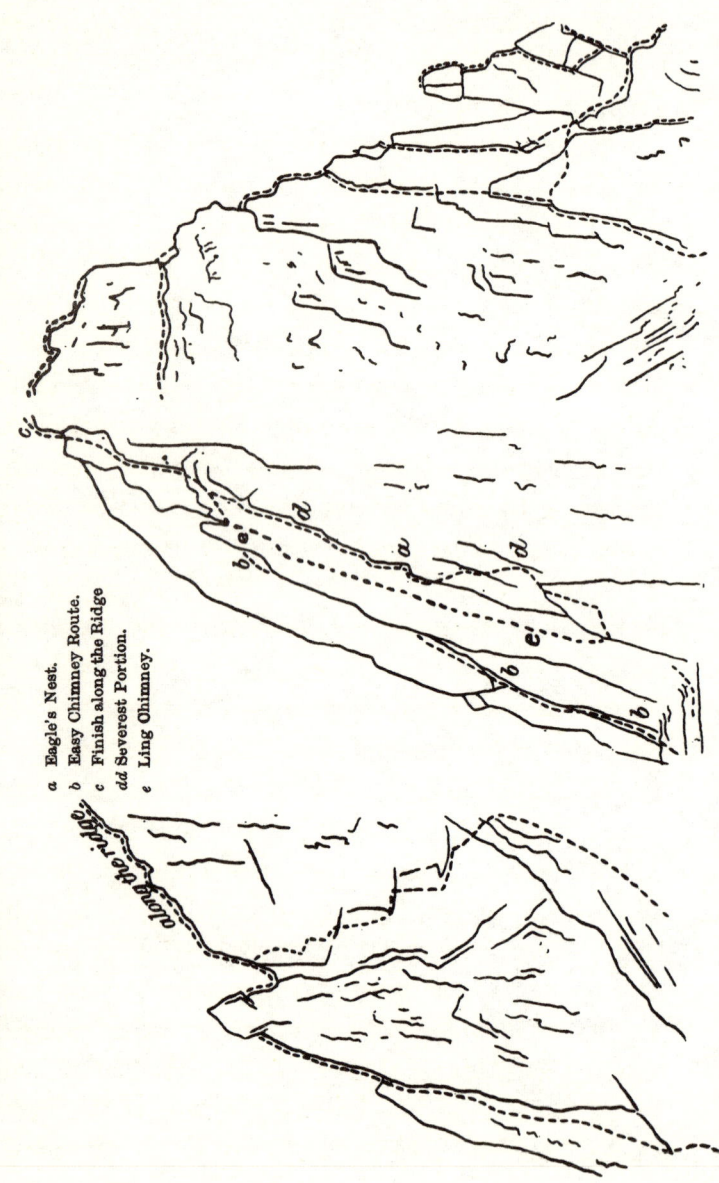

THE ARROWHEAD RIDGE.

From the South-east.

THE EAGLE'S NEST RIDGE.

From the South-east.

THE NEEDLE RIDGE.

From the North-west.

a Eagle's Nest.
b Easy Chimney Route.
c Finish along the Ridge
dd Severest Portion.
e Ling Chimney.

part first ascended is scarcely twelve feet high, but is exceptionally severe if the leader takes it without the assistance of a second.

The consequences of a slip in the next portion of the climb are more serious, but probably it is technically less difficult than the lower bit. The Eagle's Nest is barely large enough for the leader to brace himself firmly when helping the second man up on the rope, and he may naturally prefer to mount higher without assistance rather than peril the safety of both for the sake of a helping shoulder up the next piece. There are no belaying pins, and traversing to either side of the buttress is seemingly impossible. If he cannot be certain of holding on to the rope when a slip occurs to his follower, he had better decide to advance another fifty feet before the second man moves from his secure position below. The first ten feet above the Nest are remarkable for steepness and smallness of holds. If the rocks are cold and the finger tips benumbed, the holds cannot be appreciated at all, and the place becomes horribly dangerous. Yet there is a sufficiency of grip for hands and feet, and bootmarks can now be detected on the chief ledges. With perfect coolness and the exercise of his best judgment, the solitary leader will gradually mount the ridge step by step, and the tension on his nerves and muscles will be relieved when the level of the narrow pinnacle to the left is reached, and he notices the numerous scratches on the rocks of those who have climbed to the junction

by the easy route.   Mr. H. C. Bowen and I made
the second strict ascent in April, 1898, with 100
feet of rope between us.

At the foot of the slanting chimney it again becomes possible for the leader to obtain assistance
from his companions, though he is not the sort of
man to require it if he has come up by the difficult
way.   The climbing is now delightfully safe and
interesting.   The holds are good and the ridge
varied.   From the top of the slanting chimney,
which can be ascended without trouble, the true
arête below looks desperately stiff.   The remainder
of the climb will be found to consist of alternating
horizontal and vertical passages.   It is often possible
to pass down the grassy ledges on the left, but the
ridge is much pleasanter, and in wet weather actually
safer.   The views down the vertical walls on the
right into the Needle Gully are magnificent, and the
Needle Ridge is seen at its best.

The first party took two hours and ten minutes
to accomplish their ascent.   The ridge with the
initial variation by the chimney has been climbed in
half an hour by a party of three ; hunger lent wings,
for their lunch was waiting them on Gable.

The Arrowhead Ridge derives its name from
a very prominent crag a short distance to the west
of the Eagle's Nest Ridge.   It offers a very fine speci-
men of rock architecture, though the artist photographer has been known to express dissatisfaction at
its outline, and to claim artistic license in modifying

his pictures to suit his theories. Many of those who have been attracted to the Great Napes in search of the original have been much perplexed at the discrepancy between the old photographs and the modern reality. Some in their wrath have desired to get the photographer and his camera below them in a rickety gully, where, as Dent puts it, no stone is left unturned in their struggle to reach the top.

But if the artist cuts away a few thousand tons of rock from his negative with one fell stroke of his brush, if he commands the sun to stand still and the shadows to move on, if he subjects his angles to the influence of the personal equation of the climber instead of the mere observer, these weaknesses are not to be recorded against him. Mountaineering as a sport owes its advancement far more to the inaccurate descriptions of its literary devotees than to the simple statements of facts of the scientific, and its best pictorial advertisements have been those where art has assisted nature and laughed at science.

This to some extent is what we all need, and what we all understand. From the top of the Kern Knotts' crack the evidence of a freely hanging rope as to the direction of the vertical actually contradicts one's best judgment. The Kern Knotts wall is perhaps 15° from the vertical, but looking down it one would judge it perpendicular. Yet we never fancy a foothold horizontal when it is at a slope of 15° to our disadvantage, else the Eagle's Nest Ridge would lose much of its terror. Rather are we then inclined

to magnify the angle, and the actual slope plus our
own inclination make together something like the
30° that would figure in a fancy sketch or a popular
article.

Education is a marvellously fine thing, and in
mountaineering it works wonders. It enables men
to interpret the barren truth in accordance with
their own experience. Notes of new ascents in the
'Alpine Journal' they can enjoy and assimilate; but,
as in eating caviare, the taste needs cultivation, and
many remain unequal to such food to the ends of their
lives. Now because there are many false trans-
lations possible of the one true original, it must be
easy with a knowledge of the truth to interpret it
variously, and correspondingly difficult to get at the
correct version from a bad translation. Even the
mountaineering education fails to help us. All it
does is to give us the taste for truth, and the sense
of right to demand the genuine article. It might be
printed in italics at the beginning of the chapter,
like the usually inappropriate and obscure poetical
references, and so isolated from the author's personal
exposition. This text and sermon notion has not,
so far as my little library of Alpine books can tell
me, been adopted by any popular writer on mountaineering, though the difficulty has been grappled
with in other ways. Thus the Alpine historian or
geographer may find the required facts neatly
gathered together in a brief appendix, or still more
briefly summarised in a letter published simul-

taneously with a review of the book in the 'Alpine Journal.'

The sale of caviare is strictly limited, and the demand for 'Alpine Notes and New Ascents' confined to the few. Hence mountaineering books intended to sell well are written for the uneducated many, not for teaching purposes, but for the satisfaction of their desire for tales of adventure. So long as climbers tolerate this professionalism introduced into mountaineering—and there is every reason why they should in all cases where the professional is recognized as such—they must necessarily give the artist a free hand, whether he writes or paints or takes photographs. Personally I should ask for information as to the treatment of any negative that has been employed for reproduction of pictures. 'From a photograph by,' nowadays suggests a bad camera, a shaky tripod, an amateur operator, a cunning artist, and a long purse. But 'truth is mighty and will prevail,' so we may as well get on to the Arrowhead.

Viewing this Arrowhead from the easy ground near the Bear rock, it is seen to bear some resemblance to the Gable Needle (see Chapter XI.). In each case the rock forms the lower extremity of a Napes ridge, and its sides are remarkable for their steepness and smoothness. The outside edge of each is broken by a well-marked shoulder, and the head of the Arrow may be fairly well likened to the top overhanging boulder on the Needle. Here,

perhaps, the resemblance ends. Certain parts of the
climbing on the Arrowhead must be characterized as
insecure, whereas the Needle is firm throughout.
The former may easily be attacked from the notch
behind it, the Needle cannot be similarly treated.
The original climb up to the shoulder on the Arrowhead was by a recess on the east side, that up the
Needle by a narrow crack on the west. (See photograph facing page 153.)

The first ascent dates from April, 1892, when a
large party attacked the rock on the lines just
indicated. The lower part of the buttress was
mounted by a steep and open recess on the western
side, a good climb leading directly to the shoulder
half-way up, where the route was joined by the
upper end of a corresponding chimney on the other
side of the buttress. Thence the climbing was
straight up the corner. It was not very difficult,
but at a point a few feet below the final bit the
rocks were insecure and the situation alarming.
The stones are better now than formerly, but great
caution must be used. In 1893 another party repeated the ascent, and showed that it was possible
by passing round to the gap at the back to continue
the climb along the ridge. The usual route nowadays is to reach the ridge by the scree gully between
the Arrowhead and the Eagle's Nest *arête*, climbing
up the side wall to the notch, and so avoiding the
Arrowhead itself. The wall is steep, but its ledges
are conveniently disposed, and no trouble should be

experienced in the ascent. Once on the ridge the climbing is delightful. The holds are good, and the narrowness of the crest along which we pass gives the spice of sensationalism that at all times offers an apology for easy climbing. The actual ascent of the ridge need take but twenty minutes, the descent about half an hour for a party of three, when conditions are favourable. There is one *mauvais pas* of moderate quality : a wall of ten feet must be mounted to reach the crest of a tower on the ridge. Then follows a long stride across the gap on the other side, and it is sometimes amusing to watch the timid climber who fears that he may not be able to swing the hind leg over when in the colossus attitude halfway across. Above this all difficulties soon disappear ; the gullies on either side rapidly rise to our own level, and the ridge ends shortly before the crest of the Napes is reached.

The view facing page 153 shows the Arrowhead at the left-hand top corner, the Eagle's Nest Ridge against the sky, the lower half of the Needle Ridge, and the Gable Needle itself.

CHAPTER XI

THE GABLE NEEDLE

THE best-known rock problem in the district is offered by the Gable Needle. Its position has already been defined. As we walk towards Styhead from Esk Hause the Needle stands out from the west face of the Gable very plainly; but from Wastdale it is almost invisible against the background of the indistinguishable Napes rocks, and only those who know exactly where it should be are bold enough to say where it is. Very few people seem to have seen it before 1886, when Mr. Haskett Smith reached the top, though Mr. Wilson Robinson made a pencil outline-sketch of both the Needle and the Bear rock as long ago as 1828. Many even who were acquainted with the crags of the Napes had not noticed it. The fact is that a face of rock is very apt to look flat and void of detail at a short distance; and it is the joy of the rock-climber to discover its thousand beauties when he engages with it at close quarters.

The Needle is indeed a fine fellow as rocks go— just the sort of ornament for one's back garden in town, a gymnasium in itself. It has now many admirers. The few footholds on the top boulder

THE GABLE NEEDLE

(Face page 168)

bear the marks of many nailed boots, even its
smooth face is scored by futile scrapes of the
nervous, but it retains its charm for the Wastdale
enthusiast.   In his dreams he takes a hammer and
chisel, and chips away an important hold, and with
the dreamer's ease swarms up the rock unaided.
Again a hold is chipped away confidently with the
faith that removes mountains, and again he glides
up and down ; till at last its small top draws him up
without effort and he hastens down to Wastdale to
invite the attention of climbers to the new edition
of the Needle.

Mr. Haskett Smith climbed it alone in 1886 and
left a handkerchief on the top.   Those who have
been once on the Needle will readily believe that
this first ascent is one of the most daring things
that have been done in the Lake District.

He pointed it out to Mr. John Robinson one day
when they were traversing the face of the Napes
on to the Needle *arête*, and they both agreed
that it had a future before it, that their successors
in the field of climbing would make it their resort
and perhaps even build a diminutive shrine on its
crest to the discoverer.   Nearly three years elapsed
before Mr. Geoffrey Hastings made the second
ascent.   Then, in June, 1889, Mr. F. Wellford
climbed it, and Mr. Robinson made the fourth
ascent in August.   In the following year Professor
Marshall's party attacked the climb, spending three-
quarters of an hour in flinging a rope over the

summit for the benefit of the leader. On that occasion Miss Koecher reached the top—the first lady, at any rate in modern times, to succeed in doing so.

Dr. S. and I travelled down to Drigg one night. We breakfasted there early and walked the twelve miles to Wastdale, halting only for a plunge into cold Wastwater. After the manner of our kind, we inquired at once for the Climbing Book, to learn the latest news from the Fells. The 'Pall Mall Budget' article of June 5, 1890, on the Needle, had been inserted, and we read how it might be vanquished. In the afternoon we worked our way up to the Napes. Being the more enthusiastic, I found the Needle first, and was breathless on the top of the crack when Dr. S. arrived. He threw a rope up from the small platform (seen at the bottom of the picture facing page 168) and came after me. The crack up the face seemed difficult that first time; most people find it so. The first movement obliquely up to the left is easy, but the next part is a trifle too safe for the new comer. He gets his left thigh almost hopelessly jammed into the crack, and can move neither up nor down. The best plan is to work more with the left foot and knee in the crack, both hands on the edge of the leaf of rock, and the right leg getting general support by pressure outside, until the most constricted bit half-way up is passed. Then the leaf of rock can be swarmed up with much greater ease, and the climber soon finds himself looking down the other side of the crack.

From here the route for ten feet is directly up the right edge. The holds are not numerous, but good enough when the rocks are dry, and we find ourselves on a platform or shoulder, very conspicuous in most aspects of the pinnacle, that serves as an excellent take-off for the last struggle. The terrors of the crack often scare off people from the final piece. They almost did our little party. I found my watch-chain broken—some links still remain in the heart of the Needle—and my watch badly dented. The ' Pall Mall' had promised us that the last bit was the worst, and we thought for a moment that a little preliminary training for a few days would be the correct thing. However, I took off my boots, for they had no nails, and, standing on a shoulder of Dr. S., stepped on to the right end of the ledge on which the top block rests. This corner is difficult to climb alone and exceedingly daring work, for the climber drags his body on to it over a sheer drop of a hundred feet, and feels no certainty of safety till he is up. It is like climbing on a narrow mantel-shelf five feet high, that is only just wide enough to allow standing room. An ice-axe offers a useful take-off in the absence of a sufficiently responsible shoulder. The disposition of one's centre of gravity must be carefully considered, and there is a sense of alternate peril and safety in inspiration and expiration. Once on the ledge the game was evidently in our hands, and traversing along it to the left I found a rounded boss of rock eighteen inches higher that offered good hold for both feet. Then the left was brought well up to a little ledge nearly an inch wide, the right hand gripped the right edge of the boulder, and on straightening out the top edge could be grasped. An arm pull was helped by sundry roughnesses for the toes, and I sprawled half across the top triumphantly. In a couple of minutes Dr. S. was by my side. We had no intention of climbing higher that day, and willingly spent half an hour in examining the routes of the Napes' ridges, two of which are seen to advantage from this spot.

We descended without serious difficulty, Dr. S. going first. I half decided to fix our rope round the top block and use it for my own descent, but it would have been an awkward matter to detach it afterwards. Moreover, others had not found a fixed rope necessary, and we did not wish to have anything to reproach ourselves about subsequently. Dr. S. placed himself firmly on the shoulder, drawing in the rope as it came down. If I fell it would have been on to the rocks a few feet below him; he would experience no great shock, and could easily hold me in. The descent was by the exact route of the ascent. On reaching the crack again we re-adjusted our boots and slid down easily, the remembrance of the leg-clasping constriction preventing our jamming in the descent.

Two or three days later we took other men up the Needle. It was like introducing an old friend. Though I had lost no respect for him, he was easier to manage and offered new features for inspection.

The side of the Needle facing Lingmell exhibits an obvious alternative route to the shoulder. The climbing is twelve or fifteen feet longer, and rather more interesting. Facing the Needle at its foot with our backs to Lingmell, we bear to the right into a square corner. We pass up this on the left to a little level platform, reached best by an armpull and a foothold well away on the buttress. I have seen good men in much trouble on this corner. From here the route is straight up the wall, with a halting-place ten feet higher in a huge slit on the right. Then we climb the same cleft whose other side constitutes the first part of the old route. This side, however, is wider, and contains sundry jammed stones for convenience of passengers. The old route is joined without difficulty, and the shoulder reached as before.

To effect the ascent of the top boulder without help it has always appeared to me easier to start by standing on the small shelf just under the left-hand end of the overhanging part—the shelf, in fact, that is occupied by the sitting figure in the view facing page 168. Practice on ordinary strong mantelshelves enables one to mount up this corner with a certainty of success, the right hand being thrust into a thin horizontal cleft rough enough to offer some friction for the back of the hand as well as the palm.

If people are at the Needle and wish to explore it, they may like to know that Mr. W. H. Fowler has shown that the ' outside edge ' can be followed

from bottom to top.   Also, that it is not so difficult
to work from the foot of the ordinary route round to
the other side of the cleft that splits the Needle.
To photograph the Needle we usually get up the
other side of the Needle Gully at the foot of the
Eagle's Nest *arête*.   Indeed, this grass ledge is so
popular for the observation of a performance that it
is known as the 'dress circle.'   One photograph exists
of the Needle in which nearly all the climbing
details are masked by a crowd of daring maidens
swarming up it.   Two have reached the top, and are
supporting a terror-stricken man, who, poor fellow,
had rashly undertaken to lead up.   The picture
suggests the old problem of the mediæval theo-
logians—how many angels can balance on the point
of a needle ?

CHAPTER XII

KERN KNOTTS

Kern Knotts Chimney.—This is one of the prettiest things in the neighbourhood, and it photographs well. The small bunch of hard rock that crops out of the wilderness of scree on this side of the Gable was at one time rarely visited, though so near the actual Styhead path. Its name was almost unknown. I confused it with the Tom Blue crags higher up on the fell. Nowadays the good quality of the chimney attracts many visitors, and several come to see it who do not actually climb. The Knotts are in three parts—Raven Crag, and Upper and Lower Kern Knotts. The middle part is the steepest and longest. A prominent nose or buttress springs down its centre, and is visible in profile at a great distance. The buttress is split off from the main mass by a vertical crack extending from side to side, varying in thickness from three or four inches to a foot.

The chimney had been inspected by earlier climbers before I had ever heard of it. The uninitiated of Wastdale often lament the secretiveness of those who know where new things exist but who keep the knowledge to themselves. Nestor is very reticent, and it is to be counted unto him for righteousness that one Christmas week, after bad weather had deprived us of all the ordinary climbing, he announced to the engineer and me that there was a fascinating little thing, the fancy of an ' off ' afternoon, lying conveniently close to the hotel, that he would show us how to climb.   I was lying on the billiard table just then thinking of the different kinds of nothing.   ' Where is it ? ' I asked.   ' In Tom Blue ' was the reply, and as this was yet but a name to me I wondered whether Tom's blueness measured his difficulty.   The engineer was enthusiastic, and declined to allow me to remain longer on the billiard table after hearing this news.   So in the gentle rain we marched out of the inn that afternoon, and worked our way up the Styhead path till we had passed the little spring that crosses it near the zig-zag.   There we saw the great rocks looming up on the left and were told that Tom Blue awaited us there.   The steep slope leading up to our climb was strewn with huge boulders in chaotic confusion.   We could either keep to these or else make for an interesting crack in the Lower Kern Knotts that stood directly in our way.   To give us a foretaste we took to the crack, finding as usual that its aspect from a distance gave no clue to the wealth of useful detail in the shape of handholds.   Then a few yards more of mercurial skipping from boulder to boulder and we reached a little terrace at the foot of the fine wall of the Upper Kern Knotts.   Since that day a huge cairn has grown up on this terrace at an astonishing rate of development, to mark the beginning of the climb. Perhaps by the date of publication of this volume the cairn will have grown to rival the crags in height, the climb may be *via* the cairn, and Kern Knotts Chimney blocked up for ever. But for the sake of the afternoon strollers from Wastdale we pray that this may not be. The ascent is apparently in two portions, the lower one being the easier. Actually there is a third pitch, the one of perhaps greatest intrinsic difficulty, starting at the top of the split buttress and quite unnoticeable from below. For this reason the climb must be regarded as deceptive ; it is one thing to struggle up the middle pitch with the impression that the worst piece is being tackled, and quite another to find a part of exceptional severity higher up. With that portion impossible the only alternative is to descend again, and that does not commend itself to many men who climb more for amusement than for instruction.

To return to our narrative, we roped up with hopefulness and took to the lowest chimney. The rocks were streaming with water which rapidly discovered that its line of quickest descent was along our arms and bodies, with only a slight delay at the boots while they were filling up. The chimney was sufficiently well provided with small ledges, first in the middle, then on the right-hand side, to enable us to draw up easily. Then we worked round to the foot of the second pitch on a level platform large enough for us all to rest ourselves comfortably. The chimney now became much narrower, just sufficiently large to receive the right thigh. With dry rocks the slight holds on the left wall now facing us would have been ample for the pull up to the level of a jammed stone in the crack; but they were now doubtful, and the obvious course was to insert the right hand beneath the jammed stone and utilize the grip it afforded. A loose block thus handled from within is much less liable to come out than when held by its projecting parts. In a climb where every jammed stone has been tested scores of times, sundry small precautions such as this may be omitted; but a new route should always be attacked with respectful caution, otherwise it may exact a speedy vengeance, and promptly repulse the careless climber.

Just above the level of this useful block, which was immediately proved to be safe enough, the footholds were a short way out of the crack on the left wall, and were not particularly good in the heavy rain. The next ten feet appeared to be very hard, for the only hold was to be by the grip of the right thigh in the crack, and the next jammed stone (on which a climber is standing in the opposite illustration) seemed insecure. It was desirable to pass this without clinging to its outer edges, and to test it when its dislodgment could do no harm. The motion upwards in such a case is rather slow; the leg that does the work must not be thrust too far into the recess, or else the business of balancing is awkward, and the lift at each 'stroke' is insufficient.

Kern Knotts Chimney

(Face page 178)

The unemployed foot, as the skater calls it, can often help by a momentary purchase on a minute ledge; even the width of an eighth of an inch will suffice to steady the lift.

The jammed stone offered a fair grip underneath, but the ledges were now on the right wall, and the turn towards them was difficult under the circumstances. If we had known that the stone would hold we could have pulled straight up over it; but, out of desire to play the scientific game, I swung round by the hands so that the left leg was in the crack and the upper handholds visible just above my head. Next a pull-up enabled me to get the left knee well on to the stone, and finally to ensconce myself safely in the recess above it. Then our Nestor came up in splendid form, but with some anxious thought for the upper part of the climb. He asked me to mount up to the bridge above and see whether the remainder were feasible, for if not the best plan would be to descend at once. We disagreed over this, but being grateful for the introduction to 'Tom Blue,' and not knowing that it was Kern Knotts, I clambered up to please him while he was negotiating the engineer's rope, and committed myself to the opinion that it was 'all plain sailing from there.'

From the jammed stone which Nestor was now testing, the route was out over the right face of the chimney, and round again to the left where the top figure is shown in the photograph. A big block forms a bridge, beneath which meet the two chimneys from the opposite faces of the buttress.

We all reached the top of the bridge, and examined the final ridge that springs up for another hundred feet. The angle is not an easy one at first, and there is a scarcity of holds. The stylist who works only with fingers and toes would have much difficulty in getting up, even in dry weather. We one by one surmounted it by offering as many points of contact as possible to the rocks. They were streaming with water, and in a much more slippery condition than we should have preferred for a first ascent. The leader accepted a shoulder at the start, but he felt rather insecure till he was about twelve feet up, when a fine hold was found on the right. From that point the ground is more broken, and easy scrambling led to the top of the crags.

I have been told since then that it is easier to work round to the left from the bridge, and then up to the right; but a recent visit convinces me that both ways have their difficulties when the rocks are wet. Both are safe in dry weather. The direct route up from the bridge has lately been simplified by an artificial step, evidently cut with a chisel. It is a pity the timid mason did not go round another way.

To reach the main shoulder of Gable from here we may keep on towards Raven Crag and strike up a short chimney in its centre. It is not difficult, but its exit from the top takes time if the climber attacks the problem incautiously. Thence to the summit of Gable is a glorious walk.

From the ledge at the foot of the Upper Kern
Knotts there rises another buttress a little nearer
the Styhead. Between the two buttresses a short
gully is found which offers a satisfactory route
of descent from the crest of these crags. The
entrance to the gully is difficult if tried from the foot
of the buttress, but easy and suitable for beginners
if taken on the left. It was from this spot that our
party had the first view of the 'crack' that was to
offer such sport a year or two later. Nestor with
his characteristic caution vetoed the whole affair,
and vowed he would never speak to me again if I
attempted to climb it. The engineer, on the other
hand, thought that it could not be much worse than
the chimney which we had just climbed in safety,
and that it might be a good thing to keep in mind
for settled weather.

In December, 1895, I went up the chimney with
Mr. and Mrs. F. W. Hill. The rocks were slightly
damp, the weather misty and unpleasant. On the
natural bridge I halted, and looked down the smooth
wall of rock facing the Styhead. The crack was
straight beneath, and Hill nerved me to the sudden
resolve to descend by the rope and prospect the
middle portion of the climb. We had only sixty
feet of rope, but I was let down carefully and
at full distance found myself in a splayed-out
portion above the first pitch. The bit beneath looked
very awkward, so awkward indeed that it seemed
impossible to effect a descent on to the boulders

below. There was only one course available, that of climbing up again. This was not so hard as I had fancied it would be, for with the sense of the perfect security in the rope that Hill carefully manipulated, came freedom of movement and a bolder style. This is the reason why many Alpine climbers who know not the joys of leading are entirely ignorant of their own powers; they as often err in underestimating as in overrating their skill; they can gauge their strength only by practice without rope from above. Emerging from the crack I joined up on the rope again and finished the rest of the climb, wondering the while whether a chance would ever come of penetrating the crack from below.

Before leaving the ordinary chimney, let it be added that the climb may have an initial variation by pulling up the vertical rocks to the west of the foot of the nose; the distance to the first big platform is increased about fifteen feet, but the way is pleasanter thus.

Kern Knotts Crack.—One fine morning in April I started off for Keswick, grieved to leave Wastdale and feeling strong after a fortnight's scrambling. Surely if the crack could be done at all now would be the time, with weather and physical fitness corresponding. Our party was small; two men were coming with me to look at Kern Knotts, and subsequently to exploit the Oblique Chimney, the whereabouts of which had puzzled them the previous day. It was a bargain between us that they should help

me in the crack and I should lead up the Oblique
Chimney afterwards. The advantage was thus all
my own, and their brotherly kindness drew me
to them. It was in the preceding winter that Hill
had let me down from the top of the crack for a
distance of fifty feet to a small loose platform of
rock, and I had with extreme effort managed to
return without tugging the rope. Since that time
there had been opportunity to reflect and decide
that if I could get up to the platform from below
and then help another to the same level, we could
jointly manage the ascent of the crack without
further aid. If the platform could not hold two, it
would be a case of ascending the worst part of the
crack, the splayed-out portion some twelve feet high,
without assistance.

On reaching the spot things looked cheerful
enough. The rocks were dry, and I found that
imagination had somewhat magnified my early impressions of the wall. But the reality is bad enough.
The wall is one side of a buttress about one hundred
feet in height, and marvellously smooth to look at.
It is cut down from top to bottom by a clean-edged
slit passing right through the buttress and forming
on the other side, as I have already explained, the
now familiar Kern Knotts Chimney. At a height
of thirty feet or so from the foot is the little platform, the niche at the back of which looks as though
carved out for the reception of a piece of statuary.
The portion of the crack that leads up this first part

has a slightly different outlook; it is more open, and is provided with holds of a shaky description. Getting a companion to hold himself in this, I mounted his shoulder and felt about with the hands. There was nothing at all that seemed firm. So I called for the axe, and, remembering certain tactics in an awful rock climb in Northern Italy some years before, I rammed the axe longitudinally into the crack and endeavoured to use it as a hold. The plan is sometimes effective; it is not sufficiently often adopted *in extremis;* but on this occasion it would not act; the loose stones in the cleft were simply levered out of place, and I had to pass the axe down again. Then ensued a few moments' fatiguing suspension from one arm with but poor foothold to ease the strain. It was no go this time; I had to let myself down and rest awhile. Next we sat on a boulder opposite the wall, and stared at it silently for a space. Surely that must be a foothold ten feet up on the edge of the crack. If, while I mounted his shoulder, the second man could hold the ice-pick in a minute fissure in the face, I might manage to step on to the axe-head and reach the edge of the platform. It would at any rate prove safer than the crack route. The plan commended itself to all, and we placed ourselves in position. It turned out that the axe was scarcely necessary, for with a little delicate balancing I reached the top hold with both hands and dragged up to the lower step in the ledge. Thence to the platform was an easy matter, and we all began to breathe freely.

KERN KNOTTS CRACK

(Face page 184)

It never occurred to me that I had made no mental note, in my previous ascent of the crack, of the method of getting up the next part. It was certainly a stiff struggle that Christmas, but I was then out of form, and might reasonably hope to succeed more easily now. Nevertheless, when it came to the test I found it impossible, three times in succession, to get my head above a certain projecting block at the top of the niche. Each time it caught me by the back of the neck, and would not release me till in desperate extremity I let myself down again—no easy matter with exhausted arms. After the first try my two friends went round to the other side of the buttress, and hastily climbed the chimney so as to be ready to help me. I could hear their every word through the fissure, and rather surprised them by making a quiet remark. On a small scale we were having the Funffingerspitze incident repeated. Neruda was climbing that famous Dolomite, the scene of his tragic death in 1898, by a new route and heard another party ascending by the older way on the other side of the mountain.

My pockets had been emptied out before the start. After these failures I flung away my coat and tied on to the rope that had been let down from above. With renewed confidence the fourth attempt was successful. When the first twelve feet were passed I found two wedged stones a short distance above my head. These forced my body out of the crack altogether, but they offered respectable holds during the process. Above these the next pitch involved a process of backing up, though the chimney was much too narrow to brace firmly across from side to side.

I joined the other men at the top after a few more struggles, breathless and exhausted. Resting a few moments we descended the Kern Knotts Chimney and went down to lunch near the spring. Later on, when I effected the ascent without a rope, a rapid passage of the worst bit left me with enough reserve strength to climb up the rest of the way comfortably. The eighty feet and the descent by the chimney on the other side were then disposed of in seven minutes.

The remaining passage upwards from the cave is by the *mauvais pas* of the ordinary route.

The account of this crack has been given in much detail. It is the sort of thing for a strong party to climb on their way out of Wastdale, or some afternoon after a wet morning's imprisonment in the hotel. The danger of the first pitch can be minimised for the leader by holding him with the rope from the right-hand recess of the wall. In fact there is a pinnacle in this recess at about the level of the niche, which could be utilized as a holding-place. A shoulder to start from and an ice-axe support in continuation are certain to be appreciated. Messrs. Reade and McCulloch have lately shown that the niche can be reached by the crack. On the worst bit which immediately follows I expect a steadying hand from below will be generally necessary.

When a man can go up this without assistance from above he may well be regarded as fit for the Grépon crack. This latter is of the same length and general character. It is easier, but harder to enter, and it comes after more climbing ; moreover, there may be ice in it to create trouble.

Kern Knotts, West Chimney.—A note may here be added concerning the only remaining chimney on these crags that can claim to be a distinctive feature visible at a distance. It is about sixty feet to the north-west (or Wastdale side) of the ordinary route, and is plainly discernible from the lower part of the Styhead path. A diminutive cairn now marks the foot of the chimney ; another stands on a flat ledge a couple of yards above the narrowest and hardest portion of the climb.

There are two or three ways of reaching the foot of the main difficulty in the ascent, all converging to a point about twenty-five feet above the lower cairn. Here a vertical crack rises abruptly, varying from ten inches to nothing in width, and terminating ten feet higher in a right-angled corner of the rocks that will on no account permit any ' backing-up.' For some distance the recess looks as difficult to tackle as the corner of a room, and it is only when the climber gets to a height of fifty feet that his troubles appear to moderate. One wet day some twelve months ago our party could make nothing of the ascent, but shortly after last Easter (1897) I made another attempt on it. To help me on the difficult pitch a second man was persuaded to scramble up to the foot of the crack, as I anticipated the need of a sturdy shoulder.   But the platform on which I was waiting proved to be much too small for two, and when, by elevating myself a few feet, it was safe for him to follow, I was too high to use his shoulder and had to manage with his encouraging suggestions and the little excrescences on the right wall.   The first pull up the crack was by an excellent hold for both hands on the left, using a narrow ledge with the inner side of the left foot, and the crack itself for the right thigh.   It then became desirable to turn round so that the outer edge of the left foot should grip it without losing its support during the process of turning.   This accomplished, the method of ascent became obvious.   Small holds for hands and feet were distributed regularly up the right wall, perhaps three ledges for a rise of ten feet.   During the latter part the left hand sought support in the grassy corner of the chimney, which here began to open up again.   Then a long pull with the arms brought me up to the flat ledge that marks the finish of the difficulty.   There a cairn was built with the loose stones that needed shifting, the second man coming up like a lamplighter to help in the operation.

Thence our route was partly up the buttress, by rather exposed ledges, and partly in the chimney. The rocks were excellent and the open mountain side was reached in another fifty feet.   The climb is worthy of Kern Knotts. It is more risky than either the chimney or the 'crack,' but with a steady party and dry rocks it will go perfectly well. Nevertheless, I am far from willing to give it an unqualified recommendation. A slip of the leader on the awkward part would almost certainly cause the second to be pulled away from his hold, and the two would have an objectionable fall over twenty-five feet of steep rock. But the striking appearance of the difficult pitch is enough to keep away all weaklings.

CHAPTER XIII

THE WASTWATER SCREES

WASTWATER, the deepest lake in the district,
occupies a flat-bottomed depression in Wastdale. It
is just three miles long, and its very regular shores
somewhat detract from the prettiness of its scenery.
But the wild character of the hills that inclose it
gives it a grandeur that is not possessed to an equal
extent by any of the other lakes in the country.
Its direction is north-east and south-west; Upper
Wastdale is at its northern end. The road up the
valley from Strands runs close to the lake along its
north-western side, and is good enough for driving
or bicycling as far as Wastdale Head. There it
terminates as a driving-road, but paths lead to the
north over the Black Sail Pass and eastwards over
the Styhead. As we walk up the road, Buckbarrow
towers in steep crags a mile away to the left ; then
on the same side we skirt the gentler slopes of
Middle Fell, and after crossing Nether Beck, Yewbarrow exhibits a singular change of outline, from
that of a steep and narrow pyramid to a long level-
topped grassy ridge with no architectural pretensions
whatever. On the other side of the lake is the ridge

G. P. Abraham & Sons, Photos.

Keswick

The Wastwater Screes

of the Screes, one of the most singular mountains in
Britain. Its highest point is by no means striking to
look at, a matter of 2,000 feet above the sea. For a
length of three miles the ridge is broken away in a
line of cliff of almost uniform height, towering
1,500 feet over the lake. The character of the rock,
and perhaps also an unusually great exposure to
weathering influences, has caused an enormous wear
and tear of the face of the cliff. Thus it is that
huge screes have been formed that flow straight
down into the lake. The action is still going on.
If we take a walk along the edge of the cliff, and
this way of enjoying the round of Wastwater may be
strongly recommended to tourists, we cannot help
noticing that at the heads of the big gullies which
indicate the regions of maximum erosion, slight
preliminary landslips have already occurred. The
grassy ridge is marked in many places by curved
terraces, showing definite subsidence and taking
the general shape of the gully head. A few years
ago a great mass of rock detached itself from the
top of the cliff near its highest point, and thundered
down towards the lake. It happened at night and
nobody was there to see, but the terrific noise gave
serious alarm to the inhabitants of the valley.
It has been estimated that the volume of rock that
broke away was as great as the Manchester Town
Hall, but the comparison is perhaps worth little,
for to many a north-countryman there is nothing
greater than the Manchester Town Hall, and the

expression may have been used merely to denote that the rock-fall was very big. The scar may still be seen on the face, if one knows where to look for it ; the scree below it appeared fresh for many months. The rich colouring of red and yellow in the rocks has caused the scree itself to assume an astonishing variety of tints, and when viewed in sunlight the effects are most remarkable.

From the climbing point of view this continual weathering is altogether unsatisfactory. The rocks are too uncertain, and in most cases the gullies are too much occupied by scree. But towards the lower end of the lake we find that certain different conditions obtain. The rocks are firmer, there is less scree at their base, and it shows plainly by its grass covering that the fresh supply is strictly limited.

The last great bastion of the high ridge rises opposite Wastdale Hall. It is cut off from the crags on the left by the Great Gully, which runs up to the sky-line through a height of a thousand feet. On the right a slighter gully practically indicates the end of the precipitous portion of the face. Cutting deeply into the centre of the bastion itself is a third gully that is continued straight on to the sky-line ; if anything it is a few feet shorter than the Great Gully, though much more difficult to climb. I propose to describe these two only. From all accounts it would appear that they represent fully the satisfactory routes up the Screes. The sketch in Haskett Smith's book shows them as B and C (the reader can let B stand for 'big' and C for 'central'). That which is marked A in his sketch is no climb at all. It is just a gully and nothing more, but it was not quite so worthy of being labelled as the next great one to the left.

The B gully was first climbed in the winter of 1891-2 by Messrs. Collie, Hastings, and Robinson, and an interesting account of the ascent, contributed by Dr. Collie, appeared in the 'Scottish Mountaineering Journal' for January, 1894. A year later Mr. Mummery made the second ascent. Not so long afterwards Robinson showed me the way up with a large party of enthusiasts, whose strength and nerve were pretty well exhausted by the time we dragged ourselves over the last pitch.

Concerning the early history of the attempts on the C gully I have not been able to gather much information. Many parties have started up it with the impression that they were undertaking the Great Gully, but they never succeeded in finishing it. On April 19, 1895, Messrs. Lawrence, Simpson, and Patchell, made a magnificent assault on it, and by the merest accident they had to give in almost at the moment of success. They climbed seven pitches, the gully getting harder at each successive pitch. Then, when worn out with fatigue and exposure to wet and cold, they misjudged the difficulty of the ninth pitch. It is certainly most formidable to look at from below the eighth, but on closer examination its difficulties vanish: That is to say, they become

insignificant for a party that can get over the
seventh pitch. They saw two more huge obstacles
looming above the ninth, and were completely dis-
heartened. There happened to be an easy exit on
the left, and they took to it. Once or twice since
that date others have tried the gully again, but
without effecting any further advance. In April,
1897, Mr. H. C. Bowen accompanied me from Wastdale in an attempt. Circumstances favoured us
throughout, and the gully yielded to our attack. I
believe it is one of the hardest climbs that either of
us has yet effected in Cumberland, but that may be
because it is one of the most recent. Before
attempting it visitors to the district should see first
if they can comfortably manage the B gully.

The Great Gully of the Screes (B).—The
usual way of reaching it from Wastdale Head is by
the road as far as the second field beyond Wastdale
Hall. There a path across the bridge can be found,
and the course of the stream followed up to the lake
side. The foot of the gully is reached in fifteen
minutes by bearing obliquely upwards across ancient
scree. Its aspect is such as to directly face the
small peninsula across the water a trifle to the left
of the Hall. The right edge of the gully extends
further downwards than the left, and a small stream
of water is usually finding its way down the rough
scree bed.

A few feet up we reach the first obstacle, in the
shape of a broken waterfall altogether about thirty

feet high. It is usual to take to the steep grass on the left, a route that looks easier than it actually is. When the soil is damp the earth comes away like sand, and there is little reliability in the holds all the way up. We step with relief into the bed of the gully again, and look up to see what the prospect is. An easy slope leads towards a second waterfall, considerably higher than the first. Ordinarily there is no chance of surmounting it directly, but a way of avoiding it discloses itself as we approach. The gully divides into two, the main portion being to the left, and a fine branch passing up to a height of 150 feet on the right. We start by climbing the first pitch in the branch gully—a narrow vertical corner in the wall down which a vigorous spout of water jets like a hydrant. There are a few ledges on the left side which enable us to avoid some of the water, but if there has been much rain before our expedition it is impossible to keep dry during the ascent.

It was here that I saw a sinful act of revenge that grieved me much at the time. My companions had been with me up the Scawfell Pinnacle by the Deep Ghyll route on the previous day, and one had kept the others in painful attitudes on the cliff while he leisurely proceeded to photograph us. The partner of my woes vowed vengeance, and exacted it here on the Screes. His turn it was to manipulate the camera, and his wicked malice prompted him to insist on taking a photograph when his brother was half-way up the corner. We had given him the right of choosing his subject and could not complain, especially as he was loud in his praise of the view and in his grief at his brother's cramped and drenched condition. But he was in good humour for the rest of the day, and that was worth paying for.

The position now is that a buttress separates us from the main gully. We have to clamber a few feet up this, next along a shallow, sloping scoop as far as it goes, and then traverse across to the head of the big fall. The leader is not able to derive much help from the rope in case of a slip, but it is as well for the second man to climb thirty feet up the right wall of the branch gully, so as to be higher than the pioneer. The buttress looks much broken from below, but the general slope is to our disadvantage, and the final traverse is along a crumbling ledge of earth and grass. Frost occasionally makes the climbing easier, by binding the earth firmly to the rock.

The view across the lake from the top of the waterfall is very beautiful. The rich dark green of the pines that grow down to the water's edge on the other side form a striking contrast to the gaunt and barren walls of black rock that close in the view. Buckbarrow fills up the background, the severity of its seamed precipices softened by distance.

The branch gully, it may here be mentioned, has never been climbed throughout. It ends on the bastion at no great height above us, and is probably not very stiff. I tried it one Christmas Day with Messrs. Robinson and Fowler, but we rose no higher than the little notch on the thin curtain of rock that forms its right boundary. We got soaked in the little waterfall, and the bitter cold drove us back unsuccessful. We had difficulties with the awkward chimney above the narrow corner.

Keeping up the main gully, an easy stretch takes us to the third pitch. It is a water-slide, and we must hurry up quickly if dryness is still any consideration. The best way is on the left. There are many holds under the water, and our efforts to prevent its trickling down our arms will be futile if we get flurried by nasty remarks from those behind. Almost before we can gain breath again we are confronted by a similar difficulty. The water-slide here is taken first on the right, until a slanting crack leads across to the other side. The climbing is rather stiff near the top, and careful search should be made for the safest footholds.

The fifth pitch that we now approach is generally regarded as the hardest. It is undoubtedly difficult when taken by the route first discovered. A long wet slope of rock divides the gully into two parts. On the right there seems little likelihood of finding a way up. The great overhanging slabs are fifty feet high, and water is continually pouring down them. On the left the chance of success is greater. A slanting crack lies between the rock slope and the side wall. It leads straight up to a hole underneath a huge overhanging boulder that dominates the pitch.

There we can see a choice of route. The way first adopted is to wriggle up the chimney between the boulder and the left wall; but it is preferable to crawl out of the hole to the right and make an exit over rounded boulders to the top of the obstacle. The chimney is extremely stiff, the main difficulty being to make a start from the hole. If the cave had a level bottom the difficulties would be much moderated. There are no holds on the boulder itself and very few on the side wall, but those few make it worth while starting with the face to the wall. Six feet higher, when the climber is in the most exposed situation, he must turn half round and use both sides of the chimney. If the leader cannot get into the crack unassisted, it is a good plan for the second to hitch himself to a jammed boulder at the back of the cave and proffer a shoulder as a take-off. The first explorers had ice to contend against and proceeded in a still more cautious manner, all three combining their strength at the awkward corner. I have three times seen men swing off on the rope when half way up the chimney, and am bound to admit that there is too much touch-and-go for the way to suit any but very strong climbers. The easier way out of the hole— first taken, I think, by Messrs. Whitaker and Thorp —seems to reduce the difficulty considerably, and will probably become a favourite exit.

Above the fifth pitch we step out into a huge amphitheatre of rock. It is difficult to decide which is the main gully, and many men are willing to con-

clude that there is no more hard work in front,
and that a speedy passage out of the hollow will
conduce most to their happiness.

The real gully passes up on the left. A branch
starts pleasantly enough to the right, but after one
or two fairly easy pitches we are confronted by a
blank, wet wall. The sides are steep and spiky and
rotten; it was a most miserable hour I once spent
getting over forty feet of this dreadful *cul-de-sac*, and
ever since I have solemnly warned others from any
such attempt to shirk the final part of the Great Gully.
If they wish to get out, they should keep still more
to the right, over steep grass and occasional slight
rock. Traversing in a westerly or south-westerly
direction, they pass across the heads of several gullies,
above the worst portion of the C gully, and then out
on the fell side, whence an easy run takes them down
to the bridge.

The three or four pitches that must be overcome
in mounting to the head of the true Great Gully are
short but difficult. The ghyll is narrow and wet
and it is almost impossible towards the finish to
avoid a drenching by the slender stream that
monopolizes the direct route. The last pitch is
ordinarily circumvented by passing up the nasty
wall of loose earth and rocky *débris* on the left.
This diversion leads on to an easy broken buttress
from which we can walk into the gully again and up
its scree finish to the crest of the precipice.

On the occasion of my first ascent we were four
and a half hours in the gully. A second expedition to

the top of the fifth pitch took three hours ; and half that time was spent at photography.

The Central Gully (C).—Bowen and I had been climbing together for some days last Easter (1897), and were reserving an attempt on the C gully for the latter end of our holiday, to give ourselves the chance of getting into good form and the place an opportunity for drying up.

One fine morning we heard that another party were driving down the valley on their way to the Great Gully. They offered us seats in their wagonette. We gladly accepted, and had a pleasant drive along the lakeside as far as Wastdale Hall. The walk round to the foot of our climb occupied us the best part of half an hour, and we then left our friends to continue their journey, arranging to look out for them at the top of the Screes a few hours later.

The gully was easy at the outset, but far up above us we could see difficulties in plenty, and we began the scramble with a sense of future bliss that rather detracted from our present enjoyment.

We passed up on the left-hand side of the first pitch at 11-18, over fifteen feet of steep grass and rock. The holds were fairly good beside the water-fall. A few feet further on the gully narrowed at a second pitch—a steep gutter down which the stream endeavoured to smooth a way. We could use ledges on either side, and at the top a tree-stem that has lain there for some years gave us assistance. The pitch is about twenty-five feet high.

Then there followed two easy ten-feet bits before we found ourselves compelled at the fifth pitch to quit the bed of the gully. This obstacle sent us off to the left up a steep grass bank before we could traverse back into the narrow chimney at an assailable spot. We were obliged to use our knees for wedging safely in the V-shaped corner, and thus had our introduction to the water-way. The ledges were few and slippery. Ten feet up the corner a jammed stone and a slippery slab guarded the head of the pitch. We reached the former actually behind the water, and hastened out to the left with but slight steadying holds for the hands.

Then we halted a little and looked about us. We had gone through the preliminaries, and realized that our gully was now getting stiff. The view upwards showed the great seventh pitch, but nothing higher. Far below we could see the end of the lake. The prospect was not nearly so fine as that from the Great Gully ; the rocks were not so boldly carved out, nor the outlook so fair.

The next obstacle was formed by a jammed boulder thirty feet high, impossible to climb direct. It would perhaps have been best to take it on the right, but we advanced tentatively up the other side, and then, seeing that it would just go, kept on to the top. Our route lay up the narrow crack between the boulder and the side wall. A shoulder was useful for the leader at the start, but he had a bad six feet just above. The only hold for the right hand was obtained by clenching the fist inside the crack so as to form a wedge. A far-away notch in the wall gave an oblique push-off for the left foot, the struggle being mainly to keep close to the crack.

The difficulties now became almost continuous, and we were unable to define exactly the beginning of the seventh pitch. Some twenty feet of steep climbing up the bed of the ghyll first followed and we reached a little platform whence a branch gully of steep grass led out on the buttress to our left. The main gully was thirty feet across, narrowing a little higher up. An almost vertical rib of rock some six feet thick divided the gully into two parts. That on the right was a wide recess roofed in by a great stone nearly a hundred feet overhead. From our little platform we could see the water streaming over the edge of the roof, and forming a thin veil at the entrance to the cave. The left-hand side of the rib was a narrow crack sloping back at an angle of about 45°, but after the first thirty feet continuing to the top perpendicularly. The route we chose lay first up the crack, then across the rib and into the cave. A second start being made from there, we proposed to climb up the vertical rib, taking to the crack on its left whenever the difficulties became extreme. At the level of the roof of the cavern we were to traverse across on to it and make directly up its smooth slope and round by the left of a higher jammed block that overhung the finishing portion of the pitch. I think

PLATE VI.

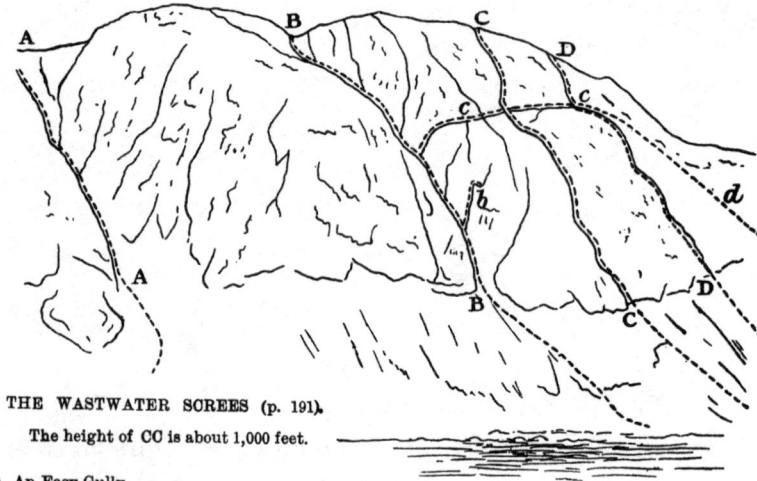

THE WASTWATER SCREES (p. 191).

The height of CC is about 1,000 feet.

A An Easy Gully.
B The Great Gully (1891).
C The Central Gully (1897).
D A Minor Gully, not very difficult.

b The Curtain.
c The Easy Traverse.
d Descent from Traverse.

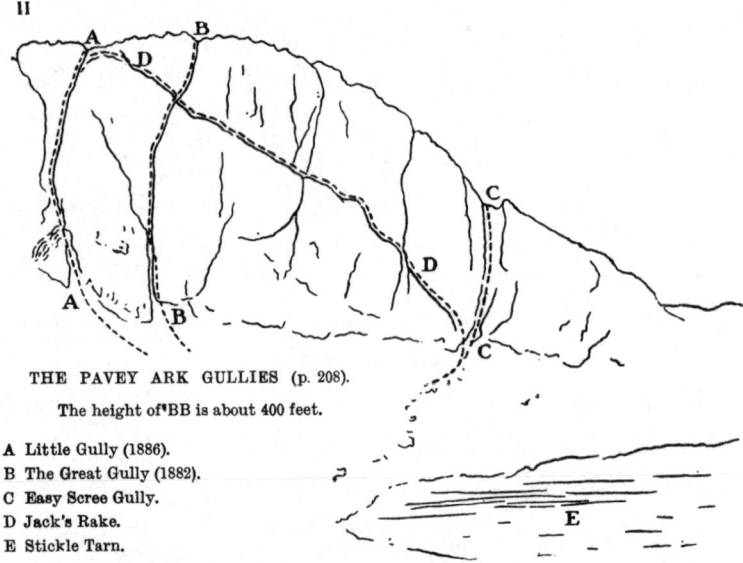

II

THE PAVEY ARK GULLIES (p. 208).

The height of BB is about 400 feet.

A Little Gully (1886).
B The Great Gully (1882).
C Easy Scree Gully.
D Jack's Rake.
E Stickle Tarn.

the route differs a little from that of the first party, who were somewhat assisted by a jammed stone then in the crack. In fact one member considered the stone essential for a successful ascent, and that its untimely removal closed the upper half for ever. But there can be no doubt that in a dry season the obstacle can be overcome by a moderately strong party, and that in the normal ' streamy ' state of the gully the climber needs but the knowledge of a route and the nerve to follow it without hesitation and without regard to dryness.

We found the way easy up to the cave. There Bowen braced himself firmly amidst the bright green ferns and endeavoured to reconcile himself to the prospect of a long wait. He could not trace out my route upwards, for the curtain of water was between us, but now and again when troubles were thickest he would inquire feelingly after my condition.

It was straightforward climbing out from the cave and up to the vertical buttress. But the absence of suitable holds in the crack on the left made the next twenty feet very severe, and I was glad to find at last a series of ledges across to the top of the cave. The holds were wet and my fingers benumbed. If the ledges had been anything but satisfactory the traverse would have been highly incorrect, not to say immoral. Then the rope had to be lengthened out and the wait was unpleasant. But the rock slope was a much simpler matter than it had appeared to be from below, and the rest of the pitch was scarcely more than a walk. I drew up over the last block with much relief, and paused to recover warmth and feeling before drawing in the rope for Bowen. He climbed with great rapidity and practically left out the traverse; it was rather vexatious to find that he emerged fresh and comparatively dry. It was now 12-34 P.M., and so far we had advanced rapidly.

A few feet in front was a long thin crack, looking easy but proving awkward at close quarters. We found it best to traverse up the smooth slab on the left and then crawl along a rickety ledge of grass and rock back to the gully again. Were we nevermore to find an easy piece? Almost at once a ninth pitch faced us, looking somewhat like the eighth. The gully suddenly narrows to a V-groove which springs up vertically for twelve feet, then slopes away at 45° for twenty feet, and finally is blocked by a few boulders before widening out again. Just before the constriction occurs, the walls of the ravine slope outwards at an easy angle, and the tangle of thickly-matted grass disguises the treacherous character of the rock underneath. This has been splintered and loosened by frost and sturdy vegetation. Great masses in many steep places are ready to fall at a touch, and scrambling is robbed of its pleasures by the sense of possible insecurity of every available hold. I tried at first to keep up the crack, but just at the corner where it trends obliquely upwards the difficulties of holding on proved too great and a cautious descent had to be effected. Then we looked to the left up a steep little gully fifty feet high. It ended abruptly in the main wall of the ravine, but a great splinter of rock at the highest corner gave us a chance of belaying. Bowen clambered gingerly over the broken ground and tied himself to the rock. Then, slipping my rope round it, he prepared to hold me during the next move. Our plan was to clamber up the loose face on the left of the awkward pitch and traverse into the gully twenty-five feet higher. My rope was dragging along the wall, and would have dislodged a good deal if suddenly called upon to break my fall. The worst bit was the last six feet of traverse, which I very much loosened during the passage. The gully was then bestridden and both sides used for the finishing portion of the pitch. When Bowen came along, the traverse broke away at his touch, and it was rather alarming to see him start falling backwards. But the rope was tight above him and he simply swung round into the gully; it was the most expeditious mode of entering, but he bruised his leg a little at the final bump. We afterwards agreed that the second man ought to take the whole obstacle direct. Trying to repeat the ascent again in April, 1898, by exactly the same manoeuvres, the slight remnant of traverse broke away with me and I had a bad fall. I was saved, of course, by the rope. The direct ascent of the watercourse has been proved to be possible, and is now much the better way.

Such was the ninth pitch, probably the one misjudged by Dr. Lawrence's party on April 9, 1895. They had taken four hours to climb to the eighth, remarkably good going when one considers the bad condition of the gully during their ascent and the amount of new ground they managed to cover. We had mounted in a little less than an hour and three quarters; but we were only a small party and the circumstances very favourable. They saw a hundred-feet pitch following on a few yards higher and endeavoured to estimate its difficulties. From below the aspect is terrifying, and after a slight survey they decided to work out of the ravine by an easy exit up the left wall. Thence they saw a few more pitches higher up beyond the tenth, and were convinced that they had done right. But they were mistaken, as our experience proved.

A little direct scrambling up the bed of the gully took us to the foot of the great obstacle. A water-shoot splashes on to the left wall eighty feet up, and is deflected into the cavernous depths of a black recess formed in the gully by a long buttress that divides it into two parts. The climb up through the splashing water appears to be almost hopeless, and a view from above of the last twenty feet shows that the risk would be extreme if the pitch were attacked on that side. But the buttress will be found on inspection to close in a sort of chimney on the right, fairly easy to reach and most comfortable to follow up to its finish three feet above the level of the top of the waterfall. This branch chimney is safe and dry. There are no loose stones about, and the occasional glimpses of the furious shoot over the way are very pleasing. They were so to us, at any rate, who had been in fear and trembling lest we should be compelled to attack the pitch through the waterfall. We were surprised at our good fortune, and none the less on seeing that the difficulties above were insignificant. A short scree and an easy twelve-feet obstacle brought us up to the well-known traverse across the face of the mountain.

We could hear occasional shouting of our friends in the Great Gully. It tempted us to work over to them and finish on the final chimneys of their climb. But we felt constrained to keep straight up, lest any further pitches should linger unclimbed. The C gully was to acknowledge itself vanquished from beginning to end, and we set ourselves to finish the task. Little actually remained. A steep climb of thirty feet, using both sides of the gully, with poor holds near the top, virtually brought us to an end of its interesting and extended series of pitches. A scramble up the last water-slide and a muddy slope led to the long scree finish, and we emerged at the summit shortly after two o'clock. The walk home over Ill Fell took an hour and a half.

CHAPTER XIV

PAVEY ARK

THE Langdale Pikes form a beautiful group of hills four miles to the east of the Scawfell Pikes. They lie at the head of Langdale, and the highest point, Harrison Stickle, is a prominent object in many a favourite landscape.

Harrison Stickle is splendidly shaped, and manages to give an impression of much greater height than it really possesses (2,401 feet). Half a mile to the west is the Pike of Stickle or the Sugarloaf. It has a little climbing on the west face. Mr. Gwynne writes of it thus : 'The Sugarloaf itself is a very fine peak, that, viewed from the valley, has very much the appearance of the Mönch. It runs down towards the Stake Pass in a spur, which must be the starting-point of most of the climbs on this mountain. There is a curious gully here, which is worthy of the climber's attention. It does not run from top to bottom, but suddenly begins about the middle of the crag. The difficulty is to get at this gully, and some pretty climbing can be obtained in the attempt.'

Somewhat south of the mid-point between Harrison Stickle and the Sugarloaf is the summit of Gimmer Crag. It overlooks the old hotel of Dungeon

G. P. Abraham & Sons, Photos.

Keswick

THE PAVEY ARK GULLIES FROM STICKLE TARN

(Face page 208)

Ghyll, and offers in dry weather a considerable amount of indiscriminate scrambling.

One of the finest little tarns of the district lies 900 feet below the summit of Harrison Stickle, on its north east side. Stickle Tarn is almost as solitary as Easedale, and its surroundings are decidedly finer. It is about an hour's walk from Dungeon Ghyll, by a small footpath keeping close to the stream that is fed by the lake waters. The view across the tarn is a delight to climbers' eyes. The great cliffs of Pavey Ark, rising 700 feet above the lake, are darkly reflected in the still waters. They are deeply cut by two gullies that immediately arrest attention. Each marks a little notch in the sky-line. A third notch further to the left indicates the head of a slighter indentation in the face of the cliff, which, so far as I know, has not yet been explored. The right-hand 'Great' Gully was first climbed by Haskett Smith in the summer of 1882. The left, called the 'Little' Gully by way of antithesis, the same climber explored in June, 1886. A lady ascended the Great Gully in 1887, and later years have seen a steady succession of visitors to these crags.

Well towards the north end of the cliff is a wide scree gully with a square notch at its crest. Near the foot of this a safe natural path may be followed obliquely across the face. This is the well-known Jack's Rake. It starts rather steeply, but soon assumes a gentle, uniform gradient. It crosses the Great Gully a hundred feet below the top; there then follows a rather awkward bit for the walker, who will need to scramble up a corner to get on to the last portion of the rake. It crosses the Little Gully within fifty feet of the summit, and ends on the buttress just beyond. Two chimneys spring from the level of Jack's Rake to the north of the Great Gully, which both look interesting. Our pleasant scramble is thus described by Gwynne : 'This ledge [i.e. Jack's Rake] offers a multitude of good opportunities to the climber. It runs obliquely across the face of the precipice, but it need not necessarily be followed throughout its length by the mountaineer who wishes for something a little more exciting. About half-way up there runs on to the ledge a chimney which —when it is not a small waterfall—forms a pleasant climb to some broken rock above, whence the summit is easily reached. If, however, the water in the chimney makes it uncomfortable and unpleasant for the climber, he may still arrive at the top of it by choosing a long bit of steep, smooth rock on the left. There are two clefts which afford fairly good hand-and-foot holds, and from there the top of the chimney is attained.'

The Little Gully.—Some six years ago I paid my first visit to Pavey Ark. The accounts of the Great Gully were very enticing. One visitor spoke of it as having only one pitch, 'but that was severe.' Another, commenting on the first, remarked: 'Yes! it has only one pitch, but that one lasts all the way up!' Then a celebrated climber had estimated its height at double the actual amount, which was a testimonial to its good qualities all the more acceptable because it was given unconsciously.

There were tales of a leader pawing about for half an hour on the second man's head and shoulders, in search of holds. Gloves and sticks and other impedimenta were understood to lie in profusion at the foot of the stiffest bit, left there by those who could climb no higher, or those who sadly expected that after their despairing attempts had failed they would have no further need for such articles. In short, there was a good deal of pernicious exaggeration concerning the Great Gully, and I went for it expecting great things. It was rather a long walk from Wastdale, over Great End and Bowfell. The descent to Dungeon Ghyll was taken for the sake of a look-in at the waterfall, and for the next half-hour hurrying up to Stickle Tarn, I felt to the full the futility of having run down from Bowfell to Langdale to save time. Arrived at the small dam that holds in the waters of the lake, I saw the two gullies on the other side, and concluding that the left-hand one looked harder, skirted the lake, and made for its foot. It was a foolish mistake, thus to confuse the two routes. The Little Gully was ascended that day, and until Haskett Smith's book came out three years later, describing the locality in some detail, I fondly imagined that I knew the best thing on Pavey Ark.

The gully is narrow at first. Its walls are red in colour, and a film of water generally covers them.

The holds are not particularly good, and the steepness of the gully renders extreme caution necessary. Both walls are used, and our advance is after the fashion of a man on a ladder. Then the gully widens, and the difficulties come in successive steps till a great overhanging boulder blocks the direct ascent. Here the right wall is sufficiently broken to offer a method of circumventing the pitch, but in wet weather the place is bad. Just above this I found a stick, conclusive evidence to the simple mind that the hard bit of the Great Gully was now being approached. It looked as though it had been there for years. The view backwards was most impressive, the tarn appearing almost beneath my feet. The second obstacle was now to be considered. The gully narrowed to a thin vertical corner plastered over with wet green moss. The take-off was earthy and disagreeably loose. The only holds were on the right wall near the corner, and were few and far between. I hesitated below for a long time, scarcely knowing how best to start operations. A big jammed stone came away in my hands as I made a first attempt, and crashed down the gully from side to side. At last I rammed the left knee tentatively into the wet corner, and edged up a few feet with the aid of sundry slight supports for the right foot. Ten feet higher an excellent hold was reached with the hand, and the chief trouble was over. Huge boulders were piled overhead confusedly, but they gave plenty of opportunities, and no longer had the smooth, almost

shiny surface that characterized the rocks further
down. The top of the gully was reached three
quarters of an hour after starting. It was half-past
five, and snow was beginning to fall; I thought it
desirable to hurry, and a steady trot westwards
round the head of Langdale Combe and the further
side of Black Crags brought me in three miles to the
path at the Angle Tarn and the foot of the up-grade
towards Esk Hause. Thence a steady two hours'
walk in the dark brought me safely to Wastdale, in
happy ignorance of the fact that I had only visited
the Little Gully. But to this day I think it as hard
as its neighbour.

The Great Gully.—Shortly after Easter, 1896,
I begged some friends to come over and climb the
Great Gully with me. It was my last day at Wastdale; I was due at Coniston the same evening, and
the Langdale Pikes offered a pleasanter walk to the
Old Man district than is given by the Eskdale and
Cockley Beck route. My friends stipulated that we
should call a halt at Kern Knotts on the way out
and attempt the 'crack.' This we managed with
expedition, and continued the journey betimes over
the Styhead and Esk Hause.

The three miles from Angle Tarn to Pavey Ark
are rather tedious, though the view of Bowfell and
of Pike of Stickle relieves the monotony. It is a
wild open moor that we have to cross, and its gentle
slope is very deceptive. For a long time the sky-
line in front of us, after rounding Langdale Combe

at the top of the Stake Pass, recedes as we advance, and it is not till the grassy ridge of Thunacar Knott is gained that we begin to see the upper crags of Pavey Ark. Nevertheless it is much better to approach the crags in this way from the Wastdale direction than to descend first towards Dungeon Ghyll. The great rocks strewn about the crest of the cliff are most singular in character. Their surface is as rough as that of the magnesian limestone in the Dolomites. If only the whole face of Pavey Ark were of this formation we should have a fine opportunity for practice with the scarpetti or rope-soled shoes used by the Tyrolese rock-climbers.

We descended towards the tarn by an easy slope between the cliff and the north-east ridge of Harrison Stickle. Then at the level of the base of the crags we crossed a water-course, and traversed over the scree to the foot of the Great Gully, passing the entrance to the other on our way. The remarks already made, and reference to the diagram on page 203, will perhaps give sufficient indication of the place at which we now found ourselves. In misty weather the locality can be identified by the branch gully to the left, that starts at once and loses itself 200 feet higher up.

The lower part of the climb very much resembles the corresponding portion in the other gully. The side walls are close together, the rock is steep, and hand-and-foot scrambling fairly continuous for about 150 feet. When the rocks are wet some special

care is necessary at a place thirty feet from the
starting-point. Then comes the first pitch, a remarkably fine piece of rock scenery. An enormous boulder
completely blocks the way, projecting at least fifteen
feet at its upper part. The left wall is practically
hopeless, but the other side shows a series of small
ledges that enable the climber to work up to the
flat corner between the boulder and the right wall.
Formerly this bit was grassy. Only a few small
tufts now remain, and the holds are therefore more
obvious. A pleasanter way lies through the cave
and out by a narrow tunnel in the roof to the same
flat corner, which is just discernible from below.
That way our party followed. The dripping water
from the roof was a trifle unpleasant sometimes, but
there was a great sense of security in adopting the
through route. The tunnel required careful going
until one's eyes got accustomed to the darkness.
Then the handholds could be distinguished and the
platform reached in safety.

The view outwards was most brilliant. Sunlight
on the distant range of Fairfield and Helvellyn, the
serpentine Windermere appearing here and there far
away to the south ; Langdale in all its loveliness,
with the watch-tower of Harrison Stickle at its
head ; and the gloomy Stickle Tarn 500 feet beneath
us. Our own situation was sufficiently striking for
the recollection of this pitch to remain impressed on
our memories. We stood (one at a time, by the
way) on the very edge of the overhanging eaves

of the huge cave beneath. The side walls of the gully seemed to cut us off from all communication with the world. We could only realize the solid platform and the enduring rock to which we hung; all the rest might have been a fantasy. Even the bold fisherman down by the shores of the tarn, slowly manipulating his rod as he cautiously waded knee-deep in the water, seemed to belong to another species. It was incredible that I should be crossing London within twenty-four hours; and the thought of it only stirred slightly in my mind, without actually shaping itself until this present time of writing.

The difficulty was not quite passed. To reach the top of the pitch we had to haul ourselves up a tight little corner between the boulder and the side wall. Formerly the headroom was so limited that it was necessary to keep out a little, and effect a rather sensational haul over the front of the boulder. Since the first ascent a piece of rock has fallen away, and the corner is easier. There is no actual danger for the leader, as his rope can be securely held in the interior of the cave. In fact, he may, if he chooses, obtain any desired assistance from the second man properly belayed on the platform. The corner is only ten feet high and the rocks are very good.

Almost immediately after the first pitch the gully undergoes a great change in appearance. It still remains narrow, but the bed has alternately vertical and horizontal stretches of wet and slippery rock. The

hardest piece is generally regarded as the second pitch.
It consists of a long slab thirty feet high, constituting
the true bed of the ghyll and the only available way
up.   It is set at a steep angle, and appears to be
singularly devoid of useful holds.   On the occasion
of the first ascent it was ' lubricated by a film of fine
mud,' and our own observations gave strength to
the conviction that such was its usual condition.
Loose gravel is being continually washed down the
incline, lodging in a most annoying manner on the
best holds. Small wonder that this ' brant and slape '
part gives pause to many climbers.   Yet it has been
climbed even when ice is about, thanks no doubt to
good nails and cool judgment.   We treated the pitch
with the utmost respect, carefully clearing away the
grit from each little ledge and working as close to
the corner as the holds would permit.   Fifteen feet
up we passed the worst spot, ugly to look at but
not bad enough to turn us back.   Then the slope
eased off and we could walk up grass and scree on to
Jack's Rake, a hundred feet above the pitch.   The
rake really terminates the gully.   To the left is a
small chimney forming a genuine little obstacle to an
advance along the rake.   That was certainly no
suitable finish to our climb.   A few yards to the
right showed what we wanted, a gully that should
lead out to the top of Pavey Ark. We found the rocks
there presented the rough surface that characterised
the boulders up above. There were several great slabs
blocking our way at first, but it was a real delight to

get over them. A short and narrow chimney followed, with such gripping powers that our clothes clung to the sides tenaciously. As Haskett Smith remarks, ' it would be quite difficult to make a slip on them.' Then we walked out to the top, three-quarters of an hour after entering the gully, and while leisurely coiling up my rope we discussed the question of tea. Should the others accept my invitation to Dungeon Ghyll and then return to Wastdale at dusk, or should they make straight for Wastdale at once ? To my sorrow they objected to the suggested extension of their walk and strode off to the west. My own course lay first to the foot of the crags, where my rücksack had been left, and thence to Dungeon Ghyll and Coniston.

The Rake End Chimney.—Besides the third chimney described by Gwynne as running half-way up on to the ledge, there is a short but excellent route up the crags starting near the foot of Jack's Rake. The following note was supplied by Mr. Claude Barton :—' The climb is in two pitches, the first being broken up into places where you can play up a second man. The *mauvais pas* is just at the top of this. A moss-grown wall and two jammed stones must be surmounted, and the leader may need some support. The second pitch is a fine chimney blocked by a large stone that is passed by the interior, and then used as a take-off for the final easy concluding portion. The climb is certainly harder than the Great Gully.'

CHAPTER XV

DOE CRAG, CONISTON

This happy hunting-ground for the rock-climber is within an hour's walk of Coniston. It forms part of the range of hills that includes Wetherlam and the Old Man, but unlike these great neighbours it has hitherto been left untouched by miners and quarrymen.

From the Old Man we may look westwards across the upper end of Goat's Water, and see the summit of Doe Crag almost at our level, some 900 feet above the lake. We are facing its grand precipices, and are in an excellent position to prospect the various gullies that cut deeply into the 500-feet wall of rock.

The first of these, as we glance from left to right, causes the greatest impression in the sky-line, but is of the least interest to mountaineers. It is an easy scree gully, possessing a rotten pinnacle that was first climbed by Mr. Slingsby in 1887. The second is generally known as the Great Gully. It is much longer, and includes a fair amount of genuine hard work in its ascent. At a distance it appears to have a Y shape, by reason of the two branches that diverge from a point about half-way up. The Great Gully was first climbed in July, 1888, by Messrs. Hastings, Haskett Smith, and E. Hopkinson, its first pitch being then taken by the 'shallow scoop' on the left of the great obstacle. Nearly a year later the brothers Hopkinson effected a direct ascent of the pitch by an ingenious utilization of the rope, to which we shall refer subsequently.

To the immediate north of the Great Gully we see a huge buttress that springs further down the scree towards Goat's Water than any other part of the crag. The lower 300 feet of this buttress exhibit a nearly vertical gully that may escape detection altogether unless viewed in a favourable light. In the view on the opposite page it is well marked by the deep black shadow of the rocks on its south side. Apparently it joins a sloping gully that leads up to the sky-line; but in reality it finishes abruptly on the face, at a small grass platform that stretches a hundred feet across the buttress. It is now known as the Central Chimney, and was first climbed in April, 1897, by Mr. Godfrey Ellis and myself. In the first edition of this book, the chimney was erroneously identified with one of Messrs. Hopkinson's ascents of April, 1895. The route cannot be recommended except to experts, by reason equally of the genuine difficulties in the chimney and of the exposed nature of the awkward situations in it.

The next gully to the right forms the northern boundary of the great central buttress. It is but

G. P. Abraham & Sons, Photos.   Keswick

DOE CRAG AND GOATSWATER

(Face page 220)

slightly marked at the lower end and possesses serious difficulties in the first half. We shall call it the Intermediate Gully. It was first climbed in April, 1·95, by Messrs. Campbell, and Edward, Albert, and J. H. Hopkinson, and described by the most experienced of their party as the severest climb he had done in the district. Mr. W. J. Williams and I went up it at Easter, 1898, when making a fairly complete survey of all these splendid, but practically unknown gullies.

The Easter Gully now needs localization. It comes next to the preceding and is easy to identify. It has a huge cave pitch near the bottom, then from a great hollow in the crags a vertical chimney springs up over a hundred feet in a right-angled corner; above this the gully divides into two branches, both of which give good climbing until we are nearly at the summit-ridge. Careful inquiry enables me to say that this was first climbed by Messrs. Haskett Smith and Robinson in 1886; they avoided a considerable amount of the trouble, inevitable in a passage of the lower half of the direct ascent, by working up the great buttress on the right, and by traversing back into the gully when the opportunity disclosed itself. The first passage of the gully by the extremely difficult second pitch, and thence directly onwards, was made on Easter Day, 1895, by Messrs. Otto Koecher and Charles Hopkinson, who, however, circumvented the comparatively simple cave pitch at the foot. They thought they were on entirely new ground; so did I when on Easter Day, 1898, Mr. W. J. Williams accompanied me over the first pitch, up a zig-zag course to left and right of the long chimney, and then along the direct finish to the summit.

The sixth and last great gully is known as the North Gully, to see which it is necessary to go well towards Goat's Hause. Three huge boulders block up the middle and form the only pitch. The gully was formerly supposed to be Messrs. Haskett Smith and Robinson's climb of 1886; actually it is the place where Haskett Smith was let down on a rope, and gave tribute to the grandeur of the region by remarking on its 'terrific aspect.' In 1895 a party went up what they called the North Gully, but they encountered no difficulty during their ascent, and it seems more likely therefore that they climbed a slighter ghyll between the real North Gully and the Easter Gully. They traversed into the latter above its difficult chimney. It is hard to say what exploration has been made here. Mr. Williams and I descended the gully in 1898, and halted there sufficiently to convince ourselves of the feasibility of its ascent. But whether the climb has ever been taken upwards throughout its whole length is an open question.

Climbers should visit Doe Crag more frequently. The rocks give magnificent sport, the scenery is more than ordinarily impressive even to the hardened cragsman, and there yet remains a great amount of exploratory work to be done. Only the gullies have hitherto been tackled. The buttresses are almost untouched.

The Great Gully.—The satisfactory part of this climb is that its greatest difficulty confronts us at the outset. Once the first pitch is accomplished we are perfectly certain that the combined skill of the party is sufficient to insure a successful ascent of the remainder. There is no gradual increase in the technical difficulty of the subsequent passages, to vex the soul of the conscientious climber with doubts as to the morality of advancing, when a critical position might be reached where descent is dangerous and further ascent beyond his powers. The first pitch is severe, and perhaps a little risky for the leader, but the remaining four are easy, and the method of tackling them obvious. This species of gully is suitable for those who tire quickly, or whose impressions of the work before them depend on the height they have attained. On the other hand, there are climbers who like to feel that there is always something serious looming ahead, who want the troubles to last them all through their climb, and rejoice in a *bonne bouche* at the most elevated situation. Such lingering sweetness they can find in the Central Chimney, but not here ; it is not surprising that many men are satisfied with one visit to the Great Gully, and never make for it a second time.

It takes us ten minutes to walk up from the lake to the entrance of the gully. Then a few yards of scree and broken rock lead into a cavern, below a chock-stone that offers much resistance to the direct passage up the pitch. A massive buttress encroaches on the left, and renders the gully almost narrow enough for both sides to be employed together; but close inspection shows that near the top of the pitch the walls are too far apart and the handholds too few. The climber does well to descend a few feet and prospect the buttress itself. This exhibits a safer route (see view on page 225). Close against the side of the vertical left wall the buttress shows a slight fissure, that starts from an easy grass platform and runs steeply up to a level some twelve feet higher than the top of the chock-stone. The difficulty lies in working up the corner, following the crack as much as possible, and taking sufficient care that the body does not swing away from the footholds. A stout individual is likely to feel handicapped at an awkward little ledge half-way up from the grass platform. The fissure can be followed straight up into the gully, but it is easier to contour round the buttress and on to the top of the true pitch. There is excellent belaying for an ascending party, the rope lying along the crack and gripping well at several points. It grips just too well for the safe belaying of the last man in a descent; he had better adopt the dangling method and work straight over the chock-stone. This latter direct route over the obstacle was tried once or twice before 1889, but without success. It was left to the brothers Hopkinson to show in that year that it

THE FIRST PITCH IN DOE CRAG GREAT GULLY

(Face page 225)

offered a perfectly safe variation, though probably most climbers will agree that it needs more muscle than is wanted for the crack route. They clambered into the cave and thrust a rope through the small aperture in the roof. When a sufficient quantity had been poked up in that way, it fell over the front of the cave and was available for climbing. But it is very severe work to swarm up a thin rope ; in this case there is slight assistance from the sides of the gully, and the transfer of hold from the rope to the rock comes when the arms are tired.

After this difficulty is passed, some yards of scree lead to the second pitch. The gully is narrow, and the block is produced by two boulders one above the other. There is no trouble in working through the cave and on to the lower block, whence an easy pull over the upper stone takes us again to a long line of scree of the impulsive variety. This part of the gully is pleasant only when snow is about, when the ankle-twisting propensities of the scree are not permitted full play.

We are near the point where the gully opens out considerably, sending a branch up on the right. But before that we have to mount two small pitches, the first taken straight up, the second by either right or left wall.

The branch exit on the right has no serious difficulties, but it abounds in loose holds that the climber may find hard to avoid. It leads on to the great middle buttress of Doe Crag, above all its dangerous parts, and within easy access of the summit. The direct ascent of the gully is interesting only at the last step, where a narrow chimney must be passed. Its right boundary is a long smooth slab, unusually deficient in holds. There are three or four wedged stones and the pitch is often wet, but by keeping close into the chimney and working up the right wall the trouble may be overcome. It is always possible, of course, to descend a little and climb out of the gully on the right.

Doe Crag Central Chimney.—This climb is known to very few people. Many are aware in a vague manner that there is splendid climbing on the great buttress of Doe Crag, but only one or two cragsmen have learnt where to go for it. So far as my own experience is concerned it was almost a matter of accident that brought me soon after Easter, 1897, to the foot of the Central Chimney. The previous day had been spent with Messrs. George and Ashley Abraham on Lliwedd, in the Snowdon district, and a tiresome cross-country night journey to Coniston had not tended to put the keenest edge on my hunger for adventure. My companion, Mr. Godfrey Ellis, and I were really intent on ascending by the 'intermediate gully of terrific aspect,' down which Mr. Haskett Smith had climbed in 1888. The Central Chimney certainly looked terrific, more so than anything else we could find about there. It was also reasonably intermediate, and we came to the conclusion that our gully was found. Later investigation showed that we had made a mistake, for Haskett Smith's chimney is at the north end of the crags.

The Central Chimney attracted the attention of Mr. Slingsby in 1887, but apparently ours was the first ascent. Messrs. Broadrick have been up it since, and I have been advised by one of their party that the top of the chief difficulty is dangerously loose.

We had heavy rücksacks to carry over to Wastdale that day, and decided to leave them at the foot of the climb, rather than suffer the inconvenience of dragging them up with us. We had eighty feet of rope, and needed it all near the top.

Our work started easily. Three obvious courses led in about thirty feet to a broad, grassy platform, from which the chimney made its proper beginning. Each of the three ways involved scrambling; they started a few feet to the left of the lowest part of the crags, and formed between them a very fair presentment of a gully entrance. But a glance upwards showed that, for some distance at least, we should have very little of the nature of a gully to guide us. From the platform sprang up the vertical wall that gives the central buttress its appearance of inaccessibility, almost unrelieved for several hundred feet. Our chimney commenced as a thin crack in the wall from the platform, only large enough for a hand to be thrust in, and so sharp-edged that one's fingers were badly cut in climbing the first five yards.

Then the crack seemed to widen gradually until from below it appeared sufficiently broad for wedging. Appearances would have been comforting but for the curious absence of retaining wall on the right-hand side of the crack. The left was excellent; on that side the rock stood out from the corner and formed the finest part of the great buttress. But the right wall was cut clean away, leaving smooth slabs that were sure to give trouble when we should find the chimney too shallow for further progress.

I started up the thin crack, and found the strain very severe on the arms. When it became wide enough to support a knee it was possible to halt and prospect a little. The next ten feet up the crack were obviously most difficult, and a glance at the north side showed that it would have been easier to work up the right wall for twenty feet from the platform before traversing into the crack again. Ellis suggested that he should come up to my level by means of a slight fissure in the right wall, and steadied by the rope that I had flung over a small projection some six feet above his head, he managed to reach a shaky, sloping ledge of grass, and then to manœuvre the rope for my own passage to the same resting-place. We next worked upwards into the chimney, and kept close in it for twenty feet or so. There were good holds on the right until some small boulders and *débris* formed a little platform, over the edge of which we were able to pull ourselves.

The scenery about here was particularly impressive. Our resting-place was scarcely big enough for both, and a glance vertically downwards showed us the spot where we had commenced operations three quarters of an hour previously. The black depths of Goat's Water formed a striking foreground to the view of Coniston Old Man across the valley, and it almost seemed as though the tarn could be reached by a stone falling from our tiny ledge. Up above us the crags loomed fearfully. They overhung considerably in places, and we saw that our only course was to follow boldly the line of our chimney till it abruptly terminated in the face. Fortunately the weather was good, the rocks dry and warm. To have attempted the chimney with much ice or water about would have been foolhardiness worthy of our wildest days.

From the ledge we found the climbing splendid, keeping up the slight rib of rock on the right that formed the nearly vertical boundary of the chimney. The holds were just sufficiently large to give ample support, especially when the back could rest on the opposite side of the crack. 'Backing up' is usually a very constricted performance, with but limited views of the scenery around. Here on Doe Crag it seems as though most of the mountain is cut away excepting those parts of obvious utility to the climber. We crawled round the rib when the crack became too thin, and worked up several feet of slabby rock until the appearances seemed to indicate that an actual gully was now about to manifest itself and commence a fresh run up the wall. We therefore traversed again to the left into a large recess, and after a little scrambling upwards found ourselves brought to a stop by a dead wall. The bed of our recess was loose and steeply sloping. Its sides were slightly iced, and considerable care was needed in settling securely down to consider the situation.

The wall was about twenty feet high and too smooth to climb. On each side of us were huge overhanging buttresses that projected considerably beyond the latter portion of our route. It was not manifest which of these would offer the best way of surmounting the wall, and it might be that neither was suitable. We could see that a traverse out of the difficulty might be made in the northern direction, but it was very exposed and it led too far away from our chimney.

Ellis braced himself firmly at the highest corner of the recess, and manipulated the rope with special care. I started working up between the two buttresses in a manner that recalled to us both the well-known picture of the Funffingerspitze chimney in Sanger-Davies' book. When some twelve feet above him, it seemed safe to quit the left-hand side altogether, and a stride effected the change of style. But the return was now almost impossible, and in the anxious five minutes that followed I had time to repent the sudden resolve. The top of the wall was within reach, but it was fringed with loose grass tufts that scarcely seemed secure enough to offer purchase in the upward heave that I wanted to give myself. However, the time spent in hesitation was sheer waste, for at the end the pull-up was perfectly safe and easy, and a little wriggling over rock and steep grass brought me to a long terrace, that naturally suggested a halt for the second man's advance. In good time his head appeared above the grass tufts that formed the limit of my foreground, and a few seconds later he was sitting at my side and speculating as to the length of the difficult piece. The whole climb so far had been veritably one single pitch ; we had had no interval of comparative ease, and were now eager to find some temporary freedom.

That we found in perambulating our terrace. It was about a yard wide and fifty feet long, and gave evidence that our gully as such had practically terminated. We found it rather awkward clambering up the wall some thirty feet to another similar terrace. This stretched horizontally from the large ravine that now disclosed itself on our right, and across the face of the mountain towards the Great Gully. The former, we could see, involved some pretty climbing a hundred feet below us. At our level it was merely a scree-walk finishing at the highest part of Doe Crag.

Our route lay up the rocks above the terrace. Two narrow clefts offered choice. We took the one to the right, about fifteen feet long and sufficiently tough to make us remember the place. Then

followed easy hand-and-foot work till we could distinguish the branch exit of the Great Gully. Down
this we carefully picked our way, and then returned
to gather up our belongings and make tracks for
distant Wastdale.   The round had taken three
hours.

The Intermediate Gully.—We had a glorious

afternoon for this climb.   The previous night had
brought us from town to Coniston, and we meant to
give ourselves an easy day.   But fearing that the
weather might change we were tempted to seize the
opportunity and start earnest business at once.
Identifying the gully as the first to the right of the
longest buttress of the crags, we entered it and began
scrambling immediately.   After five minutes of
'staircase' work, using both sides of the gully, we
came to a point where the left wall overhung a little
and the gully closed in.   A flank movement was
then effected on the right, over steep rocks and unreliable grass ledges, returning by a narrow traverse
into the gully at a point forty feet higher.   The
second man came straight up, finding two pitches
confronting him, both of which he thought we could
have taken directly if time had allowed us to risk an
attempt.   We kept in the ghyll for the next two
pitches, both of them fairly simple.   A fine flat stone
at the top of the second offered a good standpoint
for the inspection of the overhanging wall that now
faced us.   The gully had shrunk again into the
merest crack in the wall.   My friend called it the

extreme pitch of refinement.   On our left a smooth
right-angled corner that probably thought itself a
branch gully led up to the ridge separating us from
the Central Chimney.   Again it seemed desirable to
take to the right by a course that was at any rate
feasible, although it took us away from our direct
line of ascent.   After fifteen feet of traverse the
buttress looked accessible, but recollecting the poor
holds that we had encountered in a corresponding
situation lower down, we went further away still,
descending slightly to a level platform where the
leader could be belayed during his direct ascent of
the wall.   Fortunately the rocks were quite dry, as
otherwise the work that followed would have been
risky.   At first the handholds were unsafe, but in
ten feet our industrious cleaning away of the grass
and earth disclosed an excellent cleft in the wall, safe
and sound.   Thence the way was pleasanter, swinging upwards towards the left again by immovable
rockholds.   We had several yards of a narrow ledge
tilted upwards at 30° before entering our gully again,
and arrived in it just below a little pitch of the type
that tries the elbow.

Great caution was now needed.   Not that the
climbing was difficult or dangerous, but the gully
had dwindled into little more than a slight indentation in a vertical wall, and each man had to move
with the utmost deliberation.   Holds were numerous,
generally better on the left wall, but they were all
rather wet.   Soon we were engaged in a violent

struggle with a small angular jammed block that barred our way. It seemed loose at first, but we proved its stability that afternoon by many minutes' hauling and wrenching from below and above. The chief difficulty was to get the shoulders firmly fixed between the sides of the cleft above the jammed stone; with only the block to hold and no rest for the feet this manœuvre was very awkward to perform. Above this a few steps led to a narrow cave, which we climbed by its right edge and found to be a trying piece of arm work. Here the gully expanded into a large scree-bedded ravine with only two moderately easy obstacles between us and the top of the crag. To our left we could see the ledge that marks the end of the Central Chimney. Our own gully, looking backwards, seemed to be a vertical plunge straight down to the bottom, and as usual we caught ourselves wondering whether anything else could be called difficult after this.

We reached the summit in two hours from the start, and then skirting the lower edge of the crags from Goat's Hause, we made note of each gully as we passed its foot. An easy scree shoot, followed by a buttress set back at a gentle angle, but with splendid practice on it; the North Gully with its awe-inspiring middle pitch like the great obstacle in Moss Ghyll; a branch gully leading into the North Gully; a second branch, looking rather interesting but lacking definition higher up; the Easter Gully with its double centre portion; the Intermediate Gully; the Central Chimney; and the Great Gully.

PLATE VII.

ii.

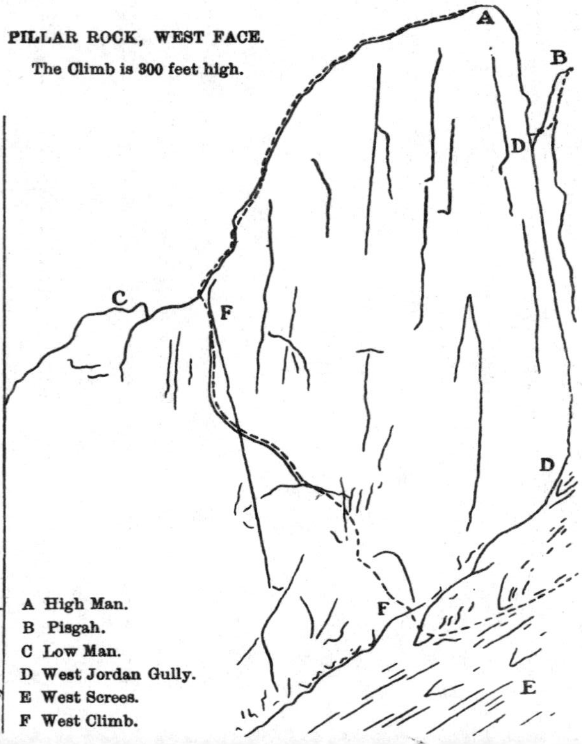

PILLAR ROCK, WEST FACE.

The Climb is 300 feet high.

A High Man.
B Pisgah.
C Low Man.
D West Jordan Gully.
E West Screes.
F West Climb.

i.

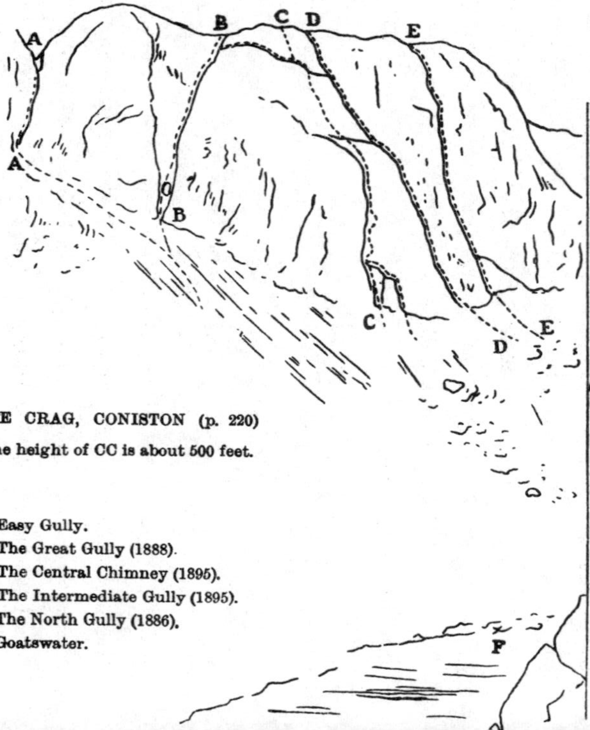

DOE CRAG, CONISTON (p. 220)

The height of CC is about 500 feet.

A Easy Gully.
B The Great Gully (1888).
C The Central Chimney (1895).
D The Intermediate Gully (1895).
E The North Gully (1886).
F Goatswater.

The Easter Gully.—The same party came two days later to examine this climb. The weather was very unsettled, and we were forced to the conclusion that the main central chimney was too wet to be approachable. The scrambling was easy up to the cave; then we worked up the vertical left wall by diminutive ledges till the level of the cave stone was ours, whereupon an awkward bit of traverse brought us safely out of the difficulty. We were in the great hollow, and were astonished to find that in addition to the main chimneys on the right and left centre, there were splendid branch gullies up to the ridges on either side.

I started up the left central chimney. It was dry, but its holds were fragile. In forty feet it divided into two parallel branches; that on the left was overhanging, and held a bunch of long splinters of rock forming a dangerous *chevaux-de-frise*, ready to fall at the slightest notice. So we left it alone, and looked to the right branch. For twenty feet it went very well, and there, where one man might safely wedge himself, it became practically impossible to mount any higher. My companion, therefore, came up while I worked out on the open face to the right. Without much trouble a small platform one foot square was reached, from which we proposed to mount the buttress that separated us from the right central chimney. I hesitated a long while before venturing on it; the place was assuredly difficult, we were not certain whether the upper portion would be feasible,

and the strong wind, swirling mist, and intermittent
rain sapped our courage and strength the more we
deliberated.

The stiff work began with a scramble up into a
grassy corner, fifteen feet above my platform. It
was too small to enter, but from it sprang a narrow
cleft to the right, very much like the well-known
'stomach traverse' on the Pillar Rock, but considerably harder to pass, and without an easy walk
out at the further end. At its highest point the
best course seemed to be up a vertical crack in the
wall, and a stiff scramble here of ten feet brought
me out on the head of the buttress. Here there was
a chance of walking over to the right central chimney
and finishing by the thirty feet or so that remained
of its special difficulty. But that portion was naturally
as wet as the lower part that we had purposely
avoided, and we chose to cross the chimney and
climb up its right wall.

CHAPTER XVI

COMBE GHYLL

MANY a pedestrian walking down Borrowdale from the Styhead pass, looking backward at the fearful descent of some 1,100 feet of rough fellside, reaches a point in the valley where he experiences difficulty in recalling his track. For the valley between Gable and Seathwaite Fell is hidden, and his choice hovers between the combe below Sprinkling Tarn, walled in by Seathwaite Fell and Glaramara, and the upland valley that nestles between Thornythwaite and Rosthwaite Fells. His perplexity is increased when he notices that neither hollow satisfies the condition of background. The one is barred by the crags of Great End, the other by the steep wall of Raven Crag, a high dependence of Glaramara; whereas the Styhead pass as seen from Grange ought to show distant Scawfell as a background, and be easily recognised. One of these two hollows the climber will do well to identify.

Combe Ghyll is the name of the course that drains the north side of Glaramara, the stream making its way down the little valley that has already been described as lying between Thornythwaite and Rosthwaite Fells. At about the 1,000-feet level in the valley the land is flat and marshy ;

with little provocation the stream could produce a respectable lake, and the tourist in wet weather feels that such absence of deception would be to his advantage.   Above this level the mountain rises abruptly, and the ghyll has to acknowledge two sources.   That which sends its supply straight down the centre of Raven Crag was the first to be regarded as Combe Ghyll.   But the other is longer and more obvious.   Looking up from the marsh the watercourse is very distinct away to the left, though the climb is equally in evidence on the right.   When a short time since three curious cragsmen (including the curious writer) penetrated to the recesses of this almost unknown country to find the climb that Messrs. Robinson and Wilson had discovered and christened as long ago as September, 1893, we were compelled by that name to tackle the east branch, but vowed at the same time to go later to the west. Our conscientiousness was praiseworthy, though mistaken, but as events developed themselves our mistake had happy consequences.   We managed both ghylls, and were probably instrumental in preventing a nasty accident to a couple of would-be mountaineers whom we discovered in difficulties.

It was on a hot day in April.   We had been disporting ourselves for photographic purposes in the Kern Knotts crack, and had sauntered down to Seatoller for some soda and milk to give grace to our jam sandwiches.   Then we walked down the Rosthwaite Road as far as the bridge over the Derwent, and went across the opposite shoulder into the combe. It was very close down in Borrowdale, and we were glad to get out of the well of warm air and follow the water for a mile or so to the marshy upland. Here the walking was soft and pleasant. Water in our boots was no hardship, and we even hoped that there would be many waterfalls in our gully. Then came the dilemma and our decision to keep to the main stream. But the aspect of the Raven Crag gully on our right, as we skirted the boggy ground below us, was magnificent. Pitch rose above pitch apparently without any easy stretches, and the whole gully seemed to form just one vertical chimney in the rocks, five hundred feet high. Moss Ghyll itself is not grander than the Raven Crag gully as it appeared that afternoon to our longing gaze, and even now that the details of the latter climb are impressed vividly in my mind I can assure myself that it was one of the finest I have ever undertaken in Cumberland.

We followed our watercourse right up to its beginning close to a little pass over towards Langstrath. In general appearance it somewhat resembled Piers Ghyll, with its slight gradient and short pitches, its rotten walls and unavoidable water. But in respect to the last consideration we were almost exempted from a wetting, for the ghyll was nearly dry, and only in the direct ascent of one pitch did we run any risk of a drenching. No doubt the normal state of the gully is very much worse than we found it.

With hazy impression of a hundred-feet pitch we came provided with two eighty-feet lengths of rope, but

managed our climb with one only. The first pitch was
about fifteen feet high ; the left wall was feasible, the
direct climb involved the passage through a dripping
cave and out by a hole in the roof, and the right
side of the gully was of steep grass and insecure rock.
We took to the latter, and with care managed the
ascent without dislodging much that might help
later climbers. Above this we had a view of a
waterfall about fifty or sixty yards further up, and
inasmuch as the rocks showed signs of nailed boots
we were for some time prevailed upon to believe that
we had really found our quest.

The bed of the stream was rough but easy for a
while. Two small pitches about six feet high scarcely
gave us pause before we reached the foot of
the waterfall that we had seen from the first
pitch. It was about twelve yards high ; the walls
were four or five feet apart, and glistening with
the wet. They did not appear to offer very excellent holds, but I found it possible to face the fall
and utilize as footholds sundry diminutive ledges on
either side. It was a case of spanning the gully and
walking up. About twenty feet from the bottom the
holds on the left wall were somewhat greasy, but a
yard higher the ledges on the right had so much
improved that it was a safe venture to pull over
to that side and effect a traverse to the top of the
double obstacle over which the water was falling.
While the others were rapidly following, we were
surprised to hear voices from above. I advanced a

little, and discovered two young men perched precariously on the face of the steep wall to the right. Almost at the same moment a large stone fell from their feet towards us, and, in an ecstasy of fear lest they should bombard our last man, who was yet in difficulties bestriding the gully below, we shouted to them to stay still a bit and wait for us to advance to a place of safety. Then with all speed we clambered up to them, and let them down on the rope into the gully again. They were distinctly in peril ; that side of the ghyll was as treacherous, with its loose splinters of rock and steep unreliable grass, as it could manage to be without falling by its own weight. The top was slightly overhanging, and could bear no extra pulling. The men were inexperienced ; one of them had no nails in his boots ; they had walking-sticks tied tightly to their wrists with string, and when we reached them they were tired out with the physical and mental strain. We reflected on our wonderful good fortune in choosing this gully, and thought with some bitterness that this was the way that the noblest of sports acquired its notoriety for great danger. It transpired that they had scrambled down into the gully at the side of the waterfall that we had just climbed, and saw no means of getting out of the hole excepting by this loose wall.

We were now at the foot of a small pitch about twenty-five feet high. It was divided by a vertical buttress, and the water was flowing down to the left. The right-hand side seemed rather insecure, so I

climbed some thirty feet up the wall of the gully
again, and the second man clambered up the right-
hand recess, confident in the support of the rope
if his foothold gave way. He then traversed easily
to the top of the pitch, and drew in my rope as I
descended to his level and followed him. We asked
the last man how were the passengers to be conveyed
up the pitch. He replied, with perhaps just a touch
of malice, that the direct passage through the water
was the shortest, quickest, and cheapest route to the
top, and we at the summit were of the same mind.
Then our tourists were tied separately to the rope, and
hauled up through the fall. It was very uncomfortable for them, but we got as wet ourselves later on.
We hoped that their bedraggled condition would
prompt them to a speedy descent and a relinquish-
ment, for that day at least, of the joys of crag-climbing.
That pitch was the last in the gully of any magnitude,
and our friends were able to walk out easily on to the
open fell and so down to Borrowdale. We ourselves
gave one last look around for the hundred-feet fall
that was to finish Combe Ghyll, and then, finding it
not, we bore rapidly westwards across the mountain
in search of the genuine article.

As we skirted the foot of the crags we passed
two small gullies that rose steeply above us, and that
for a moment made us stop to consider their qualifications. In twenty minutes from the top of Combe
Ghyll we came to the first deep and well marked
watercourse. It was our Raven Crag Gully, and when

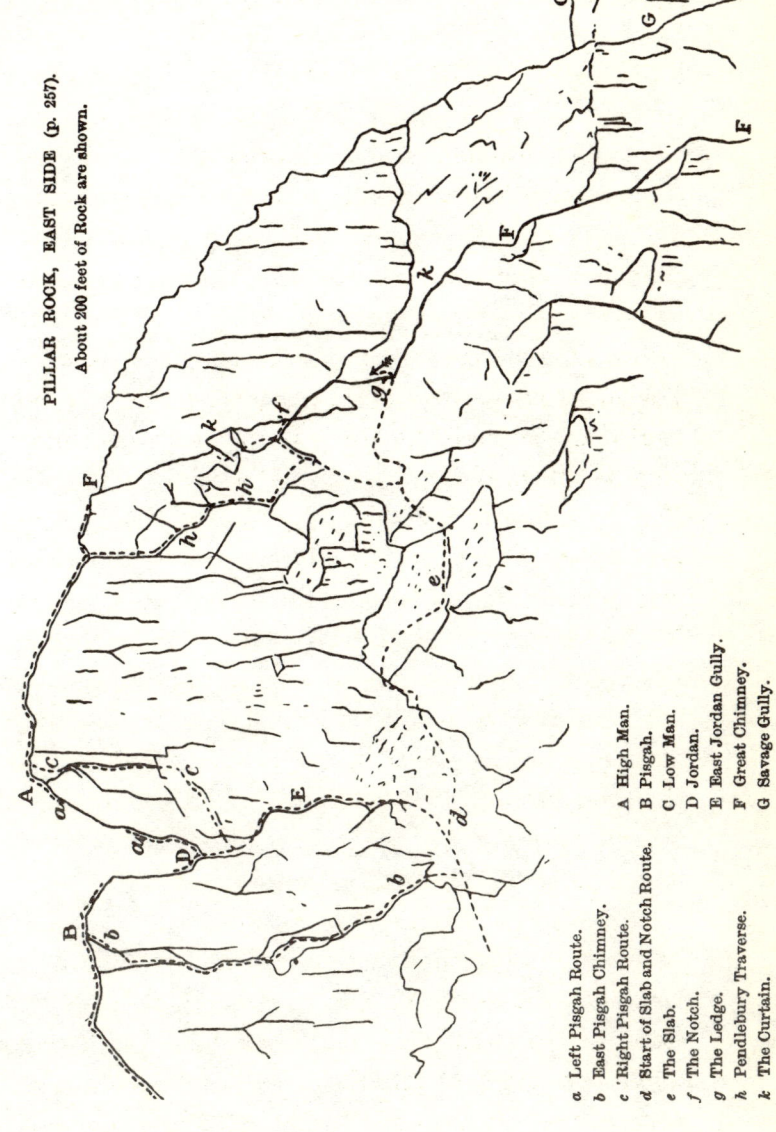

PLATE VIII.

PILLAR ROCK, EAST SIDE (p. 257).

About 200 feet of Rock are shown.

a Left Pisgah Route.	A High Man.
b East Pisgah Chimney.	B Pisgah.
c Right Pisgah Route.	C Low Man.
d Start of Slab and Notch Route.	D Jordan.
e The Slab.	E East Jordan Gully.
f The Notch.	F Great Chimney.
g The Ledge.	G Savage Gully.
h Pendlebury Traverse.	
k The Curtain.	

we peered up into its dark recesses we felt that good
sport was at last before us. We finished the rem-
nants of our lunch and drank a little water. It was
not a tempting beverage, for the rocks just above
were covered with objectionable vegetation, and the
supply was so much below the average that the pools
seemed almost stagnant. Also, I was haunted with
the recollection of a dead sheep that we had passed
in the other gully, lying on a ledge close to the
stream. Mountain water is not always free from
microbes, especially in those craggy regions where
sheep come to grief.

We started on the climb close by a little pool of
water at the foot of a short and greasy pitch. It could
have been taken direct, but we worked round the
buttress on the left and entered the gully a few feet
higher. Then, penetrating well into the recess, we
were at once confronted by the first big pitch. A
steep buttress divided the gully into two parts, the
left-hand recess being cut deeply into the mountain
and forming a long and narrow waterfall. This was
the true bed of the gully. To the right of the buttress
the recess was comparatively shallow, but its easier
inclination somewhat compensated for its exposed
position, and we found that the footholds were just
sufficient to render a rapid advance possible. About
forty feet up I craved the second man's helping hand,
but while he was advancing to offer assistance an
easy way of swarming up the buttress commended
itself; I found a resting-place at the level of the

top of the pitch, eighty or ninety feet above the foot
of the fall, where the second man could join me before
I ventured on the traverse round to the bed of the
gully.   The traverse reminded us of the steps over
the buttress from the Tennis Court ledge in Moss
Ghyll, and was no doubt a place to respect in wet or
icy weather.   Our last man came up more directly,
keeping on the inner side of the buttress for the first
half of the climb and then working straight up the
pitch.   Excepting for an awkward bit of some three
feet at the middle of the ascent, his route had
advantages over ours.   The rocks throughout were
splendid, and their warmth and dryness made the
scrambling easy.

A yard or two further, over great boulders
bestrewn in the bed of the gully, and we were
brought up at the foot of the second great obstacle.
Here the two side walls approached to within a
distance of four feet of each other, and straight down
the centre from a height of seventy feet dripped the
weak promise of a second waterfall.   Close to the
water it was impossible to ascend, but some ten feet
away from it suitable ledges on either side discovered
themselves.   These enabled me to use both walls
in a directly vertical ascent for so long as they
were within four feet of each other.   Then I pulled
over to a crack on the right and performed a safety
wriggle to more open ground above, whence it
was easy to clamber over the big boulders at the
top of the pitch.   The second man was asked to

prospect the route on the other side of the left wall,
and came up with the report that the traverse out
of the main gully was easy and that the rest of the
ascent, about eighty feet of solid rock, was just comfortable hand-and-foot work all through.   While the
third was adopting the same tactics which we afterwards remembered had been employed by a previous
party from Keswick, I went on to inspect the next
obstacle.   It certainly was the worst-looking pitch
in the whole ascent.   A large cave was formed by
two massive boulders jammed between the narrow
walls seventy feet above our heads.   The first-floor
of the cave was fifty feet up, and from its roof dripped
the inevitable water-supply to damp our daring
ardour.   The walls of the gully were close together
and covered with wet moss.   Holds were very scarce,
and for a moment we considered the advisability of
working out on the right as others had done
before us, and traversing into the gully above the
cave.   But a tentative backing-up in the main
chimney gave some hope of success in the direct
attack ; and abandoning all idea of making a final
exit with dry garments, I cautiously worked up the
inner face of a leaf of rock on the right wall, the
others steadying my feet on sundry infinitesimal
ledges so long as I was within reach, and then
supporting me with words of encouragement and
approval.   When within six feet of the floor of the
cave it became necessary to wedge well into the
chimney, with back against the left and scanty hold

opposite. Then a desperate wriggle gave me a lift
of about eighteen inches and the handholds improved
sufficiently for haulage. Leaving the left wall, I
could just thrust my knee in a corner under the fall,
and lever up to the opposite side. Next a few easy
ledges brought me into the cave, and I paused to
wring the moisture from my coat and cap before
inviting the others to follow on. By regarding their
manœuvres and subsequent criticism it impressed me
as likely that I might have saved myself some exertion, and perhaps have better avoided the water, by
keeping up the edge of the leaf of rock instead
of attacking its inner face. But that course would
expose the leader to a greater risk of slipping at a
failing hold, and would demand more ingenious
tactics.

Our cave was large and airy; the water passed
into it at the back, so that we could easily stay at
the entrance and avoid the fall. High up above our
heads were a couple of apertures in the roof, probably
wide enough for our passage, but difficult to reach.
The right wall of the gully was well broken up, and
without ado we set ourselves at it and worked round
the edge of the nearer overhanging block as a step
to the other. Some thirty feet of my rope ran out
before the second man advanced from the bed of the
cave : not that the climbing refused to admit an
earlier start, but that he was busy wringing out his
clothes. I awaited his advance impatiently, for a
bend in the gully prevented my seeing the next pitch

above us—the last in the climb. But when he was firmly braced against the top boulder, hauling in the rope of the last man, I advanced to the end of my tether to steal an early glance at the pitch that report had spoken of so respectfully. Robinson's account in the Wastdale book was succinct enough : 'A return on to the floor of the ghyll was made near the top of the third pitch, when a little scrambling led to a very fine waterfall more than 100 feet high. Here climb in the water as little as you can ; then diverge slightly on to the right hand of the ghyll just where the water spouts over a small recess ; next traverse across a rather difficult slab into the cave under the final boulder, which is climbed on the left hand and is the last difficulty.' The only part of his prescription that I had carried in my mind was the 'climb in the water as little as you can,' and we had been applying it all day with varying success. The trouble always is to make any headway at all against a descending mass of cold water, and we had come to regard the advice as indicative solely of the fact that an available route was only to be found in dry weather. To climb in the water as little as possible meant to choose a dry season and to mount by the usual line of flow. Another account that may prove interesting was given me by Messrs. G. and A. Abraham : 'Some enjoyable scrambling in the bed of the ghyll brought us quickly to the last obstacle and certainly the finest part of the whole climb. The climber is immediately reminded here of the great

amphitheatre in the Screes Gully, for, although on a
much smaller scale, we have the same gigantic
buttresses and receding slabs, with three suggested
exits. The most obvious way out here is up the
waterfall as usual. This we attempted until the
amount of water on the steep, slippery rocks forced
us out on to the difficult right-hand wall, about
seventy feet above the beginning of the pitch. Here
we climbed straight upwards, and, traversing round
a very awkward corner, landed right on the top of
the pitch, the leader requiring considerable help for
the last twenty feet.' Our own experiences were a
little different, a consequence of our fixed intention
to force a route directly upwards without any
traversing away on to the right wall of the gully.
Also, we were relieved of the necessity of avoiding
water, because it fell too diffusely to be avoided, and
so small an area was left to any of us that could be
affected seriously by further saturation. The first
part of the pitch was perfectly simple. We could
employ holds on either side and clamber up to a
platform made by an un-jammed stone with rounded
corners that had been caught in the cleft. It was safe
enough for our purposes, and two men could lodge
themselves conveniently above it. Straight up overhead was a formidable chimney that looked feasible
in its upper portion but impossible to reach directly
from below. A long block of rock twenty feet high,
possibly part of the living mountain, prevented a
passage up the pitch to the immediate right of the

chimney; but between the smooth slabs of wet rock
that formed the right wall of the gully and this long
boulder a narrow crack wound its way up to
Robinson's cave, and it occurred to all of us
simultaneously that the crack might be negotiated
and the awkward slab-traverse thereby avoided. But
the crack was as nothing to begin with, and from our
rickety platform we could obtain but scanty notion
of its safety higher up. I suggested advancing a
little to prospect, craving a shoulder to start from, and
a steadying hand for my completer confidence on the
doubtful little ledges that we were calling footholds. The first ten feet went very well, but although
I found the crack useful for the left knee, it was
unable to accept the responsibility of my complete
stability. I sang out for another steadying hand,
and my most admirable second clambered on to the
shoulders of the last man without a moment's
hesitation. They plastered themselves flat against
the slab, and I felt my right foot cease its uncanny
trembling as the outstretched hand held it firmly in
the niche it longed to use. This was downright
luxury, and in my sense of security there stole a
moment's shame at the thought of so much dependence on the others. But there! in climbing as in
football the combination is everything in the highest
developments of the game, and though success may
now and again be due to the unaided efforts of one
man, the full satisfaction that should follow victory
will only be felt by the whole party when all have

contributed something to the manœuvring. Be it remembered that in crag-climbing two heads are better than one, even if the second head is only used as a foothold. But there we were, three links in a chain that reached from the platform to the widest part of the crack that was to lead us to the cave. The position was not to be dwelt upon, and I hastened to relieve the others of their common burden. In the crack and at arm's length above me was a well-secured angular stone round which the rope could be passed. Using it as a hold I was able to quit the precarious foothold on the right and thrust the left knee well into the crack. The position was one that could admit of no slip, the leg being sufficient to hold the body well in ; and before quitting that favoured spot I untied the rope and slipped the free end through the hole at the back of the jammed stone before tying on again. The others had descended by this time to the platform and were taking in all the slack. Whatever the difficulty of the few remaining moves to the cave, I was insured against a big fall and could trust to the belaying of the little angular block that had so neatly adjusted itself to our needs. As a matter of fact the precaution was scarcely necessary, though eminently proper under the circumstances. The ledges above me were good and firm, and with the rope gently paid out from below I reached the cave without more trouble.

The floor was sloping; but a comfortable and reposeful attitude could be indulged in, well at the

back, far from the dripping eaves of the cave. But
I had committed an error of judgment with the rope,
threading the hole from above the jammed stone
instead of from below, before tying the bowline
round my waist. At the time the importance of that
consideration had not occurred to me, but now in my
ease, hauling up the slack between myself and the
second, I felt a sudden jerk. The rope was wrapped
completely round the jammed stone, whose angular-
ity, that had before commended itself to the hands,
now introduced so much friction that the rope would
no longer slip freely round it. We were perplexed
for a while, till our enterprising middleman, who had
many times before offered a key to our difficulties,
proposed climbing up as a leader, with the second
rope attached to his waist, and the fixed rope above
him used for steadying purposes whenever necessary.
We knew that the jammed stone that fixed the upper
rope could not be dislodged easily, and indeed I
was able to hold on to my end and oppose any dangerous leverage. He climbed up with every confidence,
and reached the crack safely. Then, repeating my
movement with the left leg, he held on while disen-
tangling my rope, tying himself to its lower end as
soon as the complications were unravelled. A few
moments more gave me a companion in the cave, and
built, as it was, for two persons only, he mildly
suggested my withdrawal for the benefit of the
third man. Thence our method of advance was
practically identical with Robinson's. We had a

little walk of six feet over towards the left wall of
the gully, by ledges that lay on the very verge of a
sheer drop of eighty feet to the foot of the pitch.
Then the ascent was continued by a narrow crack
that commenced in a somewhat sensational manner,
not so much by reason of its difficulty as by the
feeling of nothingness to fall back upon in case of a
slip.   The second was at my heels, and he was firmly
braced up by the sole remaining tenant of the cave.
Lifting the left leg as high up the crack as possible,
and accepting a push from behind, I reached over a
slab on the right and dragged up on to it.   That was
to be the last big effort ; the final pitch was all below,
and the gully eased away above me to its open finish.
I shouted the tidings to the others.   With all eager-
ness they followed, the last man claiming with pride
the discovery of a grand foothold that he had un-
earthed or unmossed at the lower edge of the slab.

Well ! we had had a rare little fight ; the gully
had taken us an hour and twenty minutes of continuous work, and we voted it a piece of solid good
business.

There remained the long walk back to Wastdale
and to dinner.   I proposed getting there in an hour
and a half, and started on the journey with a pipe in
my mouth.   We had about three miles of rough, high-
level skirting along the 2,000-feet contour to Sprinkling Tarn, two miles of descent to the Burnthwaite
level, and a mile of valley walking at the finish.
The consequence was that very little smoking was

enjoyed. We were a quarter of an hour behind time at Burnthwaite, a laudable spurt in the valley being abruptly terminated by the discovery of another climbing-party on the track. We had found that if two parties were late, dinner would await their arrival ; hence our motive for haste was removed and we composed our gait and our thoughts for a more sedate entry into the hotel yard.

NOTE: In the first edition of this book, I followed Mr. Haskett Smith's nomenclature and located the climb in Eagle Crag. It seems that this shoulder of Glaramara goes by the name of Raven Crag, and I have changed the name of the gully accordingly. There are many Raven Crags and many Eagle Crags in the district, but climbers need only be warned against confusing the Raven Crag Gully on Glaramara with the Raven Crag Chimney on Great Gable.

254

CHAPTER XVII

THE PILLAR ROCK

MOSEDALE is closed in by Yewbarrow, Red Pike, Pillar, Looking Stead, and Kirkfell. These form a noble amphitheatre of dark mountains, a cordon through which it is not easy to break. Between the last two hills we can effect the passage of the Black Sail over into Ennerdale, which passes down behind the Pillar to the north-west. A more direct route to Ennerdale is by Wind Yatt (or Windy Gap), a pass 2,400 feet high, between the Pillar and the Red Pike. On the northern or Ennerdale side of the Pillar mountain is the famous Rock, beloved of climbers great and small. It springs up vertically from the steep fellside, with a north face like a cathedral-front 500 feet high. From the summit of the fell a descent of 400 feet of steep rock and scree will bring us to the nearest part of the crag. From the Liza River at the bottom of the valley we have 1,100 feet of grass and scree to tackle before reaching the lowest buttresses that support the great wall.

From below, the precipice is seen to be divided into two parts by a long, black chimney. This is Walker's Gully, named after the young man who fell there in

PLATE IX.

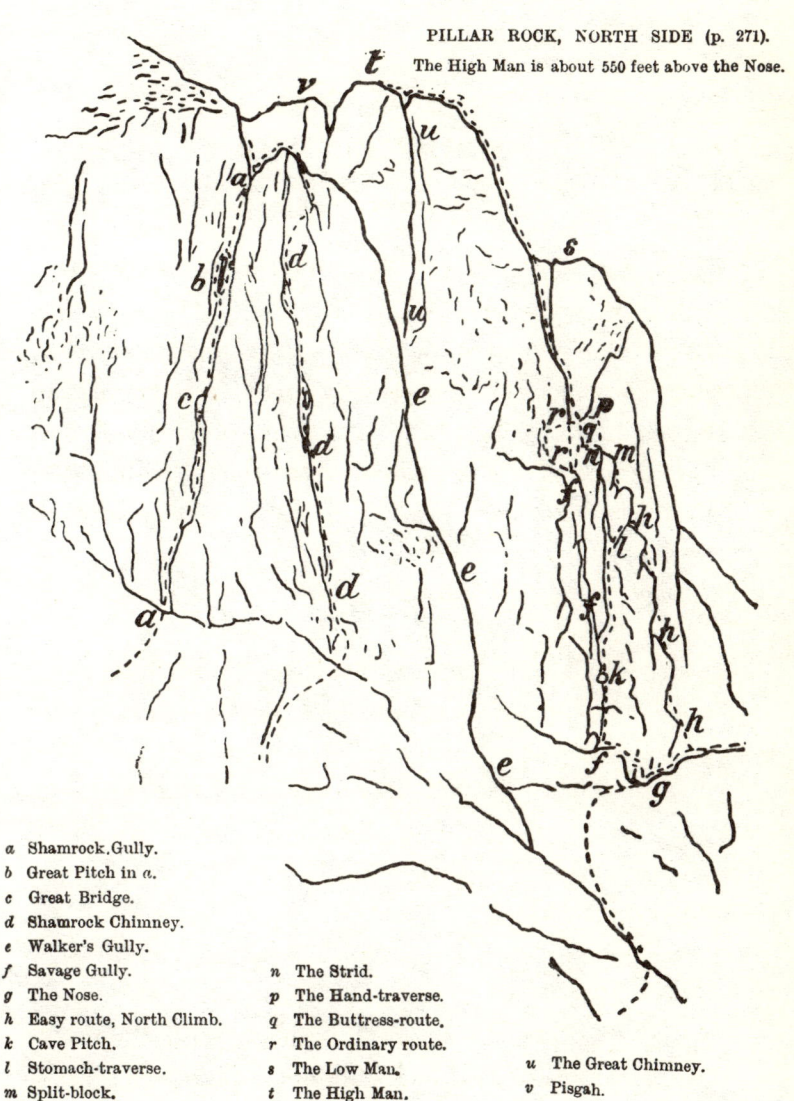

PILLAR ROCK, NORTH SIDE (p. 271).

The High Man is about 550 feet above the Nose.

a	Shamrock Gully.	
b	Great Pitch in *a*.	
c	Great Bridge.	
d	Shamrock Chimney.	
e	Walker's Gully.	
f	Savage Gully.	*n*	The Strid.
g	The Nose.	*p*	The Hand-traverse.
h	Easy route, North Climb.	*q*	The Buttress-route.
k	Cave Pitch.	*r*	The Ordinary route.
l	Stomach-traverse.	*s*	The Low Man.	*u*	The Great Chimney.
m	Split-block.	*t*	The High Man.	*v*	Pisgah.

1883. Its head is the point of convergence of sundry lines of scree from the upper fell. It suggests a funnel cut down along its centre-line, and scree frequently slides down the sides of the funnel and into the gully. This no doubt is the chief reason why Walker's Gully has never been climbed until recently, when snow and frost diminished the risk from this cause. It would prove difficult under any conditions, and the risk of a battery of stones from above is too heavy a handicap for the cautious climber.

The Pillar Rock itself is on the right of the gully, in our view from below. The crag on the left is considerably lower, and in fact scarcely rises high enough over the head of the gully to be visible from above. But from the east it presents an imposing appearance. Its outline partly suppresses that of the higher crag beyond, partly combines with it, and it is often mistaken for the actual Pillar Rock. Hence the name Sham-rock by which it has been known since 1882. It is a mere walk to reach the summit from the Pillar Fell. The climbing on the Shamrock is not quite so good as that on the neighbouring crag, but it cannot well be neglected. On the eastern side is the well-known Shamrock Gully, a magnificent looking cleft in the rocks, finishing with a huge V-shaped notch at the summit. A natural arch spans the gully half-way up, and an obstacle some few feet higher makes a pitch of unusual severity—' one of the stiffest pitches in all

Cumberland.' It was first climbed by Mr. Geoffrey
Hastings' party in March, 1887, when a bank of
snow below the pitch gave a little help. In December,
1890, the climb was repeated by a party with the
same leader, without the aid of snow, and since that
date various ascents have been made with and without snow. Among others a new route over the
obstacle was effected in December, 1896, by the
writer and three friends. It is probable that the
pitch turns back fifty per cent. of the people who
essay to climb it.

On the same eastern face, a few yards further
away to the north, is the Shamrock Chimney, a thin
crack running somewhat irregularly upwards to the
summit ridge. The credit of the first ascent belongs
to Mr. John Robinson, whose keen eye and sound
judgment made the ascent an accomplished fact, on
September 23, 1894, within a few days of his discovery of the chimney. Shortly afterwards Robinson
showed me the route, and I was convinced at once
that in difficulty and extreme interest it was far
superior to the Shamrock Gully, and equal to the best
climbing on the Pillar Rock. The third ascent was
made by Dr. Lawrence in April, 1895. Not many
parties have been up it as yet, and I am hoping that
the full account of its details here supplied will
tempt others to attack it.

I have said that the Pillar Rock lies to the right
of Walker's Gully when viewed from below. It is
bounded on the other or western side by a broad

hollow in the fell, down which a slender stream flows without any abrupt change of level till the foot of the precipice is reached. There the 'Great' waterfall disturbs the even tenor of its way, and is said to offer a formidable obstruction to our approach of the west face from below.

From the Shamrock side we can get the best idea of the shape of the Rock. We have first the Pisgah rising out of the upper fellside, a pinnacle easily accessible and only forty or fifty feet high. Then to the right comes the actual Pillar Rock, the 'High Man,' separated from Pisgah by a narrow vertical cleft, the 'Jordan,' that renders the ascent from Pisgah almost an impossibility. At the Jordan two gullies meet; one up the east side, short and easy, the other up the west side, longer and more difficult.

The outline of the rock is marked by a notch to the right of the summit, where the Great Chimney finishes, and a little further northwards it shows a sudden drop to the level of the Low Man, the immense buttress that from below hides the true summit altogether. A cairn has been erected on the top of this buttress, and the outline to the right of this falls in one vertical drop of 400 feet to the foot of the rock. This is the great north wall. It is supported at the base by a minor buttress, the 'Nose,' that stretches across the full width of the north wall, and along the top of which, immediately below the precipice, an easy terrace takes us across to the Great Waterfall from a point near the foot of Walker's Gully. From the eastern end of the traverse rises the Savage Gully, a well-marked cleft with sundry branches, reaching to the top of the Low Man.

On the western side the rock appears much more formidable. The chimney up to the Jordan looks black, and its crest is overhanging. The wall of the High Man itself is built up with long slabs of smooth rock, broken only by the smallest grass ledges, and its difficulties appear to increase near the summit. This side of the Low Man looks as inaccessible as the great north wall. Nevertheless a series of short gullies starting from the foot of the High Man lead obliquely up towards the left and offer a very easy route to the southern end of the Low Man, whence to the summit the climbing is but moderately difficult.

The best ways of reaching the Pillar Rock are given in full detail by Mr. Haskett Smith. It will here be sufficient to remark that from Wastdale the usual course followed is to ascend by the path towards Black Sail Pass until about ten minutes beyond Gatherstone Beck, then to make for the ridge on the left leading over Looking Stead and up to the summit of Pillar Fell. Thence a descent of 450 feet in a northerly direction brings us to the Pillar Rock. Sometimes Mosedale is followed straight up, and the steep slope climbed that leads to Windy Gap. Thence the ridge to the right takes us in twenty minutes of easy going to the summit of the Pillar Fell. Both these routes involve an unnecessary ascent of 450 feet, and the 'High-Level Route' was designed to avoid this waste of time and energy. Looking Stead is reached as before from Gatherstone Beck, and the wire fence followed up for a few minutes as far as the head of Green Cove. Here a cairn marks the spot where a rough path starts down the cove. We descend only fifty feet or so, and then turn round to the left and skirt along the north-east side of the fell. It is unsafe to attempt the traverse for the first time in a mist, but with clear weather the various cairns that mark successive points on the route can be easily discerned, and a half-hour's walk brings us to the wide scree gully running down by the eastern side of the Shamrock. To reach the foot of the Pillar Rock is a simple matter. The photograph facing page 271 was taken across this scree, and it will be seen that the route down to the Nose is only a walk round the foot of the Shamrock. A broad, sloping corridor in the lee of a steep rock-wall further up the fellside, enables us to steer clear of the Shamrock cliffs and to reach their head without any hand-and-foot scrambling. Thence across the scree descending to Walker's Gully we see Pisgah and the High Man, and with care we can now make the traverse to the foot of the Jordan Gully. There we are in a position to start any of the ordinary short climbs on the Pillar Rock. The west route can be reached by turning Pisgah on the left and descending the west scree for 300 feet. The long climbs up the north face are started from the Nose.

The Pillar Rock was first climbed by an Ennerdale cooper named Atkinson, who in 1826 ascended by the west side. The 'slab-and-notch' route on the east side, starting from the upper screes above Walker's Gully, was devised by Messrs. Conybeare and A. J. Butler in 1863, though it would seem that the same side was successfully attacked a year or two before. Matthew Barnes, a Keswick guide, found a route across the eastern face to the Low Man, and thence back along the summit ridge to the highest point. He was climbing with Mr. Graves, of Manchester. Mr. W. P. Haskett Smith found in 1882 a direct way up to the High Man from the Jordan, and a second route straight up the wall a few yards to the east of the first. Two years later he reached the summit by a particularly hazardous course still further to the east, passing up close to the buttress whose lower end marks the start of the 'slab-and-notch' route. In the same year he made the first ascent by the Great Chimney on the east side. Mr. Haskett Smith named the first three routes the 'West Jordan,' the 'Central Jordan,' and the 'East Jordan' climbs respectively; the latter route is never undertaken, and the other two are often termed the 'Left Pisgah' and 'Right Pisgah.'

For many years Mr. Haskett Smith made visits to the north face, endeavouring to reach the summit of the Low Man from the easy ledge at its foot. On the right his course was limited by the almost seamless wall of rock that gives the Pillar Rock its appearance of hopeless inaccessibility from Ennerdale. On the left the Savage Gully cut off all chance of traversing to the eastern side of the rock. The space between was strictly limited, and it narrowed as he climbed higher. Within thirty feet of an easy scree gully that obviously led to the summit of the Low Man, the only available course had dwindled down to a slender rib of rock in a dangerously exposed situation, much too risky to attack without guarantee of its feasibility.

In 1891 this climber, with Messrs. Hastings and Slingsby, succeeded at last in finding a way of descending into the Savage Gully at that point. Their leader then mounted its left wall and worked easily across to the foot of the scree gully. The others followed, and the 'long climb' up the Pillar Rock became an accomplished fact. No published detailed description of the route is known to the writer.

Shamrock Gully.—This is rather an unpleasant climb for those who dislike loose stones. The bed of the gully is very steep and narrow. It is followed straight up the centre, by using horizontal shelves on either side that now and again flake off in a most unexpected way. Extreme care is necessary on the part of the leader, for his followers cannot avoid any fragments that he may dislodge. The climbing is otherwise easy, and very little distance should exist between the separate members of the party.

Half-way up the gully the bridge is passed, high above our heads when no snow is about, but occasionally completely blocked by heavy drifts. Next the bed of the gully runs up into a little cave, formed by the huge jammed stone that presents the only genuine obstacle in the ascent.

The block is long and narrow. It leaves just enough room on each side, between the walls of the gully, for a thin chimney. That on the right is very difficult to enter but comparatively easy to follow up. The other is designed differently ; it leads the climber by a temptingly easy beginning into a position twenty-five feet up, that will in many cases pound him most distressingly, and his descent will be uncommonly awkward. Hence it is that the right-hand chimney was for nine years the only course adopted.

The process of backing-up is, as a rule, safe, though fatiguing. In the case of the Shamrock pitch, the leader will never find his attitudinising comfortable. If he starts from the shoulders of a companion, he can at any rate enter the chimney ; but its walls are undercut, and he needs all his strength to brace himself firmly between them. A little higher and there is risk of jamming too well. Twenty feet up he has to turn towards the block and work up over a shelf on to the scree above the pitch. It is not easy for his companions to follow on, even with the aid of the rope.

The left-hand route was climbed in winter. Sundry weak holds were frozen into position, but the rounded top of the great block was glazed completely, and the finish was of great difficulty. Dr. Collier had told me that he thought the upper portion just possible, and our party of December, 1896, decided to try it. I started up the first twenty feet and then found the glaze of ice too heavy for further advance. It was not very difficult to traverse out of the chimney into a wider gully on the left; but after rising a few feet in this, the great smooth slabs in front completely barred the way, and I attempted to return to the chimney. This could not be effected, and hitching the rope over two small excrescences on the wall I climbed down the retaining ridge and rejoined my companions. This was very unsatisfactory, though I was glad enough to be in safety again. We had a long discussion about the pitch, and referred to many engineering principles. At last I suggested that the lightest member of the party, weighing not more than nine stones, should take the lead, and that I should follow on closely as far as the difficult spot. There I proposed to brace firmly in the chimney and thrust him straight up to the frozen grass above. He looked at me apologetically and said that he would go up if I insisted on it, but would rather hear of some different plan that deprived him of the honour of leading. Then a bold but heavy man spoke up and volunteered to take his place. It was my turn to decline, and we felt completely at a loss. At last I went up again to the turning-point of the previous venture, and for the sake of safety threaded my rope through two or three jammed stones in the chimney. Then followed the longest member close behind me, likewise threading his rope. I climbed on to his head—it had been tested many times before—and then got him to steady my left foot on a frozen hold half a yard higher. An ice-axe was then passed up from the cave, and the pick rammed hard into the frozen grass above the boulder. The handle then offered enough stay to enable me to pull up over the smooth icy surface of the boulder, and the pitch was conquered. I cut steps up the snow to a safe place for belaying the others, and they then followed singly on a long rope. The rest of the gully was simple walking.

Shamrock Chimney.—This is shown very clearly in the photograph facing page 271, as a series of vertical pitches almost in a single straight line from top to bottom of the Shamrock. We take to the first set of easy rocks on the north side of the great gully, and for about 160 feet climb over irregularly disposed crags interspersed with grass. These are usually wet and slippery, and they finish at the extreme south end of the grassy terrace crossing the Shamrock face.

We keep straight up and enter the lower extremity of a narrow chimney thirty feet high. Its two pitches are scarcely separated, and require careful climbing up to the narrow cavern on the next grassy ledge. The first real difficulty now lies in front. Ten feet of steep smooth rock are to be climbed before we can enter the foot of the next chimney, and the leader will do well to accept a shoulder-up and a lift with an axe in tackling this wall. It is practically impossible in icy weather. The chimney is easy enough, with plenty of jammed stones for a distance of twenty-five feet; but it then dwindles down to nothing, and a very exposed bit of work follows for the leader, who has to crawl up some six or eight feet of rock without any respectable holds. This brings him to another small cavern just sufficiently large for him to take breath and recover his strength. He cannot see his party below, and in manipulating the rope for the second man he will need to shout his directions. Then follow a short traverse to the right, and an upward scramble over more broken ground to an interesting splayed-out chimney.

Thence a steep grass slope takes us up to an open gully with a great overhanging boulder. It may be passed straight over or by a through route, and we are then at the end of the chimney climbing. A turn to the right leads to a splendid ridge that runs to the top of the Shamrock, and offers a finish as charming as that of the Scawfell Pinnacle from the Low Man. The work is over when a perched flat-topped stone is mounted; and then we walk to the summit of the Shamrock and down by easy ledges to the screes above Walker's Gully.

Pillar Rock, Jordan Climbs.—Very easy scrambling from the upper fell will bring the climber

to the summit of Pisgah.   There is a short chimney
on the east side that leads to the same spot; it is
easy to enter, but the exit at the top is very stiff.
The view of the near wall of the High Man is interesting, and there is ample opportunity for studying
the two direct climbs before descending to the gap.
They are both difficult, but the rocks are so much
scratched by nailed boots that the difficulty does
not consist in finding the way up.   It is generally
supposed to be impossible to descend into the gap
from Pisgah, but inspection will show that there is
a series of small ledges a little to the west, down
which a safe passage can be effected.   The Left
Pisgah route starts up at once from the *col*.   The
holds are only moderately good for the first thirty
feet, and fail to give satisfaction when wet or icy.
Next it is possible to force the body into a narrow
crack, and for a little while the climber can cease his
strugglings and rest himself.   Above this the rock is
more broken and the holds are better.   A thin leaf
of rock is crossed and a downward view obtained of
the Right Pisgah final chimney.   Then the slope is
eased off, and the cairn on the High Man is but a
couple of yards away.

The Right Pisgah route is generally started low
down the East Jordan Gully.   This offers pleasant
hand-and-foot work, but no difficulty whatever up to
the Jordan.   But before reaching the gap a square
recess on the right is entered, and then a passage is
made over smooth rocks to a clean-cut right-angled

G. P. Abraham & Sons, Photos.   Keswick

"Round the Notch"—Pillar Rock.   East Side

(Face page 267)

corner forty feet high on the south-east side of the
High Man.   It is just possible to traverse round
from the Jordan to the top of the square recess, and
so up over the slabs to the corner, but the variation
is not worth much.

The crack climb that now starts straight up the
corner is one of the neatest things on the Pillar
Rock.   The right wall is used for steadying purposes
when, half-way up, a jammed stone makes it necessary to emerge from the crack.   Some of the holds
have splintered away during the last few years, but
there are yet enough to satisfy one's needs.   The
finish is a splendid pull up with the arms on to the
leaf of rock already referred to at the top of the
Left Pisgah climb.

Slab and Notch route.—The upper part of
the Great Chimney offers no difficulty to the climber.
Its southern boundary is a long narrow buttress
called the 'Curtain,' stretching from the top of
Walker's Gully, to the summit of the High Man.
Viewed in profile from the Pillar Fell, the Curtain
shows three distinct notches two-thirds of the way
up ; they are about thirty feet above a slab set at an
angle of thirty degrees, and attainable by rough
scrambling from the foot of the East Jordan Gully.
The easy route passes along this slab, directly
upwards to the middle notch and thence round the
Curtain to the bed of the Great Chimney.   The walk
along the slab is to some people a critical undertaking, for a slip would have very serious consequences.

A thin crack on the line of march makes the course safer, unless ice or snow have filled it up, but it is not an unusual sight to see men tackling the walk on all-fours.   The Curtain may be crossed at the lowest notch, the ' Ledge,' by good firm rocks, and the Great Chimney entered on the other side.   Formerly it was the usual course to reach the bed of the chimney at the lower part of the steep grass by what was called the ' Eight-foot Drop.'   But there is no need to drop at all ; an easy traverse from either the Notch or the Ledge brings the climber above the steep grass, and virtually at the end of his cragwork.   The chimney finishes with scree, and lands the climber within a few feet of the cairn on his left.

Variations on the East Face.—It is possible to make a way straight up the Great Chimney from its foot, joining the easy route about a hundred feet up.   Haskett Smith took this course in 1884, commencing the climb on the stepped buttresses of the Curtain.   Since then the rock has had time to loosen a little, and climbers very rarely enter the chimney that way,

The *Pendlebury traverse* is an excellent variation of the ordinary route, a popular scramble first indicated by Professor R. Pendlebury, of Cambridge. From the slab the way lies straight up to the notch in the Curtain, and then along a horizontal ledge in its south face as far as the corner where it meets the High Man.   Thence up the corner is straightforward chimney-work, and on emergence at the top the cairn will be visible close at hand on the left.

The traverse looks difficult until it is closely approached, when it will be found that handholds abound on the wall, and that the ledge is perfectly firm and continuous across the whole width of the Curtain.

The chimney in the corner of the south side of the Curtain can be entered much lower down. From the slab a way lies straight up into it, but the grass holds are not particularly pleasant if wet, and the first thirty feet are severe.

From the head of Walker's Gully a way may be found to the Low Man, below the immense slabs that crown the north-east buttresses. It is best to climb the Shamrock first and prospect the route. Sheep occasionally manage to get across, and the *Old Wall* was built many years ago to prevent their passage, but it is now ruined. Sometimes, ignoring Badminton, they still venture across without a rope, and their weaker members are liable to get crag-bound. Climbers can tell many tales of famished sheep found in appalling situations on the Pillar Rock. They are too weak to resist the slipping on of a rope, and are simply hauled or slung out of every difficulty till a safe pasturage is reached.

The West Climb.—This was the route first discovered. It is much longer than any of the ways on the south or east side, and possesses but few interesting details. It is more popular as a descent than as an ascent.

It is seemingly impossible to climb directly up the west wall of the High Man, but in the walk down the

west screes it will be noticed that the rocks of the
Low Man are more broken, and that several short
scree gullies sloping upwards to the left mark a
rough route straight towards the Low Man cairn.
The course is best examined from a distance, across
the great western gully ; it lies as close to the High
Man as is possible without undertaking anything but
gully scrambling.   Not infrequently climbers find
themselves astray on narrow grassy ledges too much
to the right.   I experienced the same thing myself
when first attempting to find the way up, and found
the ascent by no means so easy as report had
credited the west climb.

From the level of the Low Man the way lies very
nearly along the sky-line to the highest point.   The
High Man is struck at the end of a square corner
in the rock, and there is some excellent work for the
arms during the next thirty feet of ascent.

It is easier to turn over slightly to the east side,
and up by the great jagged boulders on the crest of
the ridge.   The *Slingsby crack* is a short but rather
stiff variation a little on the right or western side of
this route and is particularly interesting.   Formerly
a loose block at its upper end gave the climber an
occasional scare, but there is nothing unsafe now in
the form of detached boulders, and the ridge can be
followed with confidence to the High Man cairn.
Nail marks are strongly in evidence all through the
crag-work ; the leader should not attempt the route
if snow or rain prevents their recognition, unless he
is already perfectly acquainted with the way.

G. P. Abraham & Sons, Photos.

Keswick

THE NORTH FACE OF THE PILLAR ROCK

(Face page 271)

The North Climb.—For several months after the first ascent it was difficult to learn anything of the details of the route up the Ennerdale face of the Pillar Rock. The only way was to persuade some one who had been up to take the lead and act as guide; for a complicated course that had taken Haskett Smith eight or nine years to work out was not likely to be mastered easily by any one who had not made a special study of the north face.

My own chance came in the summer of 1893. Mr. John Robinson called for me at Buttermere one fine afternoon, and took me off to Ennerdale with another friend, Mr. F. W. Hill. We left the village at two o'clock, and were back again after a successful ascent by eight in the evening; whence it may be inferred that Buttermere is as good a starting-point for the Pillar Rock as Wastdale or Seatoller.

Our guide led us rapidly by the shortest route over Scarth Gap, and across Ennerdale to the foot of the Pillar Rock. Then a fifty-feet length of rope made its first appearance; it had been hidden in a bag during our walk, lest we should alarm the folks about Gatesgarth. We tied ourselves up, and made for the eastern end of the terrace across the Nose.

Robinson then started along the terrace, and in a few yards scrambled up to a shelf on the left, five or six feet high, which gave us easy access to the lower portion of the Savage Gully. This latter has never been climbed along its whole length. If the gully were moderately easy, the north climb would be far

less complex.   But for a great portion of its length
the side walls are at right angles to each other ; the
corner is nearly vertical, and the only resting places
are diminutive, grass-grown ledges placed too far
apart for any safe employment of the rope. The right
wall of the gully forms part of a conspicuous buttress
on the north face, whose western side is much more
broken and less dangerous to ascend.

The route that was being shown us lay along the
Savage Gully for about sixty feet, then across to the
west side of the buttress and up a vertical branch
gully with sundry small chimneys in it.   Higher up,
we were told, it would be necessary to round a cliff
still further to the right, by means of the *Stomach
traverse*, to render further ascent possible.   We objected to the inelegant name, but were too far advanced
to hesitate on the score of a faulty title.   Above the
traverse our climbing would be easier, until the course
returned to the Savage Gully again.   That was to
be our *mauvais pas*, and after settling it the scramble
to the Low Man, and thence to the highest cairn,
would be scarcely more than a walk.

So spoke our guide, and having delivered himself at some length, with an occasional appropriate
anecdote thrown in, he concentrated his attention
on the small pitch that marked our point of arrival
at the Savage Gully.   It was a wall seven feet
high with indifferent grassholds at the top, and in
scrambling up care was needed to avoid dislodging
loose stones near the edge.   It was then easy to

clamber into a small cave somewhat to the left, and
out again by a twisted tunnel at the back. Thence
Robinson worked upwards over broken ground for a
few yards, until the point was reached where we
were to leave the gully. The direct route looked
feasible for some distance ahead, but there was no
questioning the fact of its severity, and we had not
come out that day for exploration.

A divergence was made along an easy traverse
towards the right, to a short and narrow chimney
that already bore traces of many previous struggles.
Wherever the rocks were clean and free from scree,
we could plainly see the scratches of nailed boots
along the route. It was here that we were rounding
the great buttress of Savage Gully, and after a little
rough-ledge work we arrived at a square corner with
a grassy floor. Straight up from this floor a cleft
offered safe passage. It was plentifully supplied with
holds, though some discrimination was necessary in
selecting the firmest. The climbing was delightful,
and zest was given to it by the magnificent situation.
The corner was not so deeply impressed in the
buttress as to prevent our recognition of the vastness
of the cliff we were slowly ascending. The view
downwards just included the little grass platform,
and beyond that the wild and steep fellside at the
foot of the precipice, already some hundreds of feet
below us.

We kept up the direct route so long as we were
able. Then the cleft in the corner suddenly dwindled

down into the thinnest of cracks, and it was obvious
that a change of tactics would be necessary. The
left wall was faultlessly smooth. The right for the
most part looked just as inaccessible. The grass
ledge on which we were standing really seemed to
suggest finality, the end of our upward progress, and
I turned to Robinson inquiringly with the impression
that some wonderful engineering process with the
rope was now to be explained to us. We knew that
such was necessary on the climb, and were prepared
by the situation to see its application immediately.

But the solution of the difficulty was of the
simplest character. A few feet from the corner the
smooth right wall was split by a single crack that
passed up at an angle of perhaps thirty degrees and
terminated at a notch that broke the clean-cut outline
of the rock facing us. From the notch it certainly
seemed as though nothing could be done further,
even if we got so far. Nevertheless, we were assured
that when once we were there all doubts would
vanish, and we should have the easiest hundred feet
of scrambling in the whole day's expedition. The
crack was the famous *Stomach traverse*; it was
reached as long ago as 1884 by Haskett Smith in
his early exploration of the north face ; and the
name, which had only recently been given to it, was
intended to show how the passage was supposed
to be tackled. One of Willink's illustrations in
the Badminton, showing an intrepid cragsman
crawling along a ledge from left to right, is

sometimes criticised as an exaggeration of the difficulties that rock-climbers have to overcome. This traverse before us was not so easy as the one so cleverly depicted by the artist. It sloped upwards, and the ledge was not wide enough for the whole body. We were in no sense precariously placed, for the cleft enabled us to wedge with security; but the right half of the body was outside the leaf of rock on which we hung, and the right leg found no support on the vertical wall.

Some twenty feet of wriggling brought us each in turn to the critical corner, and there to our amazement we had merely to get up and walk away. The wall we had passed was the last obstacle separating us from a long stretch of steep grass chimneys and broken rocks. These extend from the Nose at the foot of the crags up to the final difficulty, now only a hundred feet above us, and offer the easier route up the north face. Our own course by the Savage Gully was by far the more entertaining one, and under most conditions decidedly safer than the other.

From the notch we could either walk straight up to the cave-pitch in the corner now facing us, or work easily round a rib of rock on the right and join the other route. We chose the former, and found the pitch decidedly stiff, the main trouble being to get satisfaction out of the diminutive hand-holds on the upper surface of the top boulder. However, it was time to be thankful for small mercies, and confidence carried us up safely.

A party coming up the easy way would start from the terrace on the Nose, close to its highest point. Their route would be quite straightforward, though occasionally the question as to the safest movement might introduce a slight digression. The great wall of the Low Man on their right limits in the most definite manner all westerly climbing, and their only trouble would be in negotiating two narrow chimneys and some of the grass ledges, where the tufts are unpleasantly loose and the slopes very slippery. The fact is that this way is not much to be recommended; until it joins the other there is little merit to justify the variation. If parties are certain they can finish the second half of the ascent, they can assuredly climb the lower portion *via* the Savage Gully and the Stomach traverse.

We halted for a moment above our cave-pitch and looked around at the crags. From a distant survey, such as that indicated in the photograph facing page 271, it is impossible to realize that so large an open space of easy ground can exist on the north face. But our opportunity for advance was strictly confined to one direction. Further westwards we could not go; the great wall was unassailable. To the east we could have perhaps traversed away until progress was barred by the narrow branch of the Savage Gully, which we had utilized lower down. The northerly direction of course led down the easy route, and the southerly pointed to an uncompromising extension of the great wall towards the Savage Gully.

We were led straight up the small scree to the *split block*, a huge boulder at the foot of the wall. The leader disappeared into a deep crack, and after a few moments appeared at the top of the block, having mounted by a secondary fissure that cut into the left portion of the boulder. The movement was quite unexpected, and Hill and I were rather startled at the aspect of things from the summit of the split block. It stood at the top of the narrow branch of the Savage Gully already referred to, and the view vertically down this branch was calculated to make us hesitate before taking the next step.

This was the *Strid*. Close up against the wall that blocked the head of the gully, a long stride was to be taken across to a narrow 'mantelshelf' on the other side. There was no difficulty in the step, but the consequences of any slip were so obvious that we were not surprised to learn how respectfully the Strid is usually regarded. The mantelshelf led us along under the wall for a few yards, and an upper ledge was mounted. We were now close to the Savage Gully again, and Robinson prepared to be let down into it on the rope. We were adopting the tactics of Haskett Smith's party in the first ascent. Robinson was to climb down the wall of the gully by means of an irregular crack twenty-five feet long, using the rope to steady himself during the descent. At the foot of the crack he would be able to step into the bed of the gully, and thence, after mounting it for a few feet, effect an easy passage up the opposite side. He was then to unrope, and Hill was to let me down in the same way, there being plenty of friction between the rope and the rocks to enable him to hold my weight in case of a slip. When safely landed in the gully, I was to take the rope up to Robinson and wait the issue of events.

These went off without a hitch. The crack was difficult, though not impossible for one man to descend alone; but I am convinced that a man attempting the climb single-handed would be running great risk if he proceeded without some sort of belaying with a rope. The little story is well known of the youth who could not understand why he as third and last man of his party had to be left behind on the ledge; he had examined the crack and was certain he could climb down safely without support from above. Nay more, he insisted on demonstrating the fact, and when three-quarters of the way to the bed of the gully his feet slipped and his handholds failed. Luckily the others were able to prevent a serious fall, and the young man's 'climbing down' was strictly metaphorical.

Robinson then rapidly swarmed up to the left of the gully, and, after mounting forty feet, traversed to the right into a long scree-shoot that ended abruptly some twenty-five feet vertically above our solitary companion on the ledge. Upwards the scree led straight to the summit level of the Low Man, and two of us were of course in a position to attain this point in a couple of minutes. But there was the third to manipulate, and Robinson proceeded to take out a short, spare rope from his sack and expound the method of using the ' stirrup.'

He tied a loop on to one end of his spare rope, large enough for a foot to be comfortably slipped therein, and flung that end down to Hill. I operated with the other rope, sending an end down for Hill to tie round his waist in the usual manner. The object of the process was to get the third man up with the least expenditure of energy on our part; in fact, to make Hill do all his own lifting. The wall was not so complicated in design as to render it impossible to haul him straight up like a bale of goods. But neither he nor I had till then seen an application of the stirrup-rope, and we had come out to be educated. There are many places where the method is well worth employing.

The operations commenced by Hill's fixing a foot in the stirrup and lifting it a couple of feet as Robinson hauled up his rope. Then, with Robinson simply holding on firmly, Hill straightened himself on the stirrup, using it as a foothold, while I pulled up the couple of feet of slack in the waist-rope. Next it was my turn to hold hard as Hill raised his stirrup foot, and then Robinson's to keep the foot firm while Hill lifted himself on to it. These two moves were repeated again and again alternately. All through the process the ropes were held as free from slack as possible, any upward movement of Hill's engaged foot or body being responded to

promptly by Robinson or myself respectively.   It
will be perceived, if the description is as clear as I
want it to be, that all the actual lifting of Hill's
weight he managed himself during the straightening-
out on the stirrup, and that we others were at most
called upon to hold only his weight.   Even this
much stress on our hands we could avoid by partial
belaying, though in that particular spot there were
no entirely suitable projecting rocks that could be
utilized as belaying-pins.

Bit by bit Hill worked up the wall, till at last his
head and shoulders appeared over the rounded coping
at our feet, and he scrambled on to the scree.   Then
we all sat down and Robinson told us tales about that
particular locality.   Among others he gave us one to
emphasize the practical lesson we had just been having
on the use of the stirrup-rope.   A famous climber,
indeed he was sometime president of the Alpine
Club, and in a vague, traditional sort of way years
before he had fallen some hundreds of feet down a
vertical gully hard by, without coming to any harm
except that of finding his name ever afterwards
associated with the gully; well, this famous climber
was coming up that same wall by means of the
stirrup-rope, and the zealous operatives above more
than responded to his slightest movements.   He
lifted his foot a few inches, they hauled up the
stirrup-rope a few yards, and anticipating that he
might find the alternations a little laborious, proceeded to pull him up by sheer strength of goodwill.

Thus his attached foot appeared first over the edge, and the remainder of his person followed in some confusion. So, at any rate, the story went.

Sitting as we were with our faces towards Buttermere, the great wall bore away to the left, and our scree gully marked its eastern limit. A horizontal crack extended for several feet across the wall, starting from the top of the pitch below us. Only its end could be seen, but by carefully working down to the corner on the left, and looking across the face, we could see the way it cut clean into the rock. This was the notorious *hand-traverse*, by which it was just possible to reach our scree gully from the ledge below without the preliminary descent into the Savage Gully.

A few minutes' halt and we continued our course. There was no doubt or difficulty in reaching the Low Man, and thence following the ridge to the junction with the West Climb. A quarter of an hour saw us at the High Man cairn, and another five minutes at the foot of the Central Jordan. The ropes were stowed away again in the sack, and Robinson rapidly strode across the screes and down the corridor behind the Shamrock. In a phenomenally short time we were crossing the Liza stream, and, without being allowed to halt, a bee-line was drawn for us over to Scarth Gap by our untiring leader. Luckily for his followers, the name of this pass, which is sometimes called Scarf Gap, reminded him of a very good story concerning another famous

climber who went to an evening party without a
dress-tie.   We were told the story and recovered
breath sufficiently to continue our journey to Buttermere.   I wish now that I had not been so fatigued,
so that I might have remembered the whole anecdote
and given it here in all detail.

The Hand-Traverse.—Nearly two years after
the ascent described in the previous section, Dr.
Collier showed me a way of avoiding the Savage
Gully in the North Climb by following a direct
route to the upper screes.   The plan is to work to
the extreme east corner of the ledge that succeeds
the 'mantelshelf,' and when a narrow overhanging
chimney is reached, to swarm up the steep buttress
on its left.   It looks particularly dangerous, but there
is an excellent hold for the hands just round the corner
of the buttress, and when the first three feet of ascent
are accomplished the rest feels comparatively easy.

On the same occasion we each in turn ventured
on the *hand-traverse* from above.   The place has
already been referred to ; it was known for some
time that the crack could be reached from the
terrace below, and Mr. Solly showed in 1891 that it
could be followed to its left-hand extremity at the
scree gully.   It is so named because the climber
hangs by his hands, with no footholds at all for the
greater part of its length, and traverses across the
face by sheer strength of his arms.   Collier and I
were well satisfied concerning the security of the
crack itself.   We went to the further end and back

PIERS GHYLL

(Face page 282)

again, without coming across any place where the holds were treacherous. They were probably more satisfying to the grip than an ordinary horizontal bar, on account of the acute edge of the rock. On the other hand, we had no opportunity of trying the ascent from the terrace, which promised to be rather fatiguing for the arms, and which might render them useless for the traverse itself.

On Whit Monday, 1896, a chance came for tackling the pitch in this new way. It had been successfully accomplished once, and twice had the climber's strength of grip failed him when half-way across. So, at any rate, we learnt by hearsay at Wastdale. Perhaps it ought to be added that in one case it was the leader of the party who fell off, and the rope saved him in a manner scarcely short of miraculous; in the other case the rope was held from the scree gully, and the climber only swung out on it. Our Whitsuntide party were willing that I should try, and carefully measured out just a sufficiency of rope for me to reach the crack. Then two of them stood together at the western extremity of the terrace, and shouldered me up the first bad bit. There was every reason to be quick, as resting-places were absent where the strain on the arms could be eased. In twenty-five feet I reached the crack and halted for a moment on a scanty foothold before trusting to the ledge. Then came the swing off and a hasty sliding of the hands along the sharp edge. The first bit was about eight feet long; then that particular crack terminated abruptly in the wall, and another, two feet higher, continued across in the same easterly direction. The lift of the body up to the second crack was trying, but beyond this critical point the movement was horizontal. It was somewhat clumsy—the scraping of the body along the rough surface of the rock, with the legs held clear; but my sole thought was to reach the end of the traverse twelve feet away, and no consideration of style was entertained. In a very short time, though it seemed far too long, the end of the wall was attained, and it only remained to drag myself up to the scree.

The rest of the party preferred to mount the buttress by Collier's route indicated in a previous paragraph. I think the hand-traverse has not been attempted since, and it is perhaps just as well. It is scarcely less than suicidal to try conclusions with this variation unless the climber has full confidence in his strength of grip, and unless he has already tested his powers of endurance of long-continued strain in the arms. But with the leader of the party already at the head of the pitch, no matter which way he got there, it involves no serious risk for the others to follow by this route. The last on the rope had better come up over the buttress.

CHAPTER XVIII

NOTES ON REMAINING CLIMBS

In this chapter it is proposed to deal summarily with a few remaining rock-climbs that have not yet been described. Some are rather awkward to reach, others are perhaps too slight to be worth the time spent in reaching them unless they actually turn up in the day's march. One or two I have not visited, and am reluctant to accept the responsibility of guiding people up them. But

> What he thought he might require,
> He went and took—the same as me!

is too general a motto among book-writers for me to hesitate long before incorporating other people's notes, and the attempt will be made to acknowledge the source in each case.

Piers Ghyll.—This is a fine-looking ravine on the north side of Lingmell, occasionally visited by climbers. It has four or five comparatively easy pitches before the big bend, but at the point where the main gully is bridged by a great mass of rock the whole width of the ravine is occupied by a water-fall fifty feet high, and any attempt to force a passage up this pitch is peculiarly unsatisfactory unless a rainless season has much diminished the volume of water passing down. Such a season was that of 1893, and in April of that year Dr. Collier led the first party up the whole length of the ghyll. Even under those favourable circumstances the climb was very difficult, and no other party has succeeded in repeating the ascent. Dr. Collier tells me that the hardest bit is up the narrow pitch before reaching the great fall. The latter offers a choice of two or three routes.

Piers Ghyll is conspicuous from a distance, and many a tourist knows the place. Hence it has a reputation of its own even as a climb, which it can scarcely be said to deserve. If, as Haskett Smith expresses it, it is in nineteen seasons out of twenty wholly impossible to get over the great obstacle, it cannot rightly be called a climb. The scrambling up to the bend is mostly unpleasant by reason of the water and the loose character of the rock. An exit can there be made up the wall on the right, but the friability of this wall makes its ascent positively dangerous except at one spot where a scree gully runs nearly to the top of the cliff.

A most interesting account of the ghyll, giving certain of the adventures that explorers have encountered, may be read in ' All the Year Round ' of November, 1884. It was contributed by Mr. C. N. Williamson ; other parts of this article dealing with Cumberland climbing have already been referred to.

High Stile.—The north side of this mountain is precipitous, and two or three short but interesting

The Great Pitch, Sergeant Crag Gully

(Face page 286)

gullies can be followed up to the ridge. Two of them
can easily be recognised from Buttermere village.
The central gully faces towards the north-west and
is to the right of the highest point on the mountain
It has two well-defined pitches, the second being very
severe. The writer climbed it in 1893 with Mr
John Robinson, before taking the chimney described
in the next paragraph, but seemingly it has rarely
been visited since.

To the left of the central gully a wide black
chimney can be seen, leading up close to the summit
of High Stile. It offers a short but very difficult
scramble; in pulling up over the edge of the great
pitch care must be taken to avoid the loose stones.
In the first ascent the leader had a bad encounter
with three boulders that slipped over on to his head.

A long, easy gully in the north-east shoulder of
the mountain offers a pleasant route down from the
summit to the shores of Buttermere.

Buckbarrow.—The side of this hill facing
Wastwater has sundry attractions. Climbers who
are not pressed for time, on their way from Wastdale
to the nearest stations on the Furness Railway, can
be recommended to visit the crag.

The first main gully at the northern end was
climbed at Easter, 1892; two short parallel chimneys
terminate the ascent, that on the left being supposed
to be the harder. Besides this route, there are a few
ways of tackling the face further to the west; but
details are not at hand by reason of the rarity of the
visits to Buckbarrow.

Sergeant Crag Chimney.—This was first ascended by Mr. John Robinson and the writer in September, 1893. The crag itself is reached by walking up Langstrath from the village of Rosthwaite for about a mile and then bearing to the left. Close to the stream, at the point where we leave the track, is the Gash Rock, an isolated boulder that offers considerable resistance to any one attempting to climb it. It was climbed first by the writer in 1893. A good hold has recently been cleared at the critical point on the boulder. The scramble is said to be quite easy now.

The gully in the crag is in sight half-a-mile below the Gash Rock, and is well worth the visit of a strong party. It was noticed in 1886 by Mr. Haskett Smith, but seven years elapsed before the first ascent was made. Curiously enough, the second ascent was effected a day or two later by Messrs. Phillimore and Anderson, in entire ignorance that the gully had so recently been overcome.

Information embodied in the following notes of the successive pitches has been supplied by the brothers Abraham of Keswick, whose interesting photograph of the great pitch in the middle of the ascent is reproduced facing page 286.

First Pitch.—Chock-stone about fifteen feet high, passed to the left on the face of the rock. Good hand and foot holds.

Second Pitch.—Small chock-stone. Both hands are reached up to the top of the stone and a straight pull over effected with the arms. The obstacle is about nine feet high.

Third Pitch.—Sundry boulders forming a block, about fifteen feet high. The right-hand side of the gully is ascended until the leader is well wedged under the block. Then he can pass out to the left and over at the top.

Fourth Pitch.—This is the most severe of the whole set, and the direct climb up the left wall is probably as stiff a problem as can be found in the district. Two immense boulders, one over the other, separated by a gap of four feet, form the roof of a cave. The retaining walls of the gully form the sides of the cave, and the ascent is to be effected on the left. From a short distance this appears to be a smooth vertical slab; even on close inspection the holds it offers appear to be of the most minute dimensions.

The second man on the rope should mount as high up the interior of the cave as possible. After climbing under the first boulder the leader takes a long step out to the left wall, on a sloping ledge. Then using side holds on the boulder itself, with his feet or knees against the main wall, he has to work up gradually to a little jammed boulder two feet above the lower one. This is an extremely fatiguing operation. On to this block he must lift his knees, and then he can cautiously drag up so as to stand on it.

The upper boulder is then passed by throwing

the left leg across to a slight foothold, whence a thrust forward of the body is effected through wet soil and tufted ferns. This is particularly unpleasant after rainy weather, and is probably at all times somewhat risky. The height of the pitch is thirty-two feet.

A variation has been found which makes the passage of this obstacle much more feasible. It leads first downwards to a grassy ledge on the right, and then up by succeeding shelves until the upper level of the pitch is reached, when the return traverse back to the bed of the gully can be easily managed. Hitherto all parties, except the first and third in the chimney, have preferred to avoid the fourth pitch, and their preference is most reasonable.

Fifth Pitch.—This is an easy chimney twenty feet long, lined with grass and ferns, and marked at the summit by a fallen tree.

Sixth Pitch.—Two wedged stones one above the other form a pitch about twenty feet high. The route is first into the cave between the stones, then up a short chimney and over the upper boulder. The second on the rope should ascend as high as possible in the cave and, with splendid anchorage, pay out the leader's rope carefully. Sundry loose stones are lodged on the right, and should be left discreetly alone.

Seventh Pitch.—This is a chimney thirty feet high containing many loose stones. It is crowned by a chock-stone. The ascent is directly up the first part, and then over loose and dangerous rock on the right for another twenty feet.

Steep grass leads out to the top, 500 feet from the base of the cliff.

Blea Crags and Mouse Ghyll.—The Blea Crag climbs in Borrowdale can be reached from Grange in thirty-five minutes; a fine general view is to be seen from the picturesque bridge spanning the Derwent. There are three gullies of interest; one to the south is now known as Mouse Ghyll, climbed and christened in the autumn of 1897, by Mr. W. Cecil Slingsby's party; a second less-defined gully leads up the centre of the crags; and to the north of this a third takes us by loose and rather unsatisfactory pitches to the summit ridge.

Mouse Ghyll starts very narrow, with smooth walls running up to a great height on either side. An easy pitch of ten feet brings us to a little platform, whence a steep, double staircase, with good steps for each foot, gives safe access to a great cavern sixty feet higher. Here the real difficulties begin. The pitch is formed by two huge, overhanging boulders, one above the other, with a grassy ledge between them. The leader can be well anchored by his party, and makes a start up to the left from the top of the rib of rock that supplies the 'staircase.' It is sensational work up to the grassy ledge, where again the leader requires anchoring, and perhaps also a helping shoulder for the next little chimney of some fourteen feet, between the upper boulder and the left

wall. When the first party were here, a startled
mouse sprang from the grassy ledge over the leader's
head, and dropped safely at the bottom of the staircase ninety feet below. May it live long enough to
learn that the ghyll has been named in its honour!

On emerging from the chimney three routes show
themselves. The first is up two easy pitches that
remain in the gully. To the right a chimney leads
by an open buttress to the top of the crags, and can
be ascended without trouble. But on the left a
prominent chimney, succeeded by a narrow crack,
gives seventy feet of extremely tough climbing. It
was ascended by Messrs. George and Ashley
Abraham, who made the second ascent of Mouse
Ghyll.

The central gully starts with a chimney, best
taken on the right, aud continues with short and
easy pitches until some large boulders wedged in a
vertical crack offer better fun. There are no further
obstacles.

I am indebted to Messrs. George and Ashley
Abraham and to Mr. Slingsby for the information in
this section. They assure me that the climbing in
Mouse Ghyll is of a first-rate order, and the scenery
of lake and fellside almost unsurpassable in the
country.

APPENDIX.

APPENDIX.

Walker's Gully, Pillar Rock.—The Christmas of 1898 at Wastdale was marked by heavy rain and unseasonable conditions. Several large parties of climbers had come to the hotel, and, after a day or two of smoking and grumbling, had departed; until, at the New Year, Mr. Jones and myself were the only climbers left there. To keep ourselves in training, we struggled up through the powdery snow of the Central Gully on Gable Crag, performed many rash feats on the end of the barn and the billiard-table, besides leaving a considerable quantity of our clothing on the 'Mosedale Boulder.'

Early in January we walked over to Keswick; and found, on returning, that another party had arrived, amongst whom was my friend Mr. A. E. Field. We greeted him as warmly as we could under such cold conditions; and when, later in the evening, we disclosed our intention to climb Walker's Gully, he was quite 'keen' on undertaking the very necessary duties of 'third man.' Our party was now complete; but the heavy rain-clouds still rolled up from the sea, and the weather continued persistently bad.   We were forced at last to the conclusion that, if Walker's Gully had then to be climbed, it would have to be done regardless of bad weather and personal discomfort.

As a result of this reasoning, the early morning of January 7th, 1899, saw the three of us trudging patiently up the Black Sail Pass in a tremendous downpour of rain and sleet; but, notwithstanding this, with the climber's cheery optimism, a 'fair-up' was confidently prophesied.   As an exception to the general rule, our prophecy was fulfilled; for, just as we reached the soft snow on Looking Stead, the huge banks of mist rolled up from both valleys, and far away in the north we saw 'hoary-headed old Skiddaw' bathed in sunshine, while a keen dry wind blew up out of Ennerdale.   We trudged along through the snow on the High Level, and about mid-day were facing the ice-covered slabs and snow-wreathed ledges on the north-east side of the Pillar Rock.   Little was said as we scrambled to the foot of Walker's Gully; for each of us fully recognised what was ahead, and it was better to be silent, than to utter discouraging remarks.

The rope was put on at the foot of the crags, Field being the 'anchor' of the party, whilst I, as usual, was placed next to Jones, to serve as a special buttress when hand and foot holds should become scarce.   A strong jet of ice-cold water came rushing down over the first pitch, so that, not wishing to have our enthusiasm cooled so early in the day, we

climbed up the wet, slippery slabs on our left.
About fifty feet higher we had some difficulty in a
shallow sloping chimney, down which a mud
avalanche seemed to have fallen quite recently, and
here our leader remarked 'we ought to have been
equipped with mud-guards.' We were soon facing
the main gully, with its tremendous chock-stones
rising one above the other, over which streamed
large quantities of water, suggesting a somewhat
too rapid cleansing of our mud-stained garments.
We entered the chimney and found it just wide
enough to back up, with both feet on the right-hand
wall; the falling ice-chips apprising us of the fact
that hard work was in progress higher up.

We climbed very rapidly for about fifty feet,
close together, until almost within touch of the
uninviting stream of water falling over the first
jammed boulder, which was now just above our
heads. Knowing this to be one of the most difficult
pitches in the lower part of the climb, a short
'council of war' was held, for all seemed desirous
of avoiding a cold bath as long as possible. Then,
screwing up his courage, Jones made a bold dash
through the waterfall to the back of the cave.
Knowing his objection to monopolising pleasures of
this kind, we followed him, and were soon all
gasping and shivering below the jammed boulder.
After further consideration and experiment, the
only safe course, apparently, was for me to
stand under the waterfall and give the leader a

shoulder over the *mauvais pas*. As our ablutions seemed likely now to be very thorough, we ate our lunch and watched, for a time, the falling water, which, in my opinion, to some extent spoilt the view. The discomfort of our position, however, soon impressed upon us the necessity of moving. Field therefore held me firmly from the back of the cave, whilst I stood under the shower-bath ; and Jones mounted on my shoulders, from whence he reached a hold on the top of the boulder, over which he pulled himself with an exclamation of delight. I then retired to the cave with considerable alacrity. Sounds from above warned us that the leader was scarcely yet secure, so we steadily paid out about forty feet of his rope, until he reached safe anchorage at the top of the three boulders forming the pitch. In following we wasted very little time under the waterfall, and soon joined Jones on a little snow-patch, from which we could study the situation. A hundred feet or so higher, and apparently over-hanging our present position, was the top jammed boulder. Evidence was not wanting, however, to show us that we were not safe from falling objects ; for, stuck in a curiously upright position in the snow in front of us, were three walking-sticks, with two pairs of torn gloves and some much-worn socks lying by their side. We thought at first a party of tourists had somehow reached here and forgotten their 'impedimenta ;' but our leader remembered that some friends, having climbed the Pillar Rock at

Christmas, had thrown their sticks and 'luggage down into Jordan Gap before descending themselves. The snow proved harder than they thought, their property making an unexpected descent into Walker's Gully, and here were we confronted with the opportunity of acting as a rescue party; but, not thirsting for fame, we decided to leave the relics undisturbed.

Jones now led us up several small, wet pitches, until we came to a sudden stop in a great cave, where there was no apparent way out, except through a very small hole high up in its roof; an outside route being practically impossible on account of the accumulation of ice on both walls. Jones remarked that he was not going 'to emulate the camel that failed to go through the eye of a needle;' so, to reduce his bulk as far as possible, he emptied his pockets and left his wet jacket for Field to sit upon. No holds on the side of the cave were available, so the leader climbed upon my shoulders, but he could barely reach his arms through the hole. Field, meanwhile, was smoking and making the most of his comfortable position. With somewhat insincere apologies, we called on him to form an additional buttress, and, from his shoulders, I was able to force the leader through the hole, amidst the sound of tearing clothes and muffled remonstrances from their owner.

I shall not readily forget my own sufferings in that hole. The first attempt, from Field's shoulders, was a complete failure, because the upper part of my body absolutely refused to fit the shape of the hole. After several fruitless efforts and much wasted energy, I happened to look up and saw Jones smiling down at me. "That is not right. Go down and have another try," said he. He then loosed the rope rather suddenly, whereupon I made an unexpected descent upon Field, who was standing below enjoying my troubles; and there was much confusion in the cave. After extricating ourselves, Field again kindly placed his shoulders at my service, but from a somewhat higher level than before, and this, with the aid of his ice-axe applied from below, ultimately landed me at the top of the hole feeling very roughly handled. Field then sent up our jackets, and, after the hole had been slightly enlarged by removing some loose rocks, he came up himself in good style.

We were now at the foot of the formidable top-pitch, which had never been climbed. A sudden seriousness settled on us all as we looked up at it, and remembered that this pitch had defied some of the finest cragsmen of our time. The walls on both sides were perpendicular, and the rounded appearance of the rocks suggested an unusual absence of hand and foot holds, whilst the presence of ice in several places caused us much uneasiness. There were three large flat chock-stones piled irregularly right across the chasm. Towards the upper one, which overhung considerably, the two walls converged so much that it seemed possible to 'back up' the last

part of the climb, if the leader could only reach it
safely. The only other alternative would be to
climb up on the right wall, close under the lower
chock-stone, and traverse outwards and upwards
until suitable holds could be found. A troublesome
sleet was beginning to fall; so that we were glad to
climb into the cave directly beneath the chock-stones.
A firm 'hitch' was discovered in the back of the
cave, by which Field could anchor us; and he settled
himself in a wet corner where his attention was
occupied in dodging the drops of falling water and
directing our movements.

Our first efforts were on the left wall; and by
means of an ice-axe fixed in a narrow corner, Jones
skilfully and safely wedged himself in a crack which
led almost to the top of the first boulder. However,
for the next half-hour his attempts to make further
progress were in vain, for a hand could not be spared
to chip the ice off the rocks; and it was found
necessary to abandon this left wall and to try the
opposite one, which now occupied our attention for
some time. Jones made several attempts from a
shoulder to effect a lodgment below the chock-stone.
Then, whilst enjoying a well-earned rest, we espied
a small rock, wedged high up in the crack between
the main wall and the roof of the cave. That small
rock proved to be the key of the situation, for, after
probably the finest piece of climbing I have ever
witnessed, a rope was passed through the hole behind
it, and we were in a position to attempt the climb

safely. We were all suffering acutely from cold, especially Field, on account of his inaction, though he declared that the excitement of our movements kept him warm. Notwithstanding this, our leader, taking off his boots and jacket, prepared for a long struggle on that icy wall, whilst I padded my head to gain an inch or two in height. Jones now swung up as high as possible on the hitched rope ; then, while standing on my head, he found a very small hold for one of his toes, and after ascending a few feet was hidden from our sight by the intervening chock-stone. The next few minutes were anxious ones ; we shivered with cold, and held the rope firmly in case there should be a mishap higher up. Almost immediately there was a rush of falling snow far out over the pitch, and it scarcely needed our leader's jödel of success to assure us that at last Walker's Gully had yielded to the onslaught of the climber.

We pushed the leader's boots into his jacket pockets and sent up all our 'luggage.' Owing to the half-frozen condition of our fingers, tying the various things on the rope took so long a time, that we called forth an impatient exclamation from above. Eventually we, in turn, landed safely at the top, after swinging ignominiously on the rope, in much the same way as our 'luggage' had done. However, the great hitherto unclimbed pitch of Walker's Gully was below us, and there followed the usual con-gratulations. Our progress up from the screes had been slow, something like three hours, but much

time had been spent in reconnoitring under extremely
bad conditions.

The situation was still rather serious, for we were
perched on a narrow snow-ledge on the very brink of
the upper chock-stone; and the three of us were
almost in a state of collapse from cold and the
saturated state of our clothes.   The forced inaction
of the leader, whilst we were finishing the climb,
had made him so benumbed as to be almost helpless,
and he was sitting with his feet in the wet snow,
ineffectually trying to put on his boots. We had
carefully kept some stockings and gloves dry in the
rücksack; but the opening of the sack with half-
frozen fingers proved unfortunate, for its contents
escaped, and, with the other relics which had come
down through Jordan Gap, now adorned the snow-
patch far below.   It was then agreed that this
narrow, exposed ledge was, under the circumstances,
not a suitable dressing room; so we gathered up
our belongings, including our leader's boots, and
carefully ascended the snow until we came to a safe
resting place.   Here we resorted to the usual means
of thawing ourselves, and our leader's boots were
restored to their appointed places.

The race up the steep snow seemed to revive our
spirits, and, by the time the dry rocks below Great
Doup were reached, our sufferings gave way to the
glow of success One little excitement was still in store
for us, for Jones told us that he was threatened with
frost-bite in both feet. On removing his boots we found

that his statement was true, so we rubbed his feet
with soft snow, and, before putting on his boots, the
troublesome feet were placed as far as possible in the
pockets of the warmest member of the party, until
circulation was thoroughly restored.

Night was drawing on apace ; so we bade farewell
to our ' vanquished foe,' and were soon scampering
along the High Level, bound for the well-earned
comforts of Wastdale.

Iron Crag Chimney.—Towards the head of
the Shoulthwaite Valley, which is 3½ miles from
Keswick, near the road to Ambleside, may be seen
high up on the right - hand side, a magnificent
couloir. It runs up the south side of one of the
steepest faces of rock in the district, and is called,
after the rock, Iron Crag Chimney. We had passed
in sight of the Crag scores of times, but the chimney
is so cunningly hidden away on the far side from the
road, that it was not until Mr. J. W. Robinson told
us of it, that we dreamt of there being anything
worth climbing there. He and my brother went to
prospect it in March, 1896, but found it in such a
very bad condition, that after climbing the comparatively easy first pitch, they were forced to beat
a retreat. They came back, however, with a glowing
account of the second pitch, and spoke very excitedly
about ' " a thing " at least 100 feet high, wet, mossy,
and with an overhanging stone half-way up, from
which the water dropped out four yards into the bed
of the gully, 40 feet below.' They thought, however,

that a small ledge, up to which they had climbed, would continue far enough along the left wall of the gully to enable them to traverse well out from under the stone, and so reach the top of it. Of the nature of the climbing above that they knew nothing, but were both anxious to try it and confident of success.

Continued bad weather hindered another attempt until June of the same year, when Mr. F. W. Jackson and I joined the other two and we set out to attack this formidable 'hundred-footer.' The day was fine and the rocks in perfect condition, and we succeeded in climbing the chimney throughout. I intend to give more detail of the second ascent ; but it may be as well to mention here that the second pitch only yielded after several attempts, by more than one member of the party, and only with the aid of a shoulder, given from the little ledge, was the leader able to climb to the top of the 'chock-stone.' After this another thirty feet of chimney brought us to the top of the pitch, and great were the rejoicings that we had, after a very severe struggle, mastered it. I shall never forget how white the face of one member of the party was when it appeared over the top of the pitch, how he yelled to us to 'haul in the taut,' how he 'quoth "nevermore,"' and how impolitely he spoke to the leader for having climbed it at all. Altogether this second pitch gave us a good deal of trouble, but the top part of the chimney, though very rotten and steep, and liable to come away in small quantities, was climbed with comparative ease.

After this, except some exploration of the Crags by Mr. H. W. Blunt, it was not visited again by climbers until the New Year of 1899, when Mr. O. G. Jones, with my father, my brother, and myself, found ourselves standing at the bottom of the first pitch. We had expatiated on the difficulty of the second pitch, and Jones was very keen on trying it, having, in fact, come over from Wastdale with us for that purpose. *En route* to Iron Crag we had climbed the Walla Crag Gully, which consists of a series of very interesting and somewhat difficult chimneys, the pleasures of which are greatly enhanced by magnificent views of Derwentwater. This had made us somewhat later than we anticipated, and an animated discussion was held at the bottom as to whether, considering the lateness of the hour and the bad condition of the gully, which was streaming with water, it would not be advisable for two of the party to stay below or go round and join the others at the top. This was decided against; 'all or none,' said Jones, so we roped up with him leading. He soon reached the small ledge under the stone, and then stopped to take breath and prospect. 'Shall I come up to you?' shouted my brother. 'No thanks! I'll have a try from here alone, and you would get wet through in no time up here,' returned he. This consideration for my brother was utterly unlike him, for, amongst other similar occasions, I well remember one on which, in a gully—or rather waterfall—in Wales, he got wet through on the first pitch, and insisted on our finishing with him all the eight pitches. His look of glee when we emerged from the top of each pitch with the water running down us was a thing to be remembered. However, to return, he jammed his left foot against the left wall of the gully and pressed his back against the other, and almost before we had time to see what had happened, was smiling down on us from the top of the pitch. It was very disgusting to see him just 'romp' up the place we had found so difficult the year before, and when I had climbed up to him he smiled sardonically and said, 'Is that your pitch? Well, really——!' A small handhold had weathered away since the time of the first ascent, which somewhat simplified the passing over the 'chock-stone,' but even now I think most people would find it difficult. We could only apologise and feel small, but, had we known it, there was a surfeit of excitement and difficulty in store for us higher up.

The pitch we had just climbed was composed of most excellent rock, but up above, where we now were, everything was changed, and the upper rocks, which had been rotten enough before, were now, as a result of the heavy rain, of the worst description imaginable. Great pieces as large as one's head came away at once, and every step had to be most carefully tested before we could proceed. Now was the time for us to appreciate our leader, for a less careful man would have 'pounded' us severely before we had made any progress worth mentioning. As it was, several big pieces had to be removed, and some came whizzing past in much too close proximity to be pleasant.

After the second pitch the chimney continues straight up and is fairly wide for two hundred feet or so; but there is no good anchorage until the level skyline is reached. Towards the top it narrows down to a thin, rotten and very steep crack. By slow and very careful progress we reached this crack, which had been climbed straight up on the first ascent; but after Jones had tried it a few times he evidently thought it hopeless, for he shouted down to us, 'It won't go to-day. The rain has made everything too rotten. We shall have to go back.' It was four o'clock, raining heavily and nearly dark, and to go back meant in all probability sleeping on the top of the second pitch, an idea which none of us relished. So my brother climbed up to Jones and, after consulting for a while, they decided to climb out of the crack on the right-hand side. To do this a shoulder would have to be given, from a small shelving ledge, to enable the leader to reach the firmer and less steep rock up above. This was the most obvious route of ascent, but the ledge looked very unstable and rotten, and vibrated a little on being tested. However, Jones thought it might hold if stepped on in the right way; so my brother climbed up on to it and Jones followed. By utilizing the side of the crack, they were able to put very little pressure on the ledge; Jones climbed on to his companion's shoulders, and, when he had cleared away a few of the loose rocks, was, after an anxious moment or two, able to draw himself up on to the skyline and disappear from our sight. After a few seconds he gave a cheer and called to my brother to follow him. This he had just begun to do and had left the ledge about five feet, when I heard a dull ominous crack, and, on looking up, saw the whole thing coming down. There was no time to do anything but squeeze into the chimney and warn my father. I succeeded in getting far enough inside to escape serious damage, but the heel of my left boot, which projected a little, was torn entirely away. My father's escape was more marvellous, for it seemed that nothing could save him; but on looking down I saw the great rock strike a projecting piece of the chimney only a few inches above his head, and spread out like a fan into a thousand splinters which shot far out into the air, falling again near the foot of the chimney; and thus we escaped with only a few slight bruises. One shudders to think what would have happened if the ledge had fallen when Jones and my brother were on it. It may be of interest to say here that during the whole of our climbs with Jones, this was the only approach to an accident we had, and under his leadership the possibility of anything going wrong seemed, and always was, very remote indeed.

After this we were not long in joining the other two at the top. By this time it was nearly dark and still raining heavily, and on the crest of the chimney we were faced by a bitterly cold wind. Jones, who had been exposed to this during the time we were ascending, was shaking with cold, and he shouted through the storm—'Hurry up! Coil the rope and then we'll do a sprint.' On looking round we found that he had gone. We finished coiling the rope and hurried up to where he had been, but could not see him anywhere. We shouted again and again, but got no answer. After peering about and shouting several times we came to a standstill. 'Is he subject to fits?' inquired my father in a most doleful tone of voice. We had never heard of anything of the sort, so set off down the side of the crags in the hope of finding him awaiting us below A miserable hour was spent in walking about the bottom of the crags calling his name; but the whistling of the wind in the rocks above, and the swishing of the rain were the only answers we got; so we set off down the fell-side, and, after floundering about in the dark, over the stone-walls and through the river, we found ourselves at last on the main road to Keswick. We were very anxious to know what had become of Jones, so hastened home, where we found him, 'dressed up in all his best,' toasting his feet in front of a comfortable fire. 'Where have you been?' 'Dinner has been waiting an hour,' and so on, were the thanks we got for our weary hunt among the crags for him, and the query of my father's about his taking 'fits' became one of his

favourite jokes.   After proposing the 'sprint' to us
he had run round a projecting shoulder of rock to
leeward, and started off to Keswick over the moor,
by the route we had taken earlier in the day.   We
had expected him to go down to the Shoulthwaite
Valley, and in this way had missed him.

So finished one of the most exciting days we
ever spent with Owen Glynne Jones ; and its events
are indelibly stamped on my memory.   But, full of
incident as the day had been, my pleasantest
recollection is of the evening that followed ; when,
by the fire and over our pipes, we fought old battles
over again, recalling to life happy days and exciting
moments on the fells, ending with the songs and
glees Jones loved so well to sing, and across the
space of years, taking us back into the 'dear, dead
days,' will come into our 'mind's eye' the picture of
him kneeling by the piano, singing with the keen
enthusiasm which characterized everything he did,
his favourite hymn—

> Lead, kindly Light, amid the encircling gloom,
>
> . . . .
>
> O'er moor and fen, o'er crag and torrent,
> Till the night is gone.

Engineers' Chimney, Gable Crag.—This
new and interesting climb is situated about midway
between the Oblique Chimney and the Central
Gully.   The beginning of it lies at nearly the same
level as that of the Oblique Chimney, and can be
reached by traversing some easy ledges from the

'Sheep Walk,' or by ascending directly from the foot of the Crags. Although the chimney was well known to many climbers, its ascent had, curiously enough, not been seriously attempted until July 30th, 1899, when Messrs. G. T. Glover and W. N. Ling made the first ascent. Since then it has been ascended on two other occasions, and it seems likely to become as popular as any of the Gable Crag climbs. The scenery is magnificent and the climbing throughout of a most interesting character, and in the centre of the lower part of the chimney a loosely wedged stone adds an element of risk and difficulty, which is absent from the other chimneys on this face. About eight feet from its commencement the chimney divides into two branches, but the route lies up the left-hand one. A good resting place for the second man is to be obtained in the right-hand branch, and he ought to stay here while the leader is negotiating the very difficult passage over the chock-stone. In all the ascents so far it has been found advisable to pass a rope behind and over this stone, to improvise a handhold, and even then this ten feet or so will be found quite difficult enough for most people. After this, another twenty-five feet of careful climbing brings one to a broad, sloping ledge where a rest can be taken. From here two routes are available. One is to keep to the chimney, which continues straight upward for about forty feet, and the other is to traverse out round the left-hand buttress for a few feet and then bear upwards, joining the 'Sheep

Walk' near the top of the Crags.   The former of
these involves about twenty feet of fairly easy
climbing, until the small cave, roofed over with the
stone which dominates the chimney, is reached.
From this cave the easiest method of ascent is to
utilise a thin crack in the left wall into which some
small stones are firmly jammed and which may be
reached by wedging across the chimney and traversing outwards, a slight projecting ledge affording
some help in the process.   The 'take-off' into the
crack is somewhat delicate and decidedly sensational
on account of the scanty foothold, but once gained
ten to twelve feet of further climbing practically
finishes the chimney.   The traverse route round the
buttress is much easier, but it entirely evades the
most sensational part of the climb.

West Wall Climb, Deep Ghyll.—For climbers
of Deep Ghyll who ascend the second pitch by the
right-hand exit, this new route is probably the best
way out of the Ghyll.   After thus passing the second
pitch, the West Wall Climb starts from a point about
twenty-six yards below the entrance to the Great
Chimney.   By climbing over two small ledges and
up a conspicuous thirty-feet chimney, a broad ledge
is reached, where further direct progress is not
advisable.

The best way lies around a corner to the right
and up a series of easy ledges, working gradually
back again to above the commencement of the climb.
About half-way up 'The Wall' an undercut pinnacle

is reached and ascended on the left before a lodgment can be effected on its outside edge, and some enjoyable work follows until a spacious ledge on the right can be utilised. When Messrs. J. W. Robinson, J. H. Doncaster, and H. W. Blunt first made the ascent, in the September of 1898, this portion of the climb was considered difficult, and it is probably the only part where special care is necessary. Above this the climbing can be varied considerably, but the direct ascent of a rock ridge, straight ahead, is to be recommended. The course throughout is well within the powers of most climbing parties, and the magnificent views of Scawfell Pinnacle and Deep Ghyll add additional interest to the ascent.

We are indebted to two friends for the notes on the following climbs :—To Mr. G. T. Glover for those on the Ling Chimney, and to Mr. W. R. Reade for those on the West Jordan Gully.

The Ling Chimney, Eagle's Nest Arete.— In the first edition of his book Mr. O. G. Jones mentions that there are two chimneys on the left-hand side of the Eagle's Nest Arête, ' the right of these is shallow and open . . . . whether it can be climbed or not I have never ascertained.' On October 15th, 1899, Messrs. W. N. Ling, C. E. Martineau and G. T. Glover made the first recorded ascent of it, after a preliminary exploration from above. From the top of the small grass gully which commences the *arête* climb, one traverses about ten feet across some rock to the left, being then in a

direct line below the final chimney. Going straight
upwards, by steep rock steps, an upright slab is
swarmed up with the hands and feet on each side,
until a platform is reached, on which the second man
can join the leader. About fifteen feet above this
is another platform at the foot of a narrow chimney
which needs careful climbing for about ten feet, until
a foothold can be utilised on the sharp edge of the
left wall.

From here some stiff pulls on the arms land one
out either on a broad ledge above the easy gully
route, or up a continuation of the chimney to the
right-hand side of the narrow pinnacle at the finish
of the true *arête* climb. The ascent, as a whole,
requires more care than the gully route.

The West Jordan Gully, Pillar Rock.—This
deeply cut gully, or, more correctly speaking,
chimney, is a striking feature of the Western face of
the Pillar Rock, and, together with the East Jordan
Gully, the head of which it meets at Jordan Gap,
cuts off the actual Pillar Rock from Pisgah. Probably
many climbers have examined the West Jordan
Gully, but it does not appear to have been seriously
attacked before July, 1898, when Mr. W. P.
McCulloch and the writer climbed it. Walking up
the bed of the gully we passed a tempting looking
crack on the North wall which ends in a small cave ;
above this cave the gully is ' chocked ' by several
overhanging stones which from below seem very
formidable obstacles. We, however, avoided the

crack and, mounting a series of jammed stones, reached the innermost recesses of the chimney. We were now almost on a level with the top of the crack, and, the gully being here narrow enough to brace firmly across, we backed upwards and outwards for about fifteen feet, reaching the cave without great exertion. So far we had done well, but still the great jammed stones, round which we had to pass, loomed black overhead. Holds for the traverse outward looked anything but satisfactory, so Mr. McCulloch, after passing the rope round a conveniently placed jammed stone, climbed on to my shoulders and, with considerable difficulty, dragged himself into a small cave about fifteen feet above. As this cave would only accommodate one man, I climbed to Mr. McCulloch's level, with a little assistance from the rope, and took the lead. Traversing outwards for about fifteen feet, I climbed a sensational forty-feet chimney, which we had surveyed from above several days previously, and landed safely in the bed of the gully past all difficulties. The height of the whole pitch is slightly under 100 feet, and, from beginning to end, the climbing is of a most interesting character. The second ascent was made by the brothers Broadrick, in August of the same year, but there is no record of it having been climbed since.

INDEX.

INDEX.

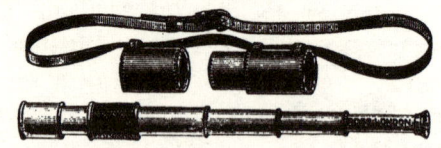

Stereo=Locoscopy.

NEW!
BEAUTIFUL!!
REALISTIC!!!

A SMALL, high-class, and very portable Stereoscope, with small glass transparent slides, $5\frac{1}{2}" \times 2\frac{1}{4}"$, free from distortion, peculiarly adapted for viewing subjects at any angle up or down. Particularly adapted to climbing views, such as chimneys, gullies, arêtes, general rock-work, etc., and when viewed at the original angle in the Stereoscope nature is marvellously repeated, whether looking up the steepest pitch or chimney, or down the deepest ghyll or ravine.

WE PUBLISH A FULL SET OF **100** SLIDES

OF THE

English Lakeland Climbs,

Also of WALES and SCOTLAND,

To which we are constantly making additions.

SLIDES, 2/- each; LOCO-STEREOSCOPES, 16/6 each,

MAY BE HAD ONLY OF

Messrs. G. P. Abraham & Sons,

Victoria Buildings,

——KESWICK.